MERCHANTMEN
IN ACTION

MERCHANTMEN IN ACTION

EVACUATIONS AND LANDINGS BY MERCHANT SHIPS IN THE SECOND WORLD WAR

ROY V. MARTIN

FONTHILL

This book is dedicated to the Allied merchant seafarers who served in both World Wars, and their families.

Cover picture: 'Bordeaux Refugees at Falmouth', Charles Ernest Cundall RA. (*IWM*)

Fonthill Media Limited
Fonthill Media LLC
www.fonthillmedia.com
office@fonthillmedia.com

First Published as *Ebb and Flow* May 2010

This edition published in the United Kingdom 2012

British Library Cataloguing in Publication Data:
A catalogue record for this book is available from the British Library

Copyright © in introduction, Fonthill Media 2012

ISBN 978-1-78155-045-8 (print)
ISBN 978-1-78155-153-0 (e-book)

Typeset in 9.5pt on 13pt Sabon.
Printed and bound in England
Connect with us
 facebook.com/fonthillmedia twitter.com/fonthillmedia

Contents

Acknowledgements

I would especially like to thank Wendy Brogden (née Watkins) for proof reading the typescript of *Ebb and Flow*, as it then was. Wendy took on this task out of regard for the Merchant Navy. As a young cadet her father spent four years (1941-45) as a prisoner of war in Milag/Milag Nord. He has recorded his experiences; the tapes are at the Imperial War Museum.

The many other people who have kindly given help, information and advice at various times are: Alan Watson, Alison and Paul Effeny, Amanda Davies, Ann Don (Prudence), Billy McGee, Bruno Comer, Derric Webster, Don Kindell, François Cersosimo, Gill and Alfred Sims, Halina Macdonald, Hazel Stringer, Hugh MacLean, Jack Mount, Janet Dempsey, John Scaffa, Joyce Murdoch, Kerin Freeman, Sue Hill, The Hon. Maurice Howard, Marek Twardowski, Mark Hirst, Peter Kik, René Allion, Terence Holland, William Oldenburg and Yves Beaujuge.

Some of the websites that have been particularly useful sources of information are: Convoyweb, (Mike Holdoway, Tony Cooper and Don Kindell); http://www.naval-history.net (Gordon Smith and Don Kindell); Mercantile Marine, (Ron (Steve) Wylie, Hugh MacLean, Roger, Billy McGee and Ray Buck); Warsailors, (Siri Lawson); www.ww2talk.com/forum/ (Diane and Hugh, yet again?). Many contributors to the forums on these and other websites have also helped. Over the years many other people have given me the benefit of their knowledge. I am most grateful to them all.

A special thank you is due to my wife June, who has put up with the many hours I have spent working on this book when there were many far more important things I could have been doing around the home! She has listened patiently to the many incidents that I have described.

Finally three people without whom this edition would not have been published: Jay Slater, who saved it from being dumped by a previous publisher, Alan Sutton, who agreed to publish it, and Jasper Hadman, for his patience and guidance while editing the book; I am most grateful to them all.

Roy Martin
Southampton, July 2012

Author's Note

When I joined my first ship in 1953, most of the officers had served through the war and had the medal ribbons to prove it. What I didn't appreciate until years afterwards, was that some of the old hands on that ship, such as the bosun and the carpenter, had served through two wars. During the eight-month trip around the world, I had the chance to read through the ship's cargo book and was intrigued to see that she had also 'done her bit'. The plans started with cargoes of bulk grain, not surprising as her owners were grain traders. From 1941 she had carried trucks, aircraft, locomotives, tanks, landing craft and barges, as well as general (mixed) cargoes.

In 1964 I joined the salvage ship *Droxford*, our task was to locate sunken ships and recover their cargoes of non-ferrous metals. Most of the shipwrecks were from the two wars. At that time all of the research was provided by the company's full time researcher, Tom Pickford. Several years later, when I worked in Risdon Beazley's offices, I started evaluating the raw research data, with a great deal of help from Tom and other senior people in the company. They had all served throughout the war, though they seldom talked about those times. As these fine men retired, I became more involved in researching targets.

By the mid-seventies I had other tasks and the research was side-lined, but it continued to be a hobby throughout the seven years that I was in Singapore. By 1986, when I left SISEA to get back to research and recovery, Risdon Beazley had ceased operations. I started to work with my friend and colleague Lyle Craigie-Halkett. We completed a number of interesting projects. In 2002 we decided to write a history of Risdon Beazley Ltd, which we published in 2006.

Over the last few years I have become interested in the part played by the British Merchant Navy during the Second World War. In 2007 I met Amanda Davies who was researching her grandfather's sea-going career, in particular his time as Chief Officer of the General Steam Navigation ship *Stork*. He was lost when this ship was torpedoed. Amanda showed me records of the *Stork* being attacked at Boulogne and then taking part in the evacuation of the Channel Islands. The Channel Islanders arrived in Weymouth about 23 June, more than two weeks after the fall of Dunkirk. This reminded me that my mother had said we were both in Weymouth at that time, when French speaking soldiers were being landed. This I followed up.

Further checking caused me to take an interest in Operations Cycle and Aerial, when well over 200,000 were evacuated from other parts of France. Little is known about this rescue, which was mainly carried out by merchant ships. Winston Churchill ordered that information on the loss of the *Lancastria* should not be released; as a result these records are sealed until 2040. A log of the Aerial Operation, found by Don Kindell, can be viewed at http://www.naval-history. net/xDKWDa-Aerial.htm.

Having lived in Singapore, I gathered information on those who escaped from there; another untold story of the steadfastness of our merchant crews. Then came the realisation that the Merchant Navy had played a very significant part in all of the successful landings in Europe, and were ready to do the same in South East Asia when the Japanese surrendered. To this, I have added chapters on Britain's dire predicament in 1941, and again in 1942. It is not possible to see how Britain would have got through this low point without the unstinting support of both the merchant fleets and the Empire.

There were ship lists at the end of each chapter, but as these may not be of interest to the general reader, they are now reproduced on www.convoyweb, with the kind help of Mike Holdoway. Readers who require more information should consult John de S. Winser's three books, which have been an excellent source. The only subjects he has not covered are the landings in Norway, the eastern Mediterranean evacuations and the flight from Singapore.

The photograph of the crew of the *Fort Dease Lake* in the picture section is from *The Illustrated London News* of 21 August 1943, © Illustrated London News Ltd / Mary Evans Picture Library. Carol and Paul at carol@sleekburnprints.com kindly first sent me the print. The *Fort Dease Lake*, built in Canada, was bare-boat chartered to the British Ministry of War Transport and managed by Buries Markes Ltd of London. Other pictures are reproduced with permission of the Imperial War Museum. Photographs of the *Empire Star* evacuating nurses, civilians and troops can be viewed at the Australian War Memorial site (also known as 'Picture Australia'). In the Singapore chapter I have quoted from www.angellpro.com.au/ women.htm, with Dr Angell's permission.

Other pictures are from Wikipedia. I have also used a few of the several hundred photographs that I have from the Risdon Beazley files. I have tried to contact copyright holders, where they are known, and I apologise if I have unintentionally breached any copyrights. It is seldom, if ever, possible to contact the photographer, so I have needed to deal with the owner of the print and in some cases there may be many prints still in existence.

The verse from 'The Streets of London' is reproduced with permission from Westminster Music Ltd. I approached the *Daily Mirror* for permission to reproduce Philip Zec's cartoon 'The price of petrol has been increased by one penny – Official', but I have not received a response.

I am especially grateful to the following individuals and bodies who kindly given their permissions without charge: The late Captain Peter Jackson for the photograph of troops on the *Bellerophon*. A. P. Watt on behalf of The Royal Literary Fund, for extracts from *Strictly Personal* by Somerset Maugham; The Society of Authors as the Literary Representative of the Estate of John Masefield, for the poem 'For the Sailors'; Pen & Sword Books Ltd, for extracts from *1940, The Last Act* by Basil Karslake. The *Daily Mail*, for the cartoon 'The Bill' by Illingworth; The National Digital Archives (NAC), Warsaw, for the *Royal Scotsman*; the Polish Institute and Sykorski Museum for the *Alderpool*; the BRB (Residuary) Ltd, for the *Alt*; The *Lancastria* Association of Scotland, for the *John Holt*; and Dr Don Cody for the *Broompark*. Information on the *Broompark*'s rescue of many items and the experts from Bordeaux, led by the larger than life Charles 'Jack' Howard, 20th Earl of Suffolk and 13th Earl of Berkshire, comes from Bruno Comer in Belgium; Lew Kowarski's story is online and the British side is in The National Archives. Ian Golding has provided a wealth of information about his father's part in the Mission and Miss Nicolle's account of the venture; this has been most helpful in providing a balanced view of what his father modestly describes as an 'interesting and unusual story'. The *City of Derby*'s voyage and the rescue by the *Thurland Castle* are from Jack Mount and Alfred Sims respectively. Details of Sub Lieut Foster's, time in command of the schuyt *Jaba* appears with the permission of his son Mike Foster. Photographs taken by Sgt Bill Lazell during the siege of Malta appear with the permission of his son Paul Lazell; Paul has put the photographs online at www.paulsww2photographs.webeden.co.uk/. For technical reasons not all of these photographs have been included.

Crown Copyright material appears under the Open Government Licence, the source being acknowledged in the text.

On the anniversary of Operation Dynamo the usual collection of private motor yachts make the trip to Dunkirk to commemorate saving the troops of the British Expeditionary Force. There is no doubting the bravery of the men who manned those small vessels, any more than those on the many hundreds of small commercial boats or the thousands of professional seamen of both sea services who answered the call. But boats and ships are not brave, the bravery is shown by the men who man them, and most of those men can no longer make the trip.

In the early stages I made several visits to The National Archives at Kew. While there I photographed hundreds of pages from files, and in some cases have not kept a record of the file numbers. I have read so many reports that I may well have unconsciously included the words or expressions of others. I apologise for this, and for any errors in the text.

Roy Martin

Have you seen the old man, outside the Seaman's Mission?
Memory fading, like the ribbons that he wears
In our winter city, the rain cries a little pity
For one more forgotten hero in a world that doesn't care

'The Streets of London' – courtesy Ralph McTell, 2006

Flight from Singapore

Singapore Island lies one degree north of the equator, at the southern tip of the Malay Peninsula. The island is about the same shape as the Isle of Wight, but bigger by half, and it is joined to the Malay state of Johore by a causeway. When Britain completed work on strengthening her military base on the island in 1938, the island became known as 'Fortress Singapore'. It lacked a resident fleet. The battleship HMS *Prince of Wales* and the battle cruiser HMS *Repulse* arrived at the colony on 2 December, the aircraft carrier HMS *Indomitable* was to have been with them, but she ran aground and was delayed.

The Japanese landed on the east coast of the Malayan Peninsula on 8 December 1941, at the same time as they occupied Hong Kong. They bombed Singapore for the first of many times the same day. The *Prince of Wales* and *Repulse*, with four destroyers, put to sea without air cover and were sunk by Japanese torpedo bombers two days later. With the loss of their two biggest ships in the East, and the withdrawal of the Royal Air Force to Palembang (carried by the Merchant Navy), Singapore had to rely largely on the Army for its defence. Neither the military nor the civilian authorities would give the order to evacuate until it was far too late and the Japanese were already on the island. In December 1941, the War Cabinet had instructed that *bouches inutiles* should be evacuated.

Once British troops retreated, the causeway was intentionally cut, and with it went the water supply pipe from Johore. On 15 February 1942, Lieutenant General Percival was instructed by his superiors to surrender. While General Yamashita had apparently outrun his supplies, the Japanese had control of the sea and the air. The records that have survived are confusing and contradictory.

The principal Singapore-based shipping company was the Straits Steamship Company, which was associated with the smaller Sarawak Steamship Company. When war reached the Malay Peninsula most of their ships were requisitioned by the Royal Navy. The vessels were hurriedly armed; the masters and officers remained with their ships and were given temporary ranks in the Royal Naval Reserve (RNR), and the crews were retained. All fifty-one of the company's ships were controlled by the government, thirty-one sailing under the White Ensign. The company also took over the management of several other vessels, including some Yangtze river steamers.

When the Japanese landed in Sarawak in December 1941, the larger units of the fleet escaped, but most of the smaller vessels of the Sarawak Steamship Company were captured or sunk. Penang was bombed on 11 January 1942 and the Company asked the Naval Authorities if they could move their ships south; permission was refused and another seven of their ships were captured. By the end of January, five more Straits Steamship Company vessels had been sunk. On 20 January, the HMS *Raub*, under the command of Captain Lawes, was bombed off Belawan and capsized alongside the quay while the crew were attempting to make repairs. At about the same time, the HMS *Larut*, under Captain Cleaver, was bombed and sunk at Sabang. The master, officers and crew set off through Sumatra, where the engineers commandeered a train in Belawan and ran it south. From there they crossed to Java.

The Sarawak Company's HMS *Jarak* and HMS *Tapah* had been employed as minesweepers. In late January 1942, the *Jarak*, under the command of Captain Hooper, formerly Chief Officer of the *Kedah*, went north to Batu Pahat to rescue 1,000 soldiers who were trapped there. WO 222/2569 says about 2,000 were rescued 'by the Navy'. The *Hai Hing* and the *Klang* sailed with refugees on 12 January 1942. The merchantmen the *Sunetta* and the *British Judge*, both tankers, and the *Talamba*, the *Aorangi* and the *Armilla*, followed independently. Some, or all, may have had refugees aboard. On 16 January 1942, the *Narkunda*, under Captain R. Lear, sailed with 407 passengers who were landed in Australia. Between then and 28 January, seven merchant ships sailed, again some with evacuees. Convoy NB 1 left on 28 January 1942; the merchant ships were: the *Cap St Jaques*, the *Darvil*, the *Ekma*, the *Ipoh*, the *Islami* and the *Pangkor*, and then the *Rohna*. All carried passengers. The *Darvil* and the *Ipoh* took 1,000 RAF personnel and their families to Palembang. The *Pangkor* is also listed as having RAF personnel aboard. The *Islami* (Mogul Line, Bombay), carrying about 1,000 Japanese women and children, succeeded in reaching her home port with her passengers.

The merchant ships, the *Abbekerk*, the *Duchess of Bedford*, the *Empress of Japan*, the USS *Wakefield*, the *Brittany*, the *Marilyse Moller*, the *Takliwa* and the USS *Westpoint* sailed on 30 January 1942. The first four ships were escorted, while the others sailed independently. These ships had arrived in Singapore only days before with 17,000 troops and their equipment. Stores and troops continued to arrive until 4 February 1942, only four days before the Japanese landed on the island. The stevedores had long gone and many of the Asian crew members had deserted. This left the weary European merchant crews to discharge their ships, in some cases helped by troops, particularly the RAF. In the final days, much of the equipment was driven off the quay to stop it falling into enemy hands.

Between them, the *Duchess of Bedford*, the USS *Wakefield* and the USS *Westpoint* carried about 4,000 evacuees, and the *Empress of Japan* just over 1,200. After loading about 1,000 women and children in Singapore, the *Duchess of Bedford* sought shelter among the nearby islands, returning alongside the following day to load a similar number. While the ship was sheltering, the purser had a heart attack. There were other deaths on the voyage home. On 1 February 1942, there was a happier event when a soldier's wife gave birth to a daughter who was named Diana, after the matron who delivered her, and Bedford, at the suggestion of the master, Captain Busk-Wood, who registered the birth. Sadly her father never saw his daughter; he drowned when his prison ship was torpedoed later in the War. The *Duchess of Bedford* made it safely home to Liverpool, unescorted, and survived the War.

There is no record of the Dutch ship *Abbekerk* carrying refugees from Singapore, though she may well have done so; she was still 'half full with ammunition'. She sailed first to Oosthaven (Bandar Lampung), and then on to Tjilatjap, where she embarked 1,500 evacuees, sailing on 27 February 1942. The ship and her passengers arrived safely in Fremantle on 4 March. The British ship the *Brittany* arrived in Trincomalee on the same day. The *Marilyse Moller* went independently to Palembang, arriving on 2 February. She may have had RAF personnel aboard. The ship then went on to Batavia, and from there to Colombo.

During the last week of January 1942, the cargo ships, the *Tai Sang* and the *Giang Seng*, were lost. The first sailing in February was the *Rochuissen*, a Dutch cattle boat with no passenger accommodation, which took 200, including fifty Malayan Broadcasting personnel. The *Rochuissen* reached Tanjong Priok, the port for Batavia, on 5 February.

On 3 February, the *Loch Ranza* was set on fire by Japanese bombers and beached, with her cargo on fire and the fire main broken. Her second officer, John Inglis, was in charge of one of the fire parties. He was blown into the air by a bomb blast, and though wounded by splinters, he refused treatment and carried on. He was later awarded the George Medal and Lloyd's War Medal for Bravery. The carpenter's good work was also acknowledged; he had remained at his post on the exposed forecastle head to operate the anchors.

The cargo ship, the *Anglo Indian*, arrived in Singapore on 31 January with a cargo of guns and ammunition; she appears to have suffered indirect bomb damage while in the port. She sailed again with an unspecified number of refugees, whom she landed at Tanjong Priok on 5 February. After making minor repairs, she sailed for Colombo on 8 February. The last convoy to Singapore was BM 12, which docked on 4 February. The merchant ships were the *Felix Roussel*, the *Devonshire*, the *Plancius* and the *City of Canterbury*. They, and the escorts, the *Encounter*, the *Exeter*, the *Danae*, the *Sutlej* and the *Yarra*, brought in the survivors from the *Empress of Asia*, which had caught fire after being bombed near the Sultan Shoal Lighthouse and had to be abandoned. The HMAS *Yarra* put her bow alongside the stricken ship's stern to carry out the rescue. When the last two survivors, the master and chief engineer, boarded the *Yarra*, she had a total of 1,804 evacuees aboard. The captain instructed the rescued to sit as he was a little dubious of the stability of the sloop. Of the 2,651 people that had been aboard the *Empress*, only fifteen soldiers and one crew member were lost.

The *Hermelin*, the *Silverlarch* and the *City of Manchester* sailed on 4 February. The *City of Manchester*, an Ellerman liner, safely reached Oosthaven on 6

February with about 700 evacuees, but was later torpedoed on 28 February while on a voyage from Tjilatjap. A report in *The London Gazette* says that the *Silverlarch* carried 1,000 from Singapore, Captain Snowling and his chief engineer were awarded OBEs.

The Shell tanker, the *Pinna*, was bombed and set on fire; many of the local crew were killed in this attack. The tanker was again bombed on 4 February 1942 and sank. Her master, Captain Thomas, was badly burnt; he and several of the officers were hospitalized in Singapore and became prisoners of war. The *Pinna* had previously rescued 900 residents from the port of Balikpapan. The balance of the crew – half a dozen survivors from the Navy and another Shell master – escaped in two small coastal tankers, the *Kulit* and the *Ribut*, and the launch, *Makota*. The masters of these ships had agreed to take as many civilians as they could. They probably would not have done this had they realised it would cause them a two-day delay and involve the loading of an unbelievable amount of luggage. All made their way to the east coast of Sumatra. After an overland journey they found a wrecked prauw which they repaired. Just as they were about to set off for Java in this vessel, it was requisitioned by a party of Dutch marines, who had spent days on the quay watching the repair work. They were eventually rescued from Sumatra by a Dutch Navy ship.

The convoy EMU sailed on 6 February. It consisted of the *City of Canterbury*, with 179 RAF personnel and their families, the *Devonshire*, with 2,400, and the *Felix Roussel* (a Free French ship with a British master) with 110, mainly women and children. The *Felix Roussel* had sustained damage before she arrived at Singapore. The convoy escorts were the HMS *Danae*, the HMIS *Sutlej* and the HMAS *Yarra*. On 12 February, the *City of Canterbury*, with the *Anglo Indian*, joined convoy SJ 1 from Batavia to Colombo. The *Devonshire* and the *Felix Roussel* stayed with the EMU convoy for what must have been a difficult trip; one spent thirteen days under repair in Bombay and the other, nineteen days. On 8 February the liner, the *Dominion Monarch*, was hastily un-docked and sailed.

On the evening of 7 February a small convoy that included the *Rahman*, the *Klais*, the *Hua Tong* and the *Changteh* – this last ship under the command of Captain C. Brown of the Straits Steamship Company – sailed from Singapore. The convoy's speed was reduced to 3 knots, because those volunteers firing the boilers of the *Klais* had packed the furnaces too tightly with coal. The passengers were landed at Palembang. Some completed their journey by rail to the south and then across to Java, others went west to the Indian Ocean by road. The Dutch Naval Command then ordered the ships to join the HMS *Jerantut* and the tug HMS *St Just* and make for Tanjong Priok. On Friday 13 February, they were attacked by aircraft. After giving a good account of themselves, they abandoned their ships and, where possible, escaped across Sumatra.

Chief Engineer Horn said in his report: 'All the engine room personnel and Chinese cooks and stewards remained to a man and I have nothing but the highest admiration for them in the manner in which they carried on cheerfully and loyally during those tragic and helpless weeks which preceded the fall of Singapore.'

Other sailings on 11 and 12 February included the *Bulan/Bulang*, the *Bagan* (or *Agan*), the *Jalakrishna*, the *Jalavihar*, the *Edang*, the *Li Sang* and the *Jalaratna*, the *Durban*, the *Kedah*, the *Stronghold* and the *Yo* (*Yoma?*). The Straits vessel, HMS *Rompin*, whose master was Captain G. R. Spaull, sailed on 10 February, towing a seaplane tender and the yacht *White Swan*. After putting into Muntok to repair the engine, the *Rompin* and her tender were captured; the *White Swan* had already sailed for Australia.

The *Antilochus, Charon, Mangola* and *Marella* arrived at Batavia on 8 February, and the tankers *Elsa, Erling Brovig, Herborg, Manvantara, Merula, Marpessa* and *Seirstad* reached Palembang on 9 February. The *Derrymore, Redang, Ipoh, Ampang, Jalakrishna, Jalavihar, Jalaratna, Oriskany, Ashridge, Hong Kwong, Sin Kheng Seng, Aquarius* and *Lee Sang* left Singapore on 11/12 February.

When the *Empress of Asia*'s crew landed, they split into three groups. Many of the engine room crew signed on other rescue ships and eventually got back to the UK. All 132 members of the catering department volunteered to serve in local hospitals, as did the ship's doctor. They helped the hard-pressed nurses by taking over the duties that had been performed by the local staff. Those who were not murdered by the incoming Japanese became prisoners of war. Many of the deck crew and a few engineers escaped on the coasters, the *Hong Kwong*, the *Sing Kheng Seng* and the *Ampang*. Between air-raids those who had been assigned to these small ships bunkered and stored them. For the crew of the *Sing Keng Seng*, this meant lugging baskets of coal aboard, and storing the ships by taking what food they could from the nearby godowns (warehouses). Royal Navy and Royal Australian Navy survivors from the *Prince of Wales* and the *Repulse* asked if they could join the *Sing Kheng Seng*, which they did, telling the gangway guard that they were from the *Empress of Asia*.

The three coasters sailed on 12 February. At first they were told to anchor to await nurses and civilians, but after several hours they received a message to get out as best they could. On the way out they passed 'an Empire type cargo ship which was getting quite a beating'. This may have been the *Derrymore*, which had left Singapore with Royal Australian Air Force personnel on the previous day. After being repeatedly attacked, *Derrymore* was torpedoed. Some accounts have claimed that the master and some of the crew abandoned the ship early, leaving the chief officer to take command, but as Captain H. Richardson was appointed to command a new ship for the same owners in 1943, this seems unlikely. Another report has a completely different account; in this the master was named as a Captain R. Doyle, who was described as a 'big bully', the chief officer, Mr E. J. Fenn was 'small in stature, a quiet but firm and excellent officer'. When the *Derrymore* was lost, Mr Fenn organised the construction of rafts to give some chance of survival. The efforts were successful and he received an OBE and Lloyd's Medal for Gallantry at Sea. Mr Fenn lost his life after abandoning the Chumleigh off Spitsbergen (See Second Low Water).

The first two ships safely made Batavia, though the *Sing Kheng Seng* ran out of coal and completed the voyage in tow of a Dutch destroyer. The *Ampang* ran short of fuel earlier on and had gone into Palembang, where she had the misfortune to arrive only 45 minutes before the invasion. The *Ampang*'s crew and passengers trekked overland to Panjang and then crossed to Java and on to Batavia. They safely made it to Australia.

Because Japanese soldiers had massacred hospital patients elsewhere, and had raped and murdered nurses, three ships were hurriedly requisitioned to evacuate as many from the hospitals as possible. These ships, in order of sailing, were the *Wah Sui*, the *Empire Star* and the *Vyner Brooke*.

On Tuesday 10 February 1942, six of the Australian nurses were told to be ready within 15 minutes to board the *Wah Sui*, a small Yangtze river steamer. Captain A. C. Benfield, who had recently retired from the Sarawak Steamship Company, was called up in the RNR and given command. Their matron told the nurses to take as many wounded men as they could and get them to safety. Matron Paschke was destined to die at sea only a few days later as one of the victims of the sinking of the *Vyner Brooke*, but those of her nurses who survived continued to obey her orders. There were about twenty nurses altogether on the *Wah Sui*, British (and Indian?) civilian nurses, and nurses from Queen Alexandria's Imperial Military Nursing Service (QAIMNS), as well as the six from Australia.

The ships stayed alongside at Singapore for two days, waiting for civilians who boarded the ship with their personal belongings. The civilians occupied the accommodation and as a result there was no room to take on any more nurses or any more of the wounded; this memory still angered the Australian nurses many years later. The recollections of the Australian and the British nurses differ, but between them they got over 400 wounded soldiers onto this small vessel.

They sailed at sunset on 10 February. The ship was displaying the Red Cross, and when a Japanese plane flew over, the pilot respected the insignia. On the night of Friday 13 February, they saw two burning ships and stopped in the hope of picking up survivors. Next day the *Wah Sui* docked in Batavia. The Australian nurses got their patients ready to transfer to another hospital ship bound for Colombo. They packed their own gear and waited aboard the *Wah Sui* to be transferred. The Straits Steamship website says 'after arriving there [Tg. Priok] he [Captain Benfield] was ordered to load 400 wounded and make for Colombo; he sailed in late February arriving in Ceylon early March, a brilliant feat of seamanship.'

On Friday 20 February, when the Japanese had already landed on Java, the Australian nurses boarded the Orient Liner, the *Orcades*, bound for Colombo. On the voyage they continued to do their duty, nursing both soldiers and civilians. The *Orcades* was the only ship in convoy SJ 6, and she carried a total of 3,768 troops and evacuees.

The *Empire Star*, a motor ship owned by the Blue Star Line, had been built to ship frozen meat to the UK. She had arrived in Singapore on 29 January as part of convoy BM 11. The ship's crew worked all day and through the night unloading guns, lorries, tanks and the 2,000 tons of ammunition that she carried. On 11 February another team of Australian nurses were chosen by their matron to board the *Empire Star*. The women objected as they did not want to leave their patients, but Matron Drummond gave them an hour to prepare. Each was allowed to take a small case. They were joined by their British colleagues from Singapore; their matron, Miss Jones, had picked those who were to go. At the wharf, their boarding was delayed by an air raid. When the sixty-three nurses and three physiotherapists did finally board, they were told to go down the cargo hold as the ship only had a few passenger cabins. Conditions in the hold would have been unpleasant, but this was the safest place to be. Miss Jones and several other British matrons lost their lives a few days later in the *Kuala*.

A letter written by the master, Captain Selwyn Capon, says there were 2,161 people on the *Empire Star*; he said later that he believed that the number was more like 2,400. There were 1,845 service personnel (including the nurses), 228 civilians, mostly women and children, and eighty-eight crew. The service personnel included a group of 139 Australian troops who were later arrested as deserters; the case against them was that they had killed a Royal Naval Captain who tried to prevent them from boarding.

Reporting to the Principal Matron of the QAIMNS, Sister Catherine Maudsley said:

> The ship [the *Empire Star*] that we boarded had many hundreds on board, including Air Force, Australians, some civilians, even babies twelve days old. We were allocated one of the holds and shared it with Australian sisters. We slept on bare boards, using gas capes, tin hats or gas masks as pillows. We only possessed what we stood up in and could carry. The Australian Sisters who had been on board for a day or so before we arrived, had all their kit and food enough for a week, but at no time did they offer us anything, not even food; it was our men who shared their rations with us.... The ship itself received four direct hits and had a fire in the stern, but it still sailed on; had it not been for the Captain and staff of that Merchant ship, we should never have reached Batavia.

Captain Capon waited until first light on the 12 February, then set course for the Banka Strait and Java. Some of the reports state that they were alone, but other records say that they sailed with the *Gorgon* and the *Kedah*, and were escorted by HM ships the *Durban*, the *Jupiter* and the *Stronghold*. The naval ships had embarked 232 evacuees between them; the other two merchant ships had over 300 each.

The *Empire Star* was attacked repeatedly and as many as fifty-seven enemy aircraft were counted. On the first day she received three direct hits. Thirteen men were killed and thirty-seven others were badly wounded. The nurses set up a camp hospital, and though they had little equipment, they tended the wounded as best they could. The second officer, Mr J. D. Golightly, sustained a severe injury to his left arm, and Able Seaman Charles P. Barber was wounded in the right thigh. The vessel, to use Captain Capon's own words, 'miraculously escaped with a series of extremely near misses on both sides'. Captain Capon took violent evasive action. He mentioned the 'invaluable assistance' rendered by the Singapore pilot, Captain G. Wright, and his third officer, Mr J. P. Smith,

> both of whom all through coolly kept the attacking aircraft under close observation ... throughout this long and sustained attack the ship's company, one and all, behaved magnificently, each going about his allocated duty with a coolness and spirit of courage unquestionably deserving of the highest praise. It was fortunate that the three direct hits did not seriously damage the ship's fire service, and prompt action and yeoman service by the fire parties under the direction of the Chief Officer, Mr J. L. Dawson, prevented any serious fire developing in the initial critical stage of the attack.

Sister Margaret Hamilton recalled:

> During the bombing there was absolutely no sense of panic or anything. In fact we sang, and sang, and sang, and sang. A lot of wartime songs but mostly 'Waltzing Matilda' which is more or less an Australian national song.

When they said goodbye to Captain Capon and thanked him, he told the nurses that his ship had been in the evacuation of Crete and Greece, but that he had never been in such a tight spot as coming from Singapore. Captain Capon asked the nurses to do two things every day of their lives: 'we were to thank God we were alive, and never to forget the Merchant Navy – as if we could!' Nurse Margaret Hamilton said, 'We knew that it was only by the mercy of God and the good seamanship of the ship's master that we managed to get home.' Captain Capon, who had been made an OBE in the First World War, was made a CBE. Others among his crew received two OBEs, three MBEs, two BEMs and nine Commendations. The *Empire Star* was torpedoed and sunk on 23 October 1942. Captain Capon's lifeboat, overloaded with thirty-nine people aboard, was not seen again.

The third ship that had been hastily pressed into naval service was the Sarawak Steamship's *Vyner Brooke*, still commanded by her peacetime master, Captain R. E. 'Tubby' Burton. The *Vyner Brooke* also sailed on 'Black Friday', 13 February, with 200 aboard, mainly civilians but including sixty-five Australian nurses. The ship had insufficient food and water, but the Australian nurses shared what they had. While heading for the Banka Strait, the vessel was attacked and three of the lifeboats were holed. One of the nurses, Jessie Blanche (Blanchie), recalled that the Captain did well.

> He zigzagged. They came over and bombed us, and missed.... They came back and it is said that they dropped 27 bombs. And eventually one hit us. Right down the funnel. The boys down in the engine room were very badly burned. We were given orders to abandon ship.

Another bomb hit the bridge and the third hit the after part, injuring scores of civilians. The ship sank in 15 minutes, capsizing towards the survivors. More were lost when the enemy pilots strafed those in the water. With the remaining lifeboat overcrowded, many survivors, including the nurses, had to stay in the water hanging on the side of the boat. They were guided towards Muntok beach by a fire lit by earlier survivors, who included Matron Drummond. Her colleague Matron Paschke, who was on one of the rafts, was presumed lost at sea, as were eleven of the sisters.

Captain Burton and others were swept in a different direction and were captured. After the War, Captain Burton was made an MBE; at the same time Captain C. E. Cleaver of the *Larut*, Captain A. B. Durrant of the *Kinta* and Captain W. Lutkin of the *Darvel* were made MBEs. Some of the survivors were reported to have been in the water for several days. In all, twenty-two Australian nurses, plus women and children, ship's crew, naval ratings and about forty British soldiers – some badly wounded – gathered together on the beach.

Mr Sedgeman, the Chief Officer of the *Vyner Brooke*, and five ratings from the *Prince of Wales*, went to a nearby kampong (village) to find food, but the villagers feared the Japanese and would not help. Then Mr Sedgeman and two Royal Naval ratings went further along the beach to contact the Japanese, so that the party could give themselves up. Matron Drummond decided that the civilian women and children should go with them; they were taken prisoner. The others sat on the beach and waited for Sedgeman's return. He returned with a Japanese officer and his troops. The Japanese separated the men from the women and then marched the men along the beach out of sight. They were lined up, facing out to sea, and machine-gunned and then bayoneted. Three who had swum out to sea were machine-gunned; only a naval stoker, Ernest Lloyd, survived, and he was badly injured.

Vivien Bullwinkel wrote:

The Japanese who had gone with the men came back wiping their bayonets. We just looked at each other. We didn't have any emotion about it. I think by this time we'd had shock added to everything else. The Japanese came and stood in front of us and indicated that we should go into the sea. And we walked into the sea with our backs to them. We knew what was going to happen to us ... we didn't talk among ourselves. It was quite silent. We were drained of emotion. There were no tears ... the force of the bullet, together with the waves, knocked me off my feet.

Only Vivien survived. An elderly civilian lady died with the nurses, her husband had been shot with the other men.

The Liverpool-based shipowners, Alfred Holt, owned several fleets which traded to the East. Their ships were among the most heavily built of all merchant ships because they were 'self-insured'. Several were in Singapore when it fell. Their

Gorgon had arrived with convoy MS 1. From 1 February, the ship was continuously bombed as her crew attempted to discharge her cargo. By 11 February, it became obvious that there was no point in continuing and Captain Marriott was ordered to sail. He then had 358 passengers on board and the Asian crew had deserted. The remaining crew got their vessel to sea, and though they were attacked by Japanese bombers six times on 12 February, and were hit three times, they reached Fremantle safely in early March. Two of the bombs caused serious fires, one adjacent to the ammunition store. These were brought under control by the ship's fire parties. The third bomb did not explode and the ship's chief officer, J. Bruce, and two soldiers manhandled it onto the deck and dumped it over the side. In his laconic report, the master said, 'only the extreme manoeuvrability of the vessel saved her'. Captain Roskill, author of *The War at Sea 1939-1945*, says, 'she was saved by the skill and coolness of the man who handled her.'

Though he was believed to have sailed overloaded with refugees (which he safely delivered), Captain J. H. Hendriks-Jansen of Holt's Dutch 'Blauw Pijper' *Phrontis* did not even submit a report! *Phrontis* had arrived on 4 February with a cargo of war materials, and four Fairy Fulmar aircraft on deck. Her master requested permission to go to Batavia to unload the balance of the cargo, but this was refused. On Monday 9 February, the master was given permission to leave, but he berthed and reloaded part of the cargo, including the four aircraft – plus one more – and another eighty passengers. The ship was camouflaged with nets, and after a stressful and exciting voyage, she arrived safely at Tanjong Priok.

The third Blue Funnel liner, the *Talthybius*, was less fortunate. Her European crew, helped by members of the New Zealand Air Force, discharged her cargo of tanks and lorries. On 3 February, as the last lorry was going over the side, the ship was hit by two bombs. The Chinese crew left, leaving the Europeans to fight the fires. As they were brought under control, another salvo punctured the ship's hull in many places. The master, Captain Kent, wrote, 'The European crew worked together cheerfully, and with a will, and I have nothing but praise for their endeavours.' They were helped by members of the Observer Corps. With the help of two harbour tugs, crewed by Europeans, the vessel was moved back alongside, but the ship was not repairable and was abandoned.

On 11 or 12 February, Captain Kent and his crew were allocated the *Ping Wo*, another of the ex-Yangtze river steamers, to make their escape. Again the crew were supplemented by Royal Navy and Royal Australian Navy sailors. They set about coaling and storing the ship, using what they could find in the burning godowns. When this was completed, they sailed, picking up about 195 refugees of several nationalities from the water. They survived several bombing attacks and arrived safely at Batavia on 14 February. At Batavia they again fuelled and stored, before setting off for Fremantle in convoy, and with the disabled Australian destroyer *Vendetta* in tow. The other ships in the convoy were the *Darvel*, and possibly the *Kinta*, and the *Giang Ann* (built in 1888, and probably the oldest ship involved in the evacuation). The HMAS *Yarra* (under Lieutenant Commodore R.

W. Rankin) escorted the convoy part of the way. Because of the *Ping Wo's* tow, the convoy's speed was limited to 4-5 knots. HMAS *Adelaide* took over the escort south of Christmas Island. When the ships encountered bad weather, the tow line parted, but they nonetheless arrived safely at Fremantle on 4 March. One report says that Captain Kent handed over 10,000 ounces of gold that he had carried from Singapore.

Another sailing on 12 February was the *Redang*, which had been put under Straits company management. Captain Rasmussen, her peacetime master, remained in command assisted by his chief officer, Mr Riemise – both were Danes. Straits provided Mr Dean as chief engineer. As so often happened in the retreat, the balance of the manning was made up by a combination of Straits staff and naval ratings. The *Redang* carried seventy-one refugees. On 13 February she was attacked by two Japanese destroyers. Captain Rasmussen survived. In his report he wrote 'I estimate that sixty-two lives were lost during the attack, either killed by splinters, burned to death or drowned ... two young ladies from Mransfield Co's Singapore office were instantaneously killed.' The chief officer and the chief engineer were also killed. Only one lifeboat could be launched and the thirty-two survivors used it to abandon ship.

The *Kuala*, the *Mata Hari* and the *Tien Kwang* were three more ships that sailed on 13 February; their complement of passengers included more nurses. About 600 passengers boarded the *Kuala*, under Captain F. Caithness. Over half of these were women and children, and in addition there were fifty nurses. There were about 300 passengers on the *Tien Kwang*. Before they sailed, they were persistently dive-bombed, and there were many casualties. On 14 February, Captain Caithness sought shelter near Pom Pong Island, together with other ships. They were attacked by about forty Japanese aircraft. The *Kuala* was abandoned when her bridge was hit and the ship caught fire. The bombing and strafing continued all morning. Even when all eleven ships had sunk, the Japanese continued to strafe both those in the water and on shore. Only about 200 who had left Singapore survived. Among those who died was the well-respected British Matron Miss V. M. E. Jones and several of her colleagues. Dr Thompson, a lady doctor, won much praise for treating the wounded. Major Nunn took charge of the organisation at Pom Pong Island, and what he did is said to have 'amounted to genius'. On 14 February, another evacuation ship, the *Kwang Wu*, was attacked. On 18 February, Captain Reynolds arrived with his fishing boat and took off sixty survivors. Lieutenant Commander Terry of the *Repulse* arrived at the *Kwang Wu* to rescue his crew from whom he had in some way become separated in the turmoil. By 19 February, 328 survivors were left on Pom Pong Island. Fifty-eight were from the Public Works Department, there were thirty-five civilians, 175 RAF personnel and sixty ship's crew. These people were all evacuated by Captain Reynolds and four tonkangs (a local coasting vessel). In all, Captain Reynolds, who was a master mariner before he became a planter, is thought to have helped over 2,000 people reach Sumatra. He was awarded an OBE, but was taken prisoner and later executed by the Japanese in 1944. Doctor Thompson and Tunku Mahmood Mohyiddeen were awarded the George Medal, and *The London Gazette* records that 'Mrs. Margaret Henderson Thomson, M.B., Ch.B., of the Malaya Medical Service was awarded the MBE.'

The *Tanjong Pinang*, under Captain Shaw, rescued women and children from the island on 20 February. The little ship was 'not much more than a barge' but it had more than 200 people on board. When the enemy sank the vessel on the following day, only about half of these people got off the ship. Of these, only fifteen to twenty adults struggled ashore.

The *Jarak* was sent to Java with Captain Hooper still in command, with a crew of ratings from the HMS *Repulse*. She sailed before dawn on 13 February, but was attacked and disabled by four enemy warships. She was then attacked by aircraft and the captain gave orders to abandon ship. The survivors rowed to nearby Saya Island where they saw their badly damaged ship drifting nearby. Though the *Jarak* was little short of a wreck, they re-boarded her, and after the engineers had raised steam, re-loaded the injured and made Singkep Island on the night of 16/17 February. There they scuttled their ship. When they arrived in the small port of Dabo, they found other survivors, including those from the *Kuala* and the *Trang*. They secured two prauws and set sail. Captain Hooper navigated his prauw using a 'compass, a small scale chart and a school atlas'. With only a few hundred miles to go to Ceylon, they encountered three Japanese fleet oilers and were taken prisoner. Mr Huntley's boat made it all the way across the Indian Ocean to Colombo. Captain Hooper and his crew were honoured with a DSC and a DCM, and five were mentioned in Despatches.

On 14 February, the HMS *Li Wo*, a shallow-draft Yangtze river steamer, was on passage from Singapore. She was still commanded by Temporary Lieutenant Thomas Wilkinson RNR, her peacetime master, who had served in the Mercantile Marine in the First World War. Before she sailed on 'Black Friday', the British part of her merchant crew was supplemented by nineteen Navy, five Army, two RAF, thirty-four Europeans, ten Malays and six Chinese. Once again, the naval ratings were survivors from the *Repulse* and the *Prince of Wales*. The captain decided to make a dash for the Banka Strait. The ship had already suffered considerable damage in four air attacks when, late in the afternoon of 14 February, she sighted two enemy convoys. The larger of the two convoys had an escort that included a heavy cruiser and several destroyers. Lieutenant Wilkinson sought the backing of his crew and engaged the convoy with the intention of fighting to the last. When all of the *Li Wo*'s 4-inch ammunition was exhausted, the commanding officer decided to ram a ship that they had damaged. The machine gunners on the *Li Wo* were said to have wiped out two guns on the Japanese vessel. After this, the British ship was hit by nine salvoes and, with her ensign still flying and her captain on the bridge, she rolled over to port and sank. At the most, thirteen survived the sinking; one of these was killed on shore and little more than half survived the War as prisoners. This scratch crew of eighty-four was destined to become the most decorated Royal Navy small ship crew in the Second World War. After the War, Lieutenant Wilkinson was awarded a posthumous Victoria Cross. Lieutenant Stanton, the *Li Wo*'s peacetime chief officer, received the DSO, Leading Seaman Thompson the CGM, Leading Seaman Spenser and Able Seaman Spendlove were awarded the DSM. Two officers and four ratings were mentioned in Despatches. Less than a quarter of her crew were from the regular Royal Navy, though the citation suggests that almost all were.

The HMS *Relau* and the HMS *Rantau* were two more Straits ships which left on 13 February. They were also manned by scratch crews, including the company's marine and engineer superintendents and the Singapore chief pilot, Captain C. McAllister. The ships picked up survivors on the way south. As they neared Banka at daybreak, they found that they were in the middle of the Japanese invasion fleets and were seized. They joined the many hundreds of men, women and children who became prisoners of war. Captain McAllister and many others did not survive. On the evening of 14 February, some of the remaining Mansfield and Straits Steamship office staff escaped on an Imperial Airways tender, but were captured off Banka.

In his record of the evacuation of Singapore, Lieutenant H. M. Lindley-Jones says of the troops:

> ... the behaviour of our men and more particularly of the deserters was very often deplorable ... this applies from senior officers to recruits.... No praise was too high for what the Dutch population in Sumatra did for the survivors.

On Sinkep Island, survivors from the *Grasshopper* were told by a brigadier that they should 'stick together', but that night the brigadier and three other officers left! After telling his Australian troops to stay at their posts, General Bennett and two of his staff officers escaped on the night of the surrender and reached Australia. But 'other officers did very good work'. Following days of desperate fighting, British Empire troops surrendered on 15 February 1942. It is said that more than 100,000 became prisoners of war, while thousands more European civilians were interned.

Had it not been for the Merchant Navy, including those who had been hastily signed up in the Royal Naval Reserve, probably 20,000 more people would have been imprisoned or killed by the Japanese. Many of the troops had only been in Singapore for a few days; they, and ratings and non-commissioned officers who survived the sinking of the *Prince of Wales* and the *Repulse*, escaped with their merchant service colleagues and in some cases died with them.

In the third supplement to *The London Gazette* of Friday 20 February 1948, Air Vice-Marshall Sir Paul Maltby says:

> Much credit is due to the Merchant Navy; it rendered the R.A.F. devoted service in bringing into Singapore reinforcements and supplies at a critical time, in

transferring units to the N.E.I., and in evacuating several thousands of personnel from Singapore and later from the N.E.I. This work was done at great hazard in waters exposed to surface, submarine and air attack. A number of ships and seamen were lost in the doing of it. I wish to record our deep appreciation to the masters and crews who did so much for us at such cost to themselves.

Part Two of the Straits Steamship history concludes with the paragraph:

> To close this chapter of the Company's history ... without paying tribute to the Officers and crews of Straits Steamship Company is impossible. Some received medals, but most didn't and yet they carried on against overwhelming odds.... There can be no doubt that they were badly let down by the Authorities ... they served both their Company and Country in the finest traditions of the British Merchant Navy and should never be forgotten.

This could be said of all of the merchant seamen who so magnificently rose to the occasion.

For their part, the Merchant Navy found the military officer class difficult: they often did not wear their badges of rank, but could produce them when they felt that it would benefit them. In the main, these were the people who wrote of their experiences after the War. Equally difficult were some of the 'mems' and 'tuans', who tried to take over what accommodation there was on the rescue ships, who carried ridiculous amounts of luggage, and expected the merchant ships crews to be at their beck and call. In the eyes of the local population, the British had lost so much face that they never re-established their hold over their Asian colonies, so the evacuation marked the beginning of the end of the British Empire.

When Batavia fell to the Japanese, the merchant ships, mainly Dutch and British, again shouldered the evacuation burden. Many of those who were rescued had already fled from Singapore and as they sailed, escapees from Singapore were still arriving. Fifty-seven ships are recorded as sailing from Java between 12 February and 26 February, most, if not all, carried survivors, including the liner *Orcades*, which carried 3,768 troops and evacuees.

The ships that sailed in convoys from Tanjong Priok in February were:

SJ 1, Batavia 12 Feb., Colombo 21 Feb. – *Anglo Indian* , *Banjoe Wangi (Du)*, *Batavia (Du)*, *City of Canterbury*, *City of Pretoria* towing HM submarine *Rover*, *Clan Alpine*, *Halizones*, *Madura*, *Malancha* towing HM destroyer *Isis*, *Rijn (Du)*, *Van der Capelle (Du)*, *Van Swoll (Du)*, *Yuen Sang*.

SJ 2, Batavia 15 Feb., Colombo 22 Feb. – *Empire Star* (for Fremantle), *Plancious (Du?)* with 970 evacuees.

SJ 3, Tanjong Priok 17 Feb. for Fremantle – *Darvel*, *Giang Ann* and *Ping Wo* (towing HMAS *Vendetta*); for Colombo – *Krian? Oriskany* and *Resang*.

SM 2, Tanjong Priok 19 Feb. for Fremantle 28 Feb. – *Cable Enterprise, Whangpu* – both independent from position 8° s, 104° e; for Tjilatjap – *Wuchang*.

SJ 4, Tanjong Priok 19 Feb., dispersed 21 Feb. – *Erling Brovig, Generaal Michiels, Generaal van Geen, Generaal van Swieten, Lee Sang, Modasa* and *Stanmore*.

SJ 5, Batavia 20 Feb., dispersed 22 Feb. – *Angby, Filleigh, Hai Lee (Nor), Jalakrisna, Lulworth Hill, Silverlarch* and *Yoma*.

SM 3, Batavia 20 Feb. for Fremantle – *Adratus, Marella* and *Phrontis* (Du); for Tjilatjap – *City of Manchester* and *Prominent*.

S 4, Batavia 23 Feb., dispersed 25 Feb. – *Deucalion, Perak, Seirstad* and *Springdale*.

SJ 6, Batavia 21 Feb., dispersed 23 Feb. – *Orcades* with 3,768 troops and evacuees.

SJ 7, Batavia 22 Feb., dispersed 25 Feb. – *Ah Kwang, Cedardale, Fu Kwang, Ho Kwang, Ning Kwang* and *Tso Kwang*.

According to Apprentice Ralph Armstrong of the *Pinna*, who was 'acting, unpaid, 2nd Mate of the *Ho Kwang*' they sailed from Batavia on 17 February, and all reached Ceylon. He says that the others were *Ah Kwang, Ee Kwang* and *Ning Kwang*.

SJ 8, Batavia 26 Feb., for Colombo – *Ashridge* (Wing Hong Co., Hong Kong) – alone.

The Dutch ship *Khoen Hoea* sailed from Tjilatjap on 26 February, with Lieutenant Commander Frank Man RNVR in command. He said 'about fifteen ships sailed independently for Fremantle and Ceylon on that day,' there was 'no convoy of any kind, in fact no warship of any description was seen.' *Abbekerk* is reported as sailing from Tjilatjap on 27 February with 1,500.

The British Merchant Navy

In 1939, Britain's merchant fleet was by far the largest in the world, with ships registered in all parts of the Empire. Various sources put the total number of British vessels at around 9,000, but only about half were ocean-going vessels of more than 2,000 gross registered tons. Many ships were twenty or more years old and a considerable proportion had been laid up for years because of the slump. In that time, seamen who had jobs hung onto them, while others trudged around the shipping offices looking for work. Master mariners signed on as able seamen and quartermasters, and many left the industry altogether.

Until after the First World War, the service had been known as the Mercantile Marine. In 1919, a standard uniform was authorized. Later it was renamed the British Merchant Navy, with the sovereign becoming Master of the Merchant Navy and the Fishing Fleets. It never was a navy, but the title was probably selected because of a problem that had occurred during the First World War. Captain Charles Fryatt, Master of the railway packet *Brussels,* had both evaded and attempted to ram U-boats. When the Germans finally captured him they held that, as he was a civilian, he was found guilty of being a *franc-tireur* and was sentenced and executed the same evening. In 1919, his body was exhumed and brought back to England; after a memorial service he was reburied at Dovercourt, Harwich.

Both the quality of the ships and the conditions of employment varied widely. At best, seamen were given continuous employment, decent accommodation and food. At the worst, living conditions were disgusting and food was inadequate; wages were stopped as soon as a ship sank. It was not until 1941 that this practice began to be phased out. For the unfortunate men on the tramp ships, conditions never really improved.

In addition to its peacetime role, which became essential for the nation's survival, the merchant fleet would be needed to move war materials and troops, and to support evacuations and invasions. At the outbreak of the Second World War, the total strength of the British Merchant Navy was only 157,000; about two thirds of the crews were from mainland Britain, with the balance coming from the Commonwealth and other countries.

Throughout this book I have referred to the men of the merchant fleets, but a small number of extremely brave women served on both British and Allied vessels. Several of these were awarded medals. One was Victoria Drummond, a god-daughter of Queen Victoria, who served as an engineer officer. Miss Drummond was awarded the MBE and the Lloyd's War Medal for Bravery at Sea for single-handedly remaining at the controls of the cargo ship *Bonita* during an attack by a German bomber. She also volunteered for service at the Normandy landings.

In peacetime, the merchant fleet brought 67 million tons of cargo into the UK annually. This included 22 million tons of food, 28½ million tons of raw materials and 9½ million tons of oil fuel. This met more than half of the country's meat requirements, 70 per cent of its cheese and sugar, nearly 80 per cent of fruits, about 90 per cent of cereals and fats and all of the oil fuel. The ships brought in all the tobacco and tea, and much of the bread flour that became so important once the War started. It is difficult to underestimate the importance of 'a cup of char, a sarnie and a fag' to the beleaguered people. One of the principal strategies of the Axis was to attack shipping bound for the UK, restricting British industry and starving the nation into submission. In order to deal with the extreme shortages, the Ministry of Food instituted a system of rationing.

Merchant ships are commanded by a master. By 1939, a foreign-going ship carried a minimum of three mates (also called chief, second and third officers); six or more engineers; a deck department of eight under a boatswain and a carpenter; another eight ratings in the Engine Room under a donkeyman; a similar sized catering department; and a single radio officer. There were usually between two and four apprentices or cadets. During the War, most carried two extra radio officers and about eight or more gunners from the Royal Artillery or the Royal Navy. On British ships, these DEMS gunners were signed on as 'sailors' and were under command of the master, one of the mates being the gunnery officer. On US ships, the Armed Guard were separate from the ship's manning and were under the charge of their own officer.

Uniform was only worn by the officers on foreign-going ships. Petty officers and ratings usually wore dungaree trousers and shirts, with an old jacket in colder weather. They wore a wide variety of headgear from flat caps to hand-made nautical caps. Few on coastal cargo ships wore any kind of uniform. Earlier in the century, some coastal masters had worn a bowler hat!

Ships leaving the UK signed on a crew at their departure port. With the exception of the master, the first mate, chief engineer and the apprentices, the crew of a tramp would have been sourced in this way. In Merchant Navy slang, they were known as a 'crowd' as in, 'she had a Glasgow crowd'. The ships of the better companies were crewed mostly, or even entirely, by 'company men'. Either way, they signed Articles of Agreement which called for them to serve for a period of two years, or until they next returned to the UK. The 'Articles' set out their working conditions and the minimum amount of food they were to receive each month, known as the 'Board of Trade whack'. Coasters and ships that called at the UK frequently signed six monthly running agreements (RA), rather than signing off each time they reached the UK.

Ratings and petty officers were paid overtime for hours worked in excess of 64 hours a week, though there were exceptions for days of arrival and sailing. Officers, engineers and apprentices were not usually paid overtime; this often resulted in the apprentices working considerably longer than the basic hours. Time spent on boat and fire drills or cleaning accommodation did not count towards the 64 hours. A seaman had to provide his own clothing, while officers had to buy uniforms for tropical, temperate and arctic service. The deck officers also bought their own sextants.

During the War, the Allies built a number of standard ships. The tramp type cargo ships built in America, Canada and the UK were based on British designs.

The British had begun developing 'Economy' ships in the early 1930s, though elements of the design came from much earlier. These were (very) basic ships that could carry up to 10,000 tons (including fuel, stores, crew etc.) at a speed of 10 knots. The motor ships consumed 10 tons of diesel oil per day, and for that reason they were sometimes known as 'ten, ten, tens'. The steamers initially burnt about 25 tons of coal per day, but with improved designs the steamers' fuel consumption was reduced to below 20 tons per day. The first ships built by the Americans – at British expense – were sixty Oceans, based on the North Sands design (a shipyard on the north-east coast of England).

When the Americans decided to build a similar sized ship to meet their own needs, they first thought of the 'Hog Islander', an American First World War design. A member of the Thompson family, British shipbuilders, made the hazardous trip across the North Atlantic with plans of the *Dorrington Court*, which his shipyard had built in 1938. That design was somewhat modified and used for the *Empire Liberty* of 1941. After some hesitation, the Americans adopted the design, though they changed the layout in a number of ways. These included a single accommodation block and a number of hull modifications that are less obvious. They chose a triple expansion steam engine for propulsion.

In all, the Americans delivered 2,710 of these Liberty ships. One hundred and seventy-seven of them were transferred to the British Registry under the Lend Lease agreement. They became known as 'Sam boats' because they were given names prefixed Sam.

They were popular with British crews because their accommodation was better than the equivalent British or Canadian ships. The Canadians also built ships of the North Sands design. Those destined for the British were Fort ships, and those that were to sail under the Canadian flag were Park ships. Thousands of Victory ships and T2 tankers were mostly manned by the US Merchant Marine. Many smaller vessels, such as the thirty-one N3-S-A1 coasters (popularly known as Jeeps) and T1-M-BT1/2 coastal tankers, were built in America. These and others were sailed across the wild Atlantic by British crews in time for the D-Day landings, where they joined US-built salvage ships.

Most of the ships built in UK shipyards for British Government account were given Empire prefixes. In this case they are not of any one type, ranging from passenger vessels to tugs. Three examples of cargo ships are shown in the picture section – *Derrycunihy*, *Empire Flag* and *La Pampa*. The most comprehensive list is given in the Mitchell and Sawyer book *The Empire Ships*. The same authors have written a number of other books, including *The Liberty Ships* and *The Oceans, the Forts and the Parks*. There are photographs of other ship types later in this book.

The Norwegian Campaign and the Fall of the Low Countries

At the outbreak of war, the Admiralty requisitioned over 100 vessels, including forty-seven to act as Armed Merchant Cruisers (fifteen were lost). Others were commandeered for services as Ocean Boarding Vessels, tugs, salvage vessels, colliers and transports. In the first few days of September 1939, the Army took forty-seven vessels to service the British Expeditionary Force. According to Winser, more than 2,000 vessels were attached to the BEF in the first ten months of the War. The Air Ministry requisitioned a few small ships to act as Barrage Balloon ships. Many others were needed to maintain the Empire and cross trades, the latter being voyages between two foreign ports. The *Athenia* was the first merchant ship to be sunk on 3 September 1939, the day that war was declared. On average, over fifty British, Allied and Neutral ships were sunk each month from then until April 1940. Then the rate doubled; from February to May 1941 it averaged 130 per month

In Europe, the winter of 1939/40 was the coldest in living memory. The Finns were fighting for their lives against Russia in the Winter War, with little more than their famed *sisu* to keep them going. By February, the Gulfs of Bothnia and Finland were covered with fast ice and most of the Baltic Sea was encumbered with pack ice. The British and French busied themselves with thinking up unrealistic schemes to 'deny the Germans possession of the Baltic' and 'to send a relief force to assist the Finns'. There has been speculation since that the real intention was for most of the force supposedly destined for Finland to remain in the Narvik area of neutral Norway, from where Swedish iron ore was shipped. With a Polish contingent, the British and French landed at several points in Norway.

On 9 April, German troops captured the British cargo ships *Blythmoor*, *Mersington Court*, *North Cornwall*, *Riverton* and *Romanby*, which were waiting to load iron ore at Narvik. The *Romanby* was alongside the jetty at Narvik and was destroyed when the jetty was blown up; her crew of thirty-eight were interned in Sweden. The light cruiser *Effingham* sank the *Riverton* when she was moored at an outlying pier; her crew of thirty-three were also interned in Sweden. The next day, Royal Navy destroyers sank the *Blythmoor*, and on the following day they sank eight German cargo ships that were waiting off the port.

Captain John Pinkney of the *Fylingdale*, a small tramp owned by Headlams, was made Commodore of the convoy HN 25. *Fylingdale* and thirty-nine ships were ordered by the Admiralty to proceed to sea, without an escort, on 9 April. The master showed 'great enterprise, determination and skill' in guiding the convoy safely through Norwegian waters to meet the escorts; all arrived safely in the UK on 12 April. Captain Pinkney was made an OBE.

On 11 April, the first expeditionary force sailed from Scotland in the liners *Batory* (Polish), *Chrobry* (Polish), *Empress of Australia*, *Monarch of Bermuda* and *Reina del Pacifico*, with twenty-two warship escorts. Admiral Layton, the naval commander, decided that it was too risky to take his destroyers into Namsos to effect the landing, so he decided to send the troops and supplies in on the *Chrobry*. Many of the soldiers were aboard the *Empress of Australia* and much time was wasted transferring. The *Chrobry*, accompanied by HMS *Vanoc*, got into Namsos just before sunrise on 17 April. In the hurry to get away before the German bombers arrived, the soldiers landed without much of their kit, but they were dispersed before a reconnaissance aircraft arrived. The liner *Orion* sailed alone to Norway on 14 April. On 17 April, the unescorted convoy NSM 1 sailed from Scapa Flow with the cargo ships *Balham*, *Blackheath*, *Charlbury*, *Inverarder*, *Lochee*, *Lombardy* and *Macgregor Laird*.

Captain William Reid, the Master of the Watts Watts ship *Blackheath*, was made an OBE for showing 'courage, resource and fine seamanship in operations on the Norwegian coast, when the Blackheath was employed as a stores carrier for the military force operating from Namsos.' Nothing more is said about the nature of the services. *Blackheath* had arrived at Harstad on 3 June in convoy, and continued to discharge alongside while under attack.

Another master who was similarly honoured was Captain Francis Butcher of the *Balteako*, a short sea trade ship owned by the United Baltic Corporation. At the same time, Mr Robert Towns, her chief engineer, was commended. *Balteako* had carried Admiralty stores to Harstad, and while discharging she was frequently bombed. Her superstructure amidships was damaged and distorted and she was holed near the waterline in thirty-six places. The master beached her and the chief engineer plugged the holes. The ship was lying at a steep angle, so she was moved to a more level beach and more lasting repairs were made. The master and chief engineer saved the ship, and with the assistance of HM trawlers, she was re-floated and brought safe home. In the same action, John Smith, Assistant Steward of the *Balteako*, was awarded the British Empire Medal. He and a naval rating tried to save the injured bowman of HMS *Delight*'s motor-boat, which was alongside *Balteako* drawing provisions. With the raid in progress they reached the motorboat before their own skiff sank, but the man was dead.

The small packet ships *St Sunniva* and *St Magnus* left Aberdeen at 0430 on 19 April, escorted by destroyers *Hesperus* and *Jackal*, who had sailed from Scapa Flow at 1400 the previous day. They were joined at sea by the *Cedarbank*, escorted by the destroyer *Javelin*, which left Scapa Flow at 1100 on 19 April. At the same time, *Hesperus* was detached and returned to Scapa Flow. At 0427 on 21 April, *Jackal* attacked a submarine contact. Before *Cedarbank* could unload her cargo of anti-aircraft guns, artillery, mortars, transport and Bren carriers, she was sunk by *U-26* in 62°49'N, 04°10'E. Her crew of fourteen and one gunner were lost. The escorting destroyers *Jackal* and *Javelin* were unable to inflict damage on *U-26*, which was returning from delivering supplies to Trondheim. *St Magnus* and *St Sunniva* arrived at Aandalsnes safely that evening with their 600 troops. The *Javelin*, escorting *St Magnus* and carrying the survivors from the *Cedarbank*, arrived at Kirkwall from Aalesund at 2230 on 23 April.

On 26 April, the troopship *Franconia*, sailing from Narvik to the Clyde without an escort, was attacked by a German submarine at 0105. The destroyers *Janus* and *Antelope* were sent to assist. When it was found that *Franconia* had escaped damage, the destroyers were recalled to Scapa Flow. It was not until 29 April, two weeks after the troops' arrival, that there were the first signs of a thaw. On that day the *Empire Ability* discharged the Assault Landing Craft and Motor Landing Craft that she carried. When the *Mashobra* arrived on 10 May, her boats were to be used, but these were reported to be unfit. This was excusable seeing the hard work the *Mashobra* had recently carried out. She had only been commissioned as a 'Fleet Air Arm depot ship' on 4 May.

On 13 May, the Irish Guards embarked in the Polish *Chrobry* which had brought three army tanks from England for the Bodo Force. On 14/15 May, while on passage, with *Stork* and *Wolverine* as escort, the *Chrobry* was bombed and set on fire. Four senior army officers were killed and thirteen of her crew lost their lives, of whom three were British. The troops were brought back to Harstad, but their equipment was lost.

On the night of 24/25 May, orders were received for the evacuation of Northern Norway. As a result 'a number of large liners were despatched from the United Kingdom, together with three store ships and one horse ship.' In Harstad, troops were moved by the destroyers, while at Skaanland, Narvik and Sorreisa, embarkation was by means of puffer (a small steam coaster) to destroyers lying off. The destroyers then went about 70 miles to load the liners, which anchored in the Fjords.

On 29 May, the *Mashobra* had to be beached as the result of bombing attacks, becoming a total loss. The *Oleander* was sunk and the disabled trawlers were destroyed. The smaller landing craft were scuttled.

The convoys assembled during the night of the 7/8 June. The *Monarch of Bermuda*, *Batory*, *Sobieski*, *Franconia*, *Lancastria* and *Georgic* were with *Vindictive*. The *Oronsay*, *Ormonde*, *Arandora Star*, *Royal Ulsterman*, *Ulster Prince*, *Ulster Monarch* and *Duchess of York* were escorted by cruisers *Coventry* and *Southampton*, plus the destroyers *Beagle*, *Delight*, *Fame*, *Firedrake* and *Havelock*. The destroyers *Firedrake*, *Fame*, *Beagle* and *Walker* sustained minor damage from near misses of air bombing on the 12 June. The boarding vessel, *Vandyck*, should have been with this group, but she arrived after it had left and was sunk by bombing off Andenes. Temporary Lieutenant Commander E. Watson RNR, Refrigerating Engineer D. Elias and five ratings were lost. The rest of the crew of 152 were able to row ashore and were taken prisoner; four died during their imprisonment.

A convoy departed Tromso at 1700 on 7 June with British tankers *Oil Pioneer* and *Yewmount* and the small ammunition ships *Arbroath* and *Ngakoa*, together with several Norwegian vessels. They were escorted by anti-submarine trawler *Juniper*. Naval whalers met the *Yewmount*, *Arbroath* and *Ngakoa* later on 7 June, and towed the *Ngakoa* (a British-owned schuyt) to Scapa Flow. A slow convoy of eight British and five French merchant ships left Harstad at 2200 on 7 June. They were the British *Acrity*, *Blackheath*, *Conch*, *Coxwold*, *Cromarty Firth*, *Harmattan*, *Oligarch* and *Theseus*, and the French *Alberte Leborgne*, *Enseigne Maurice Préchac*, *Paul-Emile Javary*, *Saint Clair* and *Vulcain*. The convoy was escorted by the anti-submarine trawlers *St Cathan* and *Loch Monteith*, which were joined by the destroyer *Arrow*, the sloop *Stork*, and the trawlers *Eldorado*, *Newhaven*, *Shandwick*, *Strathderry* and *Strathdevon*.

The convoy 'Greek', consisting of the British steamers *Heron*, *Marina* and *Balteako*, and the French steamers *Enseigne Maurice Préchac*, *Vulcain* and *Paul-Emile Javary*, escorted by the anti-submarine trawlers *St Elstan* and *Wastwater*, left Harstad on 5 June. The *Vulcain* arrived at Scapa Flow at 2220 on 7 June; the *Paul-Emile Javary* also arrived on that day. The rest of the convoy arrived safely at Scapa Flow at 1740 on 10 June. With them were the *Marina* and the *Dallington Court*.

On 8 June, the British tanker *Oil Pioneer* and escorting trawler *Juniper* were attacked and sunk off Jan Mayan Island by the German heavy cruiser *Admiral Hipper* and the four destroyers of the Juno Operation. The master and nineteen crew of the tanker were lost. Twenty-five survivors and four from *Juniper* were picked up by the German ships. Also on 8 June, the unescorted troopship *Orama* (Orient Line) was sunk by the *Admiral Hipper*, the *Hans Lody* and the destroyer *Karl Galster*. Her companion, the hospital ship *Atlantis*, was not molested. The troop ship had been bound from Scapa to Narvik; twenty of her 297 men and two gunners were killed, and all but two of the crew of the trawler were lost.

On 8 June, General Dietl retook Narvik, and on 10 June, the last Norwegian forces in Norway surrendered. The French Béthouart Division was brought back to Scotland, from where they returned to France in two convoys that sailed from Greenock on 13 June and arrived off Brest the next day. By this time, troops were being evacuated from France in Operation Aerial. Four hundred and fifty men of the Lovat Scouts were landed on the Faroe Islands on 25 May 1940 by the *Ulster Prince*. This ship was later wrecked off Nauplia, Greece, while evacuating troops, and destroyed by Stuka dive bombers on 25 April 1941.

While British, French and Polish troops were unsuccessfully trying to prevent the German occupation of Narvik, the Germans were overrunning the neutral Low Countries in what they called Blitzkrieg – lightening war.

Dotterel was a cargo coaster built in 1936 for trade to the near Continent. On 9 May 1940, when under the command of Captain I. Green, the ship was loading near Rotterdam. During the night, the master woke to the sound of gunfire. He went out on deck and realised that the port was being attacked; at first light paratroopers began dropping and aircraft started mining the channels. Captain Green destroyed the ship's secret papers and prepared the 12-pounder gun for destruction. With the chief engineer, he made plans to destroy the engines and scuttle the ship. To confuse fifth columnists, the crew made it look as if the ship intended to remain in port. They stayed alongside throughout the day as the battle raged around them.

Just before noon on 11 May, the attack eased and the crew cut the mooring lines; the *Dotterel* steamed at full speed down the waterway on the ebb tide. On reaching the Hook of Holland, the master received instructions to proceed to the port of Ijmuiden to evacuate British citizens. They reached Ijmuiden late that evening and berthed close to the lock gates, where the ship was prepared to receive 150 refugees who were to be housed in the cargo holds. The ship had no food for this number. At 1800, the *Dotterel* moved to another berth to embark her passengers, where she was repeatedly attacked by aircraft. The last refugees boarded at 0130 on 18 May and the ship sailed for Harwich. She was escorted into the port by a destroyer. The passengers were disembarked and Captain Green delivered several packages of diamonds to the naval authorities. On 7 March 1941, while on a voyage from London to Dublin, *Dotterel* was one of five vessels attacked and sunk by E-boats. Eight of her crew died.

After unloading cargo at Brussels, the *City of Brussels* was attacked in the evening by two enemy aircraft. The gunlayer, Elliot Allard, opened fire with a 12-pounder. The first shot, bursting between the two machines, caused one of the aircraft to shoot up into the air and then to fall to the ground. The second aircraft, obviously damaged, rapidly lost height and was reported also to have fallen. The gunlayer was supported by his loaders, Firemen Webster and Gallacher. The master and officers, by their unfailing courage and confidence during the attack, inspired the whole crew of the vessel. Allard was awarded the BEM and the two firemen were commended, as were the master and the two mates.

Northern Coast was attacked by enemy aircraft on two occasions. On both occasions, Captain Quirk, the officers, and all the crew behaved with the greatest courage and coolness under most trying conditions. Captain William Quirk, Master, was made an OBE, while Second Officer David Flack and Gunner Henry William Donald were commended.

M/V *Stork*, unloading at Boulogne, was continuously bombed and machine-gunned off that port. In the middle of a dive-bombing attack Gunlayer Missen, who had been on continuous duty at the ship's 12-pounder, succeeded in hitting a German bomber. The machine, on fire and out of control, swerved away, one of its crew using a parachute, falling into the sea. Further continuous raids, with dive-bombing and mine-dropping attacks, went on above and around *Stork* till her Master decided to try and save her. He was successful in this, and the ship eventually reached Southampton. Gunlayer Missen showed persistent devotion to duty and entire disregard of personal safety, and successfully replied to continuous attacks during three days and nights.

Gunlayer Missen was awarded the BEM and Captain Carey and Gunners Maryson and Kent were commended.

When the LNER packet *Malines* escaped from Rotterdam, she carried 178 British people, mostly women and children. She was attacked en route, but reached Tilbury on the next day.

On 12 May, the Master of Holt's *Phrontis* (Dutch) received orders from a director of her owners in Amsterdam to sail as soon as possible. They later intercepted a radio message to all Dutch ships, purporting to come from their owners, saying that they were not to sail. Captain de Boer ignored this, assuming that it had come from the Germans or Dutch Nazis. *Phrontis* was sent to Ijmuiden, where a British ship was loading prisoners of war. They did likewise and left Ijmuiden on 13 May with 800 POWs and forty officers, plus an armed guard of fifty-six Dutch naval ratings and a number of civilians. They were told that they would be escorted by two French destroyers, but the promised escort 'left at full speed'. Another of Holt's Dutch ships, the *Perseus*, was one of three Dutch merchant ships that carried the Dutch gold reserve to the UK. Hours before the Netherlands fell on 14 May 1940, the Dutch merchant ship *Bodegraven* left Ijmuiden. Among those she saved were eighty Jewish children, who had been brought to the ship by Gertruda Wijsmuller-Meyer. En route, the ship was machine gunned by German aircraft, but she reached Liverpool safely. *Bodegraven* is remembered as the last of the kinder transports – though this name is more generally applied to the trains that carried these children to safety.

Operation Dynamo – Dunkirk

The 'miracle' of the Dunkirk evacuation was well known to those who were alive in 1940. The accepted version is that all 338,226 members of the British Expeditionary Force were saved from the beaches near Dunkirk by the Royal Navy and an armada of 'little ships' who volunteered for the task. Churchill described the rescue of 'every last man' of the BEF as a 'miracle of deliverance'. There is no doubt that these two groups performed magnificently, but, as with so many 'miracles', the story includes some myths. One was that only Royal Naval vessels and the 'little ships' were involved; the other was that all of the BEF were evacuated. In fact, almost as many troops were left in France, most to be evacuated in the following three weeks by merchant ships. Certainly the Navy rescued the majority from Dunkirk, and it fell to the various admirals to organise all of the evacuations, but merchant ships carried more than 90,000 troops to safety. About three quarters of these were saved by railway steamers, ferries and excursion ships (generally described as 'packets'). The rest were carried by cargo vessels, coasters, tugs and barges. A further 5,548 stretcher cases were moved by other railway steamers acting as hospital carriers. In addition, the Navy operated Dutch schuyts and British paddle steamers; the paddle steamers were still manned partly by their peacetime crews and civilian volunteers. The private yachts were only involved in the final days of the operation and brought few troops back to the UK. One third of the rescued were French.

When the order to begin the evacuation was given, the hospital carriers *Isle of Guernsey* and *Worthing* were already alongside in Dunkirk awaiting casualties. *King Orry* and *Mona's Queen* were sailing as leave transports. *Mona's Queen* was first to leave with 1,312 troops at 2000 on 26 May. When she left the berth, the *Maid of Orleans* went alongside with 12,000 gallons of canned fresh water. *Canterbury* moored outside of the *Maid of Orleans* and began loading. She sailed for Dover with 1,269 troops at 0320 on 27 May: At about the same time the *Archangel* and the *Biarritz* left Dover, escorted by the destroyer *Verity*. All three were damaged by shell fire from the French coast. *Biarritz* and *Verity* suffered casualties and *Biarritz* put back to Dover for repairs. *Archangel* was unable to make Dunkirk as she had insufficient fuel. *Mona's Isle*, acting as a naval transport with 1,281 troops on board, was attacked both from the coast and by six aircraft.

Twenty-three soldiers were killed and sixty were wounded. The *Isle of Thanet* and the *King Orry* were also attacked, and there were casualties on the damaged *King Orry*. Around this time, and later, a number of merchant seamen of all ranks have gaps in their records of service possibly because they were serving on board vessels that had been requisitioned by the Navy.

The *Queen of the Channel* was one of the excursion steamers that had been requisitioned to carry troops. On 27 May, she was ordered to Dunkirk, berthing at the East Pier at 2000. After she had loaded about fifty troops, the German gunners began shelling the pier and she was ordered to move. Captain O'Dell anchored his vessel about three-quarters of a mile off, and launched four of her boats to ferry more soldiers from the beach. Two hundred were saved, but one of the boats, and its crew, was lost.

At 2300 she again went alongside the East Pier and loaded another 700 men, sailing at 0255 on 28 May. As it was already twilight, the troops were sent below, and shortly afterwards the vessel was attacked by a single aircraft. Three or four bombs straddled the ship; one near miss broke her back. There were no casualties among the troops, but the ship was sinking; having lost another lifeboat in the attack, there were insufficient boats for those on board.

The elderly coastal tramp, *Dorrien Rose*, had already had an eventful trip to France and was approaching the beaches to ground and load more troops. This cannot have been an appealing prospect as many of the merchant ships who were already beached there were under constant attack. Captain W. Thompson saw that the *Queen of the Channel* was in trouble and, after a short discussion with Captain O'Dell, went to her aid. To prevent either vessel listing dangerously, the ships were secured bow to bow, and in 35 minutes, the wounded, the equipment and the rest of the troops were transferred. With more than 1,000 people aboard (her usual crew being thirteen) the *Dorrien Rose* made for the Dover.

After discharging the troops, the coaster again set sail for Dunkirk. En route, she struck a piece of submerged wreckage, but the crew made temporary repairs and arrived on the morning of 30 May. The master reported:

> The prospect was far from pleasing, as the last ten miles to the port were littered with sunken and blazing ships. Bombers were paying us frequent visits. The port lay under a pall of oily smoke and flames. There was no one to look to for instructions so we poked into the harbour. Someone ashore gestured us alongside a battered wall.

Masters had to be especially alert as fifth columnists were at work everywhere, giving false instructions. During the next two hours 'in which it seemed there were always bombers overhead' the ship loaded 600 troops. She sailed at 1230, landing her passengers at Folkestone that evening.

The vessel was then put to anchor to make temporary repairs to her boilers. Meanwhile, the Germans dropped six magnetic mines around her, which the minesweepers detonated. The *Dorrien Rose* was then ordered to Newhaven, where she arrived on Sunday 2 June. The crew had been at work for six days with very little rest. Her engineers had had no rest at all as they coaxed the old ship's boilers and engines to give that little bit more, to ensure the survival of all on board. Captain Thompson, Mr T. O'Hanlon, the mate, and Mr B. Murphy, the chief engineer, received the DSC; Gunner W. Watson RN and Firemen W. Barnett OS, A. Gibson and J. O'Rawe AB were awarded the DSM. Boatswain P. McFadden, Second Engineer Mr J. Steward, Cook T. Barnett and Firemen J. Upperton AB, C. Barnett OS, Ali Khan and Abdul Mohammed were mentioned in Despatches. It can't be often that every member of a ship's crew is awarded a decoration!

The *Worthtown*, a coastal collier, had been sent to Boulogne with army stores. She was under attack from the moment she arrived, so her master took her to sea, where she was attacked by two Heinkels; her gunlayer shot down one. The bombed vessel was then brought alongside at Dunkirk, where they were incessantly bombed. Eventually the vessel sank after being set on fire. Throughout, the two gunners stuck to their guns. Three hundred and fifty British troops were waiting to board the vessel. After nightfall, Captain Thomas led them, and, one assumes, his crew, 4 miles away to shelter among the sand dunes. Next morning, they filed back to the port, from where they were taken back to England by a destroyer. Captain Thomas was made an MBE for 'fine gallantry'; Gunner Yates and Gunlayer Jensen were awarded the BEM.

Yewdale, another small steam coaster, and the motor vessel *Sequacity*, set off from the Downs on 27 May with orders for Dunkirk. During the night, *Yewdale* picked up five survivors from a raft, who told Captain Jones that Dunkirk had been occupied that morning; because of this, and because *Sequacity* needed to make repairs, they returned to England. They were attacked by German aircraft, which, despite being seen off by a British aircraft, damaged the *Sequacity* to such an extent that she sank at 1030 on the morning of 28 May. *Yewdale* rescued the crew, and took them to Deal. By the evening, more than 130 vessels had been assembled to sail for Dunkirk. The Cruiser *Calcutta*, twenty destroyers and an assortment of coasters and many 'little ships' were given the task of loading troops directly from the beach.

The coaster *Abukir* was managed by the General Steam Navigation Company (GSNC) for the MOWT. The ship had been built for GSNC in 1920 and sold onto an Egyptian company. She had shipped army stores to Ostend. For the return voyage she embarked a capacity load of over 200 passengers, including women and children, and six priests. After she sailed late on 27 May, she was bombed 'incessantly for one and a half hours', but was not hit; fire was returned by the ship's sole Lewis gun. At 0115 on 28 May, a U-boat fired two torpedoes at the *Abukir* – both missed. The master attempted to ram the submarine, but his ship lacked sufficient speed. The U-boat fired two more torpedoes. One hit the little ship amidships; she burst into flames, broke in two and sank within a minute, taking many with her. The Germans machine-gunned survivors in the water and 'many were killed, including the Chief Officer'. Captain Rowland Woolfenden was made an MBE; Second Officer Vere Rust was commended.

At Deal, the *Yewdale* stored and topped up with fresh water. She returned to Dunkirk with the smaller motor ships *Beal* and *Bullfinch* (GSNC). They anchored off the beach at about 0400 on 29 May and used their lifeboats to ferry troops from the shore. One of the *Yewdale*'s seamen, George McKenzie, aged 16, did great work teaching the soldiers how to row. Later, the Royal Navy helped with the flat-bottomed motor launches that had been transported by *Clan MacAlister* (see below), but George McKenzie 'retained his command'. At about 1500 the bombing became serious, and at 1600 *Yewdale* was ordered to leave; by this time she had taken aboard some 900 troops.

When the *Bullfinch* arrived, Captain Buxton was ordered to run his ship aground to enable the troops to board. He must have had considerable misgivings about beaching his ship intentionally; 1,400 (elsewhere 713) troops boarded the little coaster. The ship could not re-float until 1815, and almost broached on the rising tide. She was attacked twice on her homeward journey. The master had given permission for a Sergeant Head, who had brought one of two Bren guns aboard, to organise makeshift anti-aircraft defences. The guns under his charge succeeded in shooting down a plane in each attack. When they reached Ramsgate, the Sergeant 'walked ashore and was lost in the crowd', but he was later located and decorated.

All but one of the 640 troops on board the destroyer *Wakeful* drowned when the ship was torpedoed; many of the crew were rescued. The destroyer *Grafton* was torpedoed by the U-boat *U-62*, breaking her back and killing her captain and three others.

Fenella, under Captain W. Cubbon, belonged to the Isle of Man Steam Packet Company. She was told to bunker before going to Dunkirk. As there seemed no prospect of getting oil at Dover, and with the officers and crew keen to make the trip to Dunkirk, the master and chief engineer decided to sail with the bunkers they had on board. *Fenella* arrived off the port at 1300 on 29 May, but because of a bombing raid she was unable to enter the harbour immediately. As soon as possible, she berthed on the East Jetty and loaded troops throughout the afternoon, but with over 600 troops aboard, including stretcher cases, she was wrecked by several bombs. The troops were disembarked from the doomed ship, but the ship's gunners and two army Bren gunners kept up fire, until ordered to abandon the vessel. After he had checked that no one remained on the *Fenella*, the master joined the others on the *Crested Eagle*. Unfortunately she was also bombed and set on fire. This second attack caused a large number of casualties and sixteen of the *Fenella*'s crew were killed.

One of the few deep-sea ships involved was Clan Line's *Clan MacAlister*, which had arrived on 29 May with eight assault craft. Because of her deep draft, the vessel was anchored well clear of the beaches. While she was discharging *ALC 4*, the destroyer *Vanquisher* passed at speed, causing the *Clan* to roll. The assault craft crashed down on *ALC 18*, which was afloat alongside, making both craft unfit for service. The other six, and one towed across by the *City of Christchurch*, transported several thousand troops between them. *Clan MacAlister* then started loading troops, but was attacked and set on fire. The destroyer *Malcolm* took off some of the troops, and the wounded crew members; the *Pangbourne* rescued the rest. *Clan MacAlister* burned for days and was repeatedly attacked by the Luftwaffe.

The explosion of a magnetic mine broke the back of *Mona's Queen*. She sank a mile east of Dunkirk, taking twenty-four of her sixty-one crew with her; two more bodies were later recovered and buried ashore. Boats from the destroyers *Intrepid* and *Vanquisher* rescued the master and thirty-one crew members. The packet *Killarney* was hit by a shell from a shore battery while homeward bound with 656 troops (elsewhere 800). Eight were killed and twenty-nine injured. The fully laden *Loch Garry*, which had sailed at 1550, was disabled by a bomb, which put both her engines and steering out of action. *Canterbury* was also damaged, but she managed to berth and sailed that evening with 1,797 troops, her third load. The paddle steamer *Waverley* was hit by a bomb at 1700 and sank by the stern; it was estimated that 300 were killed. Another loaded paddle steamer, the *Gracie Fields*, was hit and abandoned in the early hours of the 30 May. At 0200, the *King Orry* capsized and sank and the *Normannia* sank by the stern, both following air attacks. The homeward bound *St Helier* was involved in two collisions.

On 30 May, the Master of the Hospital Carrier *St David* collapsed, and the chief officer took his place, but the crew refused to sail as the vessel could neither be armed or escorted. While having to wait for two hours off Dunkirk on 31 May, the *Lady of Mann* was repeatedly attacked by aircraft, flying in formations of forty. Once alongside, she loaded French and British troops and casualties from a local hospital, while under fire. On sailing, she was found to have seven holes near the waterline and three of her lifeboats were damaged.

The British decided that French troops should be given the chance to be evacuated to the UK; until then they were being moved by French ships to ports further west. This meant that shipping would be needed to move another 100,000 people. When the rescued French troops were landed in the UK they were sent by train to other parts of the south coast; 5,000 were to go to the already overloaded port of Weymouth, and no less than 25,000 to the Hampshire (now Dorset) holiday town of Bournemouth; Southampton and Plymouth were each told to expect 15,000. Later, other ships transported these men back to Western France.

It was not until 31 May that the first of the 'little ships' (private motor yachts) started landing troops in the UK; before this more than 170,000 troops had been saved. Less than twenty yachts made the trip back to the UK with survivors. Others were used to supplement the naval and merchant small craft who had been ferrying troops from the beaches to the waiting ships. In two trips, Dutch motor yacht *Demok I* brought 214 to Dover. The largest lift by a privately manned British yacht was Commander Lightoller's *Sundowner*, who brought back 107.

Commander Lightoller RNR, a Master Mariner, had had a most interesting career. He was the senior surviving officer of the *Titanic*.

The destroyers were usually the first to be attacked, but the merchant ships followed shortly afterwards. At 1009 on 1 June the packet *Prague* was attacked and disabled; 376 troops were taken off by the destroyer *Scimitar* and about 1,500 by the *Queen of Thanet*. The ship was towed back by the Dover tug *Lady Brassey*. Shortly afterwards, the requisitioned paddle steamer *Brighton Queen* was hit and her troops were taken off by other ships. Next to go was the packet *Scotia*. She was hit several times and one bomb went down the funnel. Destroyers and small ships rescued about 1,800 of the estimated 2,000 French troops who were aboard; twenty-eight of her crew were lost. At 1630, the homeward bound destroyer *Worcester* was so seriously damaged during a succession of air raids that she required the assistance of a tug. When entering Dover the damaged destroyer collided with the *Maid of Orleans*, which was out bound on what was to have been her fifth trip; she became the seventh packet to need repairs, and with eight having been sunk, only fourteen remained in service.

In all, over 200 vessels landed almost 60,000 survivors on 1 June, a slightly lower total than the 62,653 landed by 157 ships on the previous day.

By 2 June there was unrest among some of the merchant crews. Most had been operating without a break throughout Dynamo, and even before that; the officers and men were approaching a state of complete exhaustion. The Master of the *St Seiriol* refused to sail and a naval armed guard was placed aboard his vessel, under an RNR Lieutenant. After the vessel made one more voyage to Dunkirk, a doctor declared the whole crew unfit to continue. When news of the attack on the *Prague* reached those on her sister ship *Malines*, the authorities placed armed guards at the foot of her gangway. Several ships were similarly treated while in the UK, their crews let off steam by hurling abuse at the guards.

In his private papers, Captain G. G. Mallory of the *Malines* describes his escape from Rotterdam on 10 May, with 170 British refugees and how, on 28/29 May, he rescued about 1,000 troops (elsewhere 800) from the torpedoed HMS *Grafton*. On the next trip, *Malines* saved 715 British troops. Mallory also gives the background to his refusal to make a third trip to Dunkirk, and his subsequent unauthorised trip to Southampton. Key members of his crew were suffering from physical and nervous exhaustion and were 'on the edge of revolt'. From Southampton, he made two voyages to Cherbourg, being diverted to Jersey on the second trip.

The *Canterbury*, *Lady of Mann*, *Princess Maud*, HMHC *St Julien* and *St Helier* already had additional naval personnel put aboard. Most of these seem to have been replacements, and only a few supplements. Hospital Carriers were manned almost wholly by members of the Merchant Navy and the Fishing Fleets. The two engineers on the little Southampton-registered schuyt, *Ngaroma*, refused to sail, but this was sorted out and the master was later mentioned in Despatches. *The London Gazette* lists the masters of the following packets being awarded the DSC: *Canterbury*, *Isle of Guernsey*, *King George V*, *Prague*, *St Helier*, *Scotia* and

Tynwald. Those mentioned in Despatches included *Biarritz*, *Killarney*, *Lady of Mann*, *Nephrite*, *Princess Maud*, *Roebuck* and *St Andrew*. In addition, a number of the coastal masters were given awards, as were officers and men of these and other ships. In a supplement to *The London Gazette* dated 7 June 1940, the following are announced to have been awarded the DSC: Captain Gordon Dyer Walker, Captain George Johnson and Captain Thomas Aldis, with the added explanation, 'These three officers were temporarily employed as Masters of Troop Transports.'

The General Steam Navigation Company was involved in these, and subsequent, evacuations from France; their subsidiary, the New Medway Steam Packet Company, has the honourable distinction of operating the ship that rescued more troops than any other during Operation Dynamo. The excursion ship *Royal Daffodil*, more used to ferrying trippers from London to Margate and beyond, saved 7,461 men in five voyages (7,066 in seven trips according to the Navy). Had she not been damaged when she was attacked by six aircraft on 2 June, the number would have been even higher. Her sister, the *Royal Sovereign*, rescued 6,370 in six voyages (the Royal Navy figure is 6,858). The naval operated paddler *Royal Eagle*, from the GSNC fleet, rescued 4,015, while her sister, *Golden Eagle*, saved 1,751. The third sister, *Crested Eagle*, was lost with a heavy loss of life. Ordinary Seaman Frank Pattrick RNR said that the *Crested Eagle* was commanded by Lieutenant Commander Booth RNR. The other officers were also RNR; there were no regular naval personnel among the ship's company, though some Petty Officers and ratings were naval pensioners. In all, packet boats saved 74,000 troops; this does not include those who were operated by the Navy with part-civilian crews. The Navy credited the *Tynwald* with saving 7,534, while Winser says the number was 6,880.

The Hospital Carrier *Worthing*, with Red Cross markings, was attacked by aircraft at 1432 on 2 June. She put back to Dover with engine damage and slight leaks. In the evening, the Hospital Carrier *Paris* was attacked. This time the damage was more serious and her crew and nurses were forced to abandon ship. *Paris* sank early the following morning while being towed by the London tug *Sun XV*. The Norwegian ss *Hird* is credited with transferring 3,500 French troops to Cherbourg. En route she saved the captain of HMS *Wakeful*, who they landed off Dover.

By late afternoon of 2 June, with Dunkirk ablaze, the exhausted crews began one final desperate rescue attempt. Between 3 June and 5 June there were 247 UK arrivals with a total of 51,249 people rescued. At 1423 on 4 June, Operation Dynamo was declared over. It has started with the intention of rescuing 45,000 members of the British Expeditionary Force and had ended up saving more than 305,000 British and French troops. Winser lists over 500 merchant ships that were involved, at one point or another, in supplying or evacuating the BEF. About 100 of these were fully or partially manned by naval crews. In addition to the ships' rescue boats that were used to take soldiers from the beaches, shipping companies also sent sixty-four ships' lifeboats to help.

A photograph in *British Coaster*, a HMSO booklet, shows troops on the beach and the coasters lying off. Part of the caption reads:

> Under continuous attack from the Luftwaffe, usually without anti-aircraft guns and, of course, without air cover, the coasters draw into the beaches and the patient queues of the BEF. The coasters bore the main burden of the evacuation. Stoutly they answered the call. And heavily they paid.

Though the merchant ships made an important contribution, Operation Dynamo was the Royal Navy's show. Regular HM ships saved about 110,000 troops and other ships temporarily operated by the Navy probably saved another 50,000. The presence of the 'little ships' (private yachts) was largely symbolic; they brought about 1,000 people back to the UK. Yachts with naval crews repatriated another 3,000. Many other vessels made important contributions; French and Belgian trawlers saved more than 4,000 (*Lydie Suzanne Z50* alone carried 416 troops), without counting their sisters who were operated by their own navies. Thames tugs, fire-floats, mud-hoppers, sailing barges and ships' boats all contributed to the success of the operation.

War Office figures, compiled in 1947, say that a total of 197,918 British and 110,573 Allied troops were rescued, and a further 10,000 French troops were transferred to other French ports at the same time. Around 160,000 British troops were left in France; additionally there were Czech and Polish servicemen and many civilians from these and other nations.

> A message of admiration and sympathy for the heroes of the Flanders rear-guard battle has been received from the King by Mr Winston Churchill, Prime Minister and Minister of Defence. It reads:—

> 'I wish to express my admiration of the outstanding skill and bravery shown by the three Services and the Merchant Navy in the evacuation of the British Expeditionary Force from Northern France. So difficult an Operation was only made possible by brilliant leadership and an indomitable spirit among all ranks of the Force. The measure of its success — greater than we had dared to hope — was due to the unfailing support of the Royal Air Force, and in the final stages, the tireless efforts of naval units of every kind. While we acclaim this great feat, in which our French allies, too, have played so noble a part, we think with heartfelt sympathy of the loss and sufferings of those brave men, whose self-sacrifice has turned disaster into triumph.
> George RI'

Operation Cycle – St Valery, Veules and Le Havre

After Dunkirk, Admiral Sir William James, the Commander in Chief, Portsmouth, was given the task of overseeing the evacuation of about 20,000 British troops which had remained back from the coast between Dieppe and Le Havre. The 'large store ships' (merchant cargo ships) *Belgravian*, *Kyno*, *Maplewood*, *Sakara* and *Trentino*, who were at Southampton, were put on six hours' notice; each had a carrying capacity of about 1,000. There were 'at least' ten coasters: *Cameo*, *Glamis*, *Goldfinch*, *Guernsey Queen*, *Scheldt* and *Silver Coast* at Poole; *Felspar*, *Lowick* and *Sandhill* at Newhaven; and *Gorsefield* at Littlehampton. The coasters were reckoned to be able to carry about 500 men each; they were also placed at six hours' notice. The Ministry of Shipping promised that, given 24 hours' notice, they could provide another ten coasters and three personnel ships. Each of the personnel ships had a capacity of 1,500. In all, sixty-seven merchant ships and 140 small craft were to be made available. The latter included fishing vessels, tugs, excursion boats, merchant ships' lifeboats, naval cutters and other small craft. Six beach masters, each with a ten-strong beach party and wireless sets and telegraphists, were provided.

The Dutch schuyts, which had proved so useful at Dunkirk, were lying at Poole being de-stored before being handed back to the Dutch Shipping Board. It was said to be 'doubtful … if they will be available for 48 hours'. At 2000 on Saturday 8 June, the naval officer in charge at Poole was informed by the Ministry of Shipping that these vessels might be urgently required. The equipment that had been moved to the *Goldfinch* was put back on the schuyts and they were re-fuelled.

Six sub lieutenants were sent from Portsmouth to Poole by bus, each with a crew of one leading seaman, four seamen, one engine room artificer, one leading stoker and a 2nd class stoker. They had no weapons except for a revolver for each of the sub lieutenants. Fortunately, the Dutch masters and engineers arrived at Poole on Saturday night; they volunteered to help the naval ERAs with the bunkering and showed them how to operate the engines.

The schuyts were then to be brought down below Poole Bridge and watered at the Town Quay. All were ready to sail by 2000 on Sunday 9 June, when they were notified that 'Cycle' was suspended. The British withdrawal had been delayed to allow the French evacuation to proceed during the night of 9/10 June. At that time, the schuyts were at Hamworthy (above the lifting bridge) and in Brownsea Roads, near the entrance to the natural harbour. The coasters with cargoes of cased petrol had been anchored in Poole Bay, to minimise the fire risk. Only the passenger ships were equipped with wireless, this shortcoming was to make for considerable problems during the Operation.

On Monday 10 June, orders were received to collect all small craft that could be towed; because they had been used in Operation Dynamo, most were still at Dover. It was decided not to send fishing boats from Poole. Permission was given for small boats to be loaded on the schuyts' decks, and by 1600 the boats had been assembled at the Fish Dock and Sandbanks. The MT shipment was broached and petrol for the small craft was loaded onto *Pacific* and *Zeus*. At 1800, orders were received to sail immediately. When the fleet sailed at around 2000, the motor boats were left at Sandbanks; the British vessels with the derricks needed to load the boats were still out in Poole Bay.

For the ships from the Solent, Operation Cycle began early in the afternoon of 9 June. The railway ships *Amsterdam*, *Archangel*, *Bruges* and *Vienna* sailed from Southampton and the *Lairds Isle* from Portsmouth. A variety of tugs towing small craft and fishing vessels were also sailed from Portsmouth and nearby ports. The Royal Navy sent the destroyers, which were ordered to remain off Le Havre. The coasters *Corina* and *Sandhill* sailed from Newhaven on 10 June, each with a dozen boats in tow.

Admiral James went to Le Havre in *MTB 29* to assess how the situation might develop: during his absence the fast passenger ships were sailed for Havre to be ready for an evacuation on the night of 10/11 June. Indications were that up to 60,000 might need to be evacuated. The Ministry of Shipping figures were much higher, at 200-300,000.

The destroyers *Bulldog* and *Boadicea* were hit during the heavy bombing on the evening of 10 June, and orders were given not to close the evacuation beaches during daylight, except for urgent reasons. The French 9th Corps, which included the British 51st Highland Division, was cut off from escape through Le Havre. The 51st Division's withdrawal through St Valery was blocked by French mechanical transport and their evacuation had not been approved by the French High Command. At 0600 on 11 June, the train ferry *Hampton*, which was just completing naval service, landed a small beach party at St Valery. At that time there was no shelling in the area, but by 1100 the beaches were being shelled. *Saladin* reported that the 51st Division, of about 20,000 men, was formed in a hollow square round St Valery and arrangements were being made to evacuate them after dark. Ships and transports were being shelled and bombed during the forenoon of the 11 June, and Admiral James ordered them to retire to the north-west. During the withdrawal, the vessels were heavily dive-bombed. At one time, *Hampton* was attacked by thirty aircraft. With no fighter support the fleet were fortunate not to suffer loss. At some point fog added to their problems and delayed their return to St Valery when the French Admiral authorised the evacuation that evening.

Le Havre had also been heavily bombed and reports were received that four of the fifteen merchant ships anchored there were disabled; in the event only the *Bruges* had been sunk. Three bombs had been directed at the vessel, one entered her forward hold and the other two fell close by. As she was in danger of sinking, the *Bruges* was beached and abandoned. All seventy-two crew survived. The *St Seiriol* was damaged when a bomb exploded beneath her engine room. Most of the ships came under shell fire or air attack during the evacuation. The Royal Navy-manned schuyt *Twente* was hit in three places and sank. Another schuyt grounded on a falling tide and was lost. This may have been *Hebe II*, commanded by Sub Lieutenant John Pryor, which had been sent in to the beach because it seemed deserted. Pryor and his crew were captured and made to march all the way to the prison camp at Bremen (Marlag). The *Duke of York* was hit three times; her chief officer threw an unexploded shell over the side.

At 2100 on 9 June, *Cameo*, commanded by Captain S. Masson, received orders to proceed to 7 miles west of Cape Le Havre. At 2210, while underway, she was told to return to the anchorage. On 10 June at 2200 she was ordered to proceed to position off St Valery-en-Caux. She spent the night on reduced speed because of thick fog. She was stopped at 1100 on 11 June to await orders, and at 1130 the convoy was told to proceed to Fecamp. At noon a destroyer ordered the ships to put back, owing to enemy action, and several bombs were dropped near the convoy. At 1700 she was attacked by enemy planes during fog, but again escaped, and at 2130 she received orders to follow *Goldfinch*, which had boats in tow. She arrived off the beach at 0100 on 12 June and anchored a quarter of a mile off. At 0330 a drifter arrived with boats, but with no men to man them. The drifter was told to come alongside and *Cameo*'s men manned the boats and took them in to the beach. They transferred one boat load to the drifter and took the next six boat loads onto the *Cameo*; as the last boat left the beach they came under shell and machine gun fire. As they had no food and water and the troops were 'starving' the master signalled the cruiser *Cardiff* and went alongside her, obtaining stores and transferring three (elsewhere six) wounded soldiers. During this manoeuvre, *Cameo*'s side was severely damaged. At 2130 they received orders to proceed to home port. They anchored in Poole Bay at 0630 on 13 June. The pilot boarded at 0930 and they berthed at Poole Quay at 1100.

By the morning of 12 June, enemy fire at St Valery was intense and maximum air support was requested. The 51st Division were ordered to cease fire; this was the only instance during the campaign when a body of men could not be rescued. At 1821, Admiral James ordered the Senior Naval Officer to withdraw his force. The withdrawing ships were to turn back out-coming vessels, but they missed several, which were heavily attacked. *Train Ferry No. 2* was lost.

Captain H. H. Quail of the *Guernsey Queen* made a one-page report, in which the dates and times are similar to those reported by Captain Masson. At 1230 on 11 June they were attacked by Nazi bombers. They were then ordered to follow *Jade* to a position off St Valery, where they were damaged in another raid. At 0030 on 12 June, they embarked about 100 men, touching bottom at the time. They returned to a cove off Veules, where they remained under fire, receiving a hit on the starboard side aft, which damaged the water tanks, a lifeboat, the funnel and the hull. They arrived at Poole at 1030 on 13 June and disembarked the troops.

Commander H. W. Green RNR STO Poole amplified the masters' reports:

On June 13th vessels commenced returning to Poole, *Cameo* with over 400 troops, *Guernsey Queen* with about 90. The Masters' reports cover the interim. I would respectfully point out that these men are not able to write adequately of what they have done. This is particularly true of the *Cameo* and *Guernsey Queen*. The Master of the *Cameo*, Stephen Masson, the Mate, Neil MacKinnon and the crew of this vessel deserve special praise. The Master is an old gentleman of 69 years of age and whilst the crew were pulling the lifeboats he was alone on board with only the Second Engineer. The Mate, Neil MacKinnon, was on the beach preventing the overcrowding of the boats. It should be remembered that the heavy boat work was done by men who had had no rest for 48 hours. The Master was continuously on the Bridge from leaving Poole on the 10th to returning on the 13th, no mean feat for a man of his years. The *Guernsey Queen* apparently took up inshore berth as vacated by *Cameo* and Captain Quail did everything possible up to the last moment.

Roebuck, commanded by Captain Larbalestier, and *Sambur*, under Captain Sanderson, were cargo ships owned by the Great Western Railway. They normally operated a service from Weymouth to the Channel Islands. They left Weymouth together at 1405 on 12 June, bound for the Normandy coast. At 0150 on 13 June, having seen fires onshore, they eased down awaiting daylight. At 0410 they proceeded towards St Valery, and at 0415 made contact with fishermen, who were about 5 miles off the port.

The Master of the *Roebuck*, who spoke French, understood from the fishermen that it was safe to approach the coast, and he signalled the *Sambur* with the information. When they were within a mile of the port the enemy opened fire from the cliff tops with about nine guns. Both ships turned and zigzagged at full speed, but both sustained serious damage and casualties. On *Roebuck*, the second officer was killed outright and the RN signalman was badly wounded, as were the chief officer and one greaser. On *Sambur*, two of the crew were killed, and four were seriously injured. Both ships were badly damaged. With the exception of one AB who jumped over the side and was lost, the *Roebuck*'s crew behaved splendidly. The gunner, Leslie Mavey, was singled out for special praise; he took charge of the wounded, including the chief officer, whose place he took during the return passage to Newhaven. On *Sambur* the behaviour of all was very commendable. *Sambur*'s standard compass had been smashed, so the *Roebuck* escorted her sister back to Newhaven, where they landed the dead and the injured.

The dead were recorded as *Sambur*: John Jones, chief steward (two in ship's report); *Roebuck*: Richard Wills, AB; Herbert Caddy; William Williams, second officer. Those killed on the *Train Ferry No. 2* (LNER), which was shelled off St Valery-en-Caux and beached were recorded as: Reginald Barker, Fireman; Leonard Burger, Radio Officer; Douglas Catchpole, Fourth Engineer Officer; Owen Gage, AB; Donald Hambling, Fireman; William Maryan, Donkeyman; John Miller, Second Engineer Officer; Ralph Moore, AB; Walter Pells, Chief Steward; John Simmen, AB; Herbert Snelling, Fireman; George Starkey, Second Officer; William Stokes, AB; and Richard Summers, Donkeyman.

Captain Painter of the *Goldfinch* was somewhat aggrieved that his ship's contribution was ignored. The officer in charge of a party of naval ratings who were put aboard his ship expressed his complete satisfaction with the *Goldfinch* crew's performance. The situation was probably not helped by the fact that the officer, Probationary Temporary Lieutenant J. C. Thompson RNR, was awarded a DSC. When Lieutenant Thompson heard of the omission he made a supplementary report, in an effort to get recognition for the *Goldfinch*. In it he pointed out that the crew were involved in a great deal of boat work and saved between 500 and 600 soldiers, whom they transferred to the *Princess Maud* and other ships. The ship's second officer, with two seamen, took charge of part of the beach party 'under trying circumstances'. Both they and their ship came under hostile gunfire, and the vessel took two shell hits and suffered one fatality. The chief officer and the chief engineer, 'in the course of their duties', made repairs to the ship's degaussing gear.

The *St Briac*, *Amsterdam*, *Tynwald*, *Theems* and *Emerald* left St Valery for Cherbourg during the night of 12/13 June with 4,000 troops, including the rear guard; the *Lowick* carried the beach party. These ships were escorted by destroyers *Fernie* and *Vega*.

Many of the civilians from Le Havre tried to flee by sea. The French steamer *Niobe* had arrived at Le Havre with a cargo of Welsh coal. She then loaded ammunition and provisions for Dunkirk, but since that port was no longer operating, she was ordered to Caen instead. In the chaos, hundreds of refugees boarded to escape the advancing Germans. *Niobe* sailed at about 1430 on 11 June, but came under attack by German planes at 1700 (two or four aircraft according to conflicting reports); the ammunition she was carrying blew up in an enormous explosion. There were only eleven survivors, who were rescued by the small coaster *Cotentin*. The number of dead is not known, but it was believed that 800 or more boarded her in Le Havre. The French ships *General Metzinger* and *Syrie* were sunk by German bombing at Le Havre, also with heavy loss of life. The Norwegian steamer *Ellavore* was also sunk by German bombing at Le Havre; the entire crew was rescued by other Norwegian ships. The Belgian steamers *Albertville* and *Piriapolis* were sunk off the port; the *Albertville* had sailed from Bordeaux to embark troops.

The Norwegian *Ringulv* carried nearly 1,500 civilians. She also seems to have been left out of the records – there may well be others. *Ringulv*, a coal fired steamer, was one of the many Norwegian vessels at sea when their country was invaded. They were put under the management of Nortraship. *Ringulv* was chartered to the French and sent to Le Havre to load a general cargo for New York. The ships and the town were bombed constantly. Early on the morning of Monday 10 June, the ship was ordered to stop loading and to embark 500 mainly female workers from munitions factories. A couple of hours later, Captain Messel was asked if he could take more refugees. When the ship left at noon she had 1,472 women, children and old people on board. There were a number of babies, the youngest only two days old. When they sailed they could see thousands more waiting to embark on other ships. The catering department made coffee, tea and fresh bread throughout the day and night. The ship's entire supply of condensed milk was diluted and given to the children. The crew gave their accommodation and slept at their posts. No pilot was available at Cherbourg, so the Master berthed the vessel. They were then diverted to Brest, sailing on the evening of the 11 June. They berthed at Brest 24 hours later and the refugees disembarked. Before doing so they handed 1,500 francs to the master to divide between the crew. The crew agreed that the money should be given to the French Red Cross. This was in addition to the 6,050 kroner that they had previously collected for the Red Cross. They all disembarked quickly and with no problems, when *Ringulv* started to move away there were still around a thousand people on the quay 'shouting hooray.'

They were meant to go to Bordeaux, but never got beyond Verdon Roads due to the approaching Germans. *Ringulv*'s men thought that the worst was behind them once they got out of Le Havre, but on the first night at Verdon Roads they were attacked by air. The bombers came regularly day and night, dropping bombs and magnetic mines in parachutes. On 20 June orders were received to proceed to Casablanca, where they arrived on 25 June. Their ship was immobilised and the crew were sent to the first of nine prison camps in North Africa.

The last loss on Operation Cycle was the schuyt *Abel Tasman*, which hit a mine as she followed her sister *Wega* through the Swash Channel into Poole Harbour.

At the end of his report Admiral James says:

The achievement in the St. Valery area fell far short of my early hopes but embarkation of a large number of troops from such a coast once the enemy had established guns to command the small narrow beaches and the town was not possible.

He goes on to say that he could not speak too highly of the fishermen and yachtsmen who spent three days in their open boats, some enduring air attack or shelling from the coast. He finishes by pointing out the difficulty in tracing some of those who went over in these small craft as they were 'merchant service men and fishermen now dispersed'. Fourteen thousand, five hundred and fifty-seven British and 921 French troops were evacuated. Nine thousand of these were taken to Cherbourg and the rest to South Coast ports. Fourteen thousand, four hundred and eighteen were carried by merchant ships and 1,060 by naval vessels. There are no figures for civilian evacuees, or for the terrible casualties among this group.

Operation Aerial – Cherbourg, St Malo and the Channel Islands

After Operation Cycle ended, the authorities believed that there were 140,000 British troops to be evacuated from ports between Cherbourg and La Pallice. In addition, there were an unknown number of Allied soldiers, plus their vehicles, stores and equipment. Many civilians were making their way westward, mostly on foot. Reinforcements were still being moved from Southampton to ports in North West France, with the intention of establishing a 'Breton redoubt'. This toing and froing caused some wits to say that BEF stood for 'Back Every Friday'.

For whatever reason, few records about Operation Aerial are available, though Roskill and Winser must have had access to some. Were it not for the 'eagle eye' of Don Kindell, this chapter could not have been written. He found a record of this operation while reading a file in the National Archives at Kew. He has kindly provided me with a copy of the file: see http://www.naval-history.net/xDKWDa-Aerial.htm.

Because of the damage and losses sustained by the British merchant ships, Allied passenger vessels were also utilised for the work, including the Belgian *Prince Charles*, *Princesse Marie Jose* and *Prins Albert*, the *Batavier IV* supplied by the Dutch, and the *El Kantara* and *El Mansour* supplied by the French. The British cargo ships *City of Christchurch*, *Port Montreal* and *Yorkwood* reached Brest with guns and vehicles, but the situation was hopeless and the cargoes were not discharged.

Admiral James again supervised the evacuation, this time from the ports of Cherbourg and St Malo, which later included the evacuations from the Channel Islands. Completion was anticipated by 18 June, but in the event this part of the operation lasted until 23 June and overlapped with the evacuations from the ports that were further west.

Captain John Oswald, a gunner in 215 Battery, 54th Anti-Aircraft Regiment – part of 52nd (Lowland) Division – crossed to Cherbourg by troop transport and drove in convoy to Le Mans. After a few days they managed to escape the German advance and make it to Cherbourg 'relatively unhurt' and were taken off by small boats. His troop came back home on the 'London pleasure steamer *Royal Daffodil*'. The rescue ship may have been the *Royal Sovereign*, which had on board the 52nd, the remnants of the 51st and two other divisions.

The evacuation of Cherbourg started on 15 June. The operation was expected to take about six days, but was completed in four. In that time there were over fifty sailings, all but two by merchant ships. Some 30,000 personnel were evacuated, plus a considerable amount of war material. One of the schuyts, the *Jaba*, was commanded by Sub Lieutenant Foster, who confirms that they made two trips to Cherbourg. The first was on 16 June when they followed two ferries into port. After the ferries had loaded and left, the *Jaba* picked up 300 British soldiers. As they entered Cherbourg harbour on a return trip two days later, they saw German armoured cars on the quayside and had to carry out an immediate emergency turn. They were aiming for the eastern exit when they picked up a French demolition team from a rowing boat. The team persuaded the captain to use the western exit. As they left the fort, on the eastern end the detached mole blew up – the remains are visible on Google Earth.

The cargo ship *Delius* left for Southampton with the vehicles of the 3rd Armoured Brigade on 18 June – equipment that remained in Cherbourg was destroyed. The *Manxman* embarked naval staff and the military rear guard. On 18 June she cut her moorings and backed out, scraping her hull against wrecked vehicles. By this time the harbour was ablaze – there were explosions caused by the British demolition teams and German gunfire. Then the destroyers *Sabre* and *Fernie* sailed with the demolition teams and the last of the retreating soldiers.

The Norwegian cargo ship *Borgholm* may have sailed after the destroyers. A letter written later by the master says:

> When we escaped from France 18 June 1940 with a cargo of sugar, intended for Germany [?], we were heavily bombed and had no protection of any kind, nor a gun on board. Many ships were damaged and sunk around us but we managed to escape undamaged and succeeded in bringing the cargo safely to England. During this attack my Chief Officer Alf Hansen (since drowned) and Second Officer Henrik Wesenberg (now Chief) remained at their duties without any thought of personal danger and by their courage, determination and devotion to duty we arrived safely at England for whom we have had the honour to sail ever since.

The evacuation of St Malo took place concurrently with that from Cherbourg. There were forty-two sailings to the UK and an unspecified number to Jersey. Again, most of the sailings were by merchant vessels. Four Royal Navy-manned Dutch schuyts were also involved, as was the destroyer *Sabre* (and probably her sister *Fernie*).

The first sailings from St Malo were on 14 June when the *Manxman* and the *Prinses Astrid* ferried 2,500 troops to Southampton. Several of the other railway boats were short of fuel, so 15 June was spent bunkering them. At dawn on 16 June, two of the re-bunkered vessels, the *Biarritz* and the *Princesse Marie Jose*, sailed, followed by the *Royal Sovereign*, three coasters and the four schuyts. In all they carried about 6,000 men. The final sailing on that day was the *Hantonia*, carrying troops and civilians to Southampton; she maintained her schedule to the last, as did the other railway boats. En route for St Malo with a demolition team, HMS *Wild Swan* put in to St Helier and requisitioned seven coasters that had been waiting to load that season's potato crop. These vessels were sent to St Malo to load their human cargo. When the *Princess Maude* sailed at 1600 on 17 June with 2,600 troops, the main evacuation was almost complete.

When the coaster *Hodder* arrived on 18 June there were no troops awaiting passage, but the *Hodder* towed the disabled schuyt *Jutland*, which had a cargo of ammunition and fuel, to Jersey. Everard's coaster *Antiquity* also searched in vain. It was thought that the remaining evacuees were saved by the French tugs *Attentiff* and *Champion*. *Antiquity* then went to Jersey to assist there. The Jersey craft *Duchess of Normandy* and *RFC 113* embarked the demolition party and some stragglers, including two Belgian nurses. There were rumours that a contingent of 5,000 Polish troops were also making for St Malo, and *Sabre* was told to go to St Helier to escort schuyts to St Malo. When *Sobeiski* arrived at Le Verdon, she was also ordered to St Helier. *Sabre* reported that she was escorting three transports with evacuees from St Helier. On 20 June C in C Portsmouth informed *Sabre* that St Malo was still in French hands. He ordered *Sabre* to ascertain if Polish troops were still awaiting evacuation, and if so, to embark them in the eighteen Dutch schuyts then en route to St Helier. A French fishing vessel brought twenty-five French people, including three women and three children from Brittany to St Helier, and they were transferred to the schuyt *Despatch*.

Churchill had originally intended to defend the Channel Islands. The cargo ships *Clan Ross* and *Kohistan* were each retained to carry a battalion, one to Jersey and the other to Guernsey, though these vessels were probably too big to berth at the ports. On 20 June, the *Biarritz* and the *New Fawn* took the troops from Guernsey to Southampton. On the same day the *Malines* took troops from Jersey and also to Southampton; the cargo ship *Hodder* took others to Weymouth. When it was decided to demilitarise the Channel Islands, special facilities were made available for certain categories of the population to come to the mainland. *Sabre* reported that the 8,000 people who wished to be evacuated from Jersey had been embarked, and half the population of St Peter Port, Guernsey, wanted to be evacuated and were being embarked. The population of Sark remained on the instructions of the Dame, the hereditary ruler of the island (the Seigneur).

Lieutenant Commander T. G. Newby RNR Rtd was rushed by car to Weymouth on 22 June where he boarded mv *Stork* in Weymouth Bay. He was to be commodore of a convoy consisting of *Camroux IV*, *Alnwick*, *Empire Jonquil*, *West Coaster* and *Suffolk Coast*, which sailed for Alderney. They anchored off at daylight and went alongside at 0700. Newby met with the Seigneur, who announced that people could take one suitcase each. The bells were not rung, as that was to be the signal of invasion. Virtually all of the island's population of 1,800 had been embarked by noon and the small fleet sailed for Weymouth. The commodore transferred to the *Alnwick*, leaving the better accommodation on the *Stork* for mothers to be. Commander Newby said 'The legend re babies born springs from the fact that I did suggest that "mothers to be" should travel on the *Stork* as she was the most comfortable.' It has been suggested elsewhere that three babies were born en route, but this sounds unlikely as the trip only took a few hours; perhaps the ship's name gave rise to the tale?

The *Duke of Argyll* and ten Royal Navy-manned schuyts started the evacuation of Guernsey on 21 June. Later ships were not needed as only 6,600 from Jersey's population of about 50,000 decided to leave. *Jaba* was one of those who had first been to Jersey; they found that a railway ferry (*Viking?*) had taken all who wanted to leave. With the others, *Jaba* went on to Guernsey, where they evacuated about 250 civilians.

The *Viking*, under the command of Captain James Brisdon, arrived at St Peter Port harbour at 0400. The ship sailed for Weymouth at 1100 with 2,000 men, women and children. When the *Royal Daffodil* and the Belgian *Prince Leopold* called at the island on 23 June, no would-be evacuees remained. *Hantonia* and *Isle of Sark* maintained the scheduled link with Southampton until the German occupation; the *Isle of Sark*, commanded by Captain H. H. Golding, was one of the last ships to leave St Peter Port when she sailed with 647 passengers.

The Dorset port of Weymouth received a total of 25,484 Channel Islanders. Dozens of passenger steamers, paddle-boats, cement and cargo ships helped in the evacuation. Ten vessels arrived in Weymouth during one morning and in just over three days from 20 June, fifty-eight ships arrived, fifty of these from the Channel Islands. The port was used to dealing with less than five arrivals and sailings per day. The Dorset Women's Institute paper *Reception of Refugees in Weymouth* records:

> In all, over 30,000 persons were received of whom approximately 24,000 came from the Channel Islands and about 70,000 meals were provided.
>
> Thousands of French troops [came].... Then they in turn departed, shipped back to France ... to continue the fight.... For some days Weymouth was almost like a French town ... we were told to prepare for 40,000 or so *more* [my italics] refugees – and for four days they came. Our voluntary organisation dealt with 23,000 *in one day* [again my italics] ... these were Channel Islanders. The French were well received and the Channel Islanders even more so as these 'were our own people'.

This probably doubled the population of the town, at a time when there were also holiday makers! At nearby Bowleaze Cove, the local women served fried breakfasts to a group of tired and dishevelled French troops.

From the Channel Islands '22,656 persons took advantage of these facilities. In addition, a number of persons left by other means, including air transport. It is estimated that altogether 25,000 persons left the Islands.' The ships that carried them ranged from the well-appointed *Duke of Argyll* to coasters who had only just discharged their cargoes of coal; from these the passengers emerged covered in coal dust.

Weymouth had been caring for refugees since 18 May, when the *Volendam* arrived with Dutch citizens returning from the USA. After those of 'enemy origin and sympathisers' had been separated out, twenty-six remained; they were mostly Dutch bulb-growers. The next day, a Sunday, the people of Weymouth were told to prepare for 'a large number' of Belgian refugees: 'Foodstuffs were obtained from local wholesale grocers, bakers and dairymen; crockery and cutlery were hired and arrangements made for help from the Women's Voluntary Services.' There were 1,258 on the first boat and at ten o'clock a second boat arrived with 784; this was probably in the evening as the passengers were said to be 'extremely tired' so inspection was postponed till the following morning. In both cases, 'the passengers were able to wash, and those who had insufficient clothing were fitted out with garments brought in by donors. Babies were fed and had their napkins changed, while their mothers ate and rested.'

The report continued: 'Varying numbers of refugees arrived at all times of the day and night during the succeeding days and similar arrangements for feeding and shelter were made.' Supplies were sent out to ships waiting to enter the harbour and to those vessels that were too big to enter. Many ships had no food left and many were short of fresh water. One young girl from the Channel Islands recalled that she had coped with the sea voyage, but she was terrified by the sight and sound of the steam locomotive that was to haul their train to the comparative safety of the North.

Others were received and cared for. On 1 June, for example, thirty-seven shipwrecked seamen, mainly Lascars (Indian seamen), 357 naval ratings, forty-three members of the British War Graves Commission and twenty-six Dutch sailors were assisted. On 2 June, 1,500 French officers and men were cared for, before being re-embarked for France. On 5 June, haircuts and entertainment were provided, and at the end of a concert by the Salvation Army Band 'there were cries of *Vive l'Angleterre.*'

Southampton also received many of those displaced by the war in Europe. Over 6,000 Belgian, Dutch and French refugees landed at the port, as did 2,400 from the Channel Islands. The country's foremost passenger port was better equipped to handle the influx. In 1937, it had given shelter to almost 4,000 children fleeing from the hell of Guernica and the Spanish Civil War. Many of the Channel Islanders were moved to other cities in the UK, though several hundred decided to remain, and later formed the Channel Islands Association in the town. Wounded French soldiers were sent to the Royal South Hants Hospital, where their records still exist. Those who were not wounded were billeted on local schools; records show that 800 were at one school. Residents pushed cakes and sandwiches to them through the railings: 'they appeared tired and dirty and only partially equipped; other residents took them in so that they could have a bath.'

The total number of people landed at both ports from Cherbourg was about 30,000 (almost all British and Canadians from the 'Norman Force'), from St Malo, 28,000 were expected (less arrived?), and from the Channel Islands to Weymouth alone were 25,484.

Operation Aerial – Brest to La Pallice

Little information on this phase of the rescue is available at The National Archives. Winston Churchill prevented news of the tragic loss of life when the *Lancastria* was bombed and sunk. Control of this part of the operation passed from Admiral Sir William James to Admiral Sir Martin Dunbar-Nasmith at Plymouth. On 13 June, the *Batory, Duchess of York, Georgic* and *Sobieski* sailed from the Clyde to Brest in convoy FF 1; they carried French and Polish troops back from the Norwegian Campaign. Convoy FF 2 – Clyde to St Nazaire – included the *Ulster Monarch, Royal Ulsterman, Royal Scotsman* and *Ulster Prince*. The *Batory* and *Sobieski* arrived on 14 June and disembarked their troops.

By 15 June a fleet of 133 merchant vessels were earmarked for the rescue. Thirty-three of these were ordered to sail from ports in the south of England and South Wales, destined for Brest, Cherbourg, Quiberon Bay and St Nazaire. The fleet included passenger liners, railway boats, cargo ships and coasters. The *Empire Ability* and *City of Florence* were sailed from Falmouth to Brest; the *Ettrick, Koningen Emma, Royal Ulsterman* and *Royal Scotsman* to La Pallice, and the *City of Windsor* was diverted to Cherbourg from Convoy OA 168. The *Lancastria* was told to proceed to Quiberon Bay for onward passage to St Nazaire, and the *Franconia* to Brest. The *Arandora Star, Otranto* and *Strathaird* were ordered to Brest from Cardiff, and the *Ormonde* and *Oronsay* from Falmouth to Quiberon Bay (the last seven were passenger liners). The officer in charge at Southampton was told to sail the *Clew Bay, Kilrae, Afon Gwli, Hythe, Whitstable, Malrix, Marsworth, Lyroca* and *Polgrange* to Quiberon Bay. The *Mackay* and *Wincheslea* were ordered to Brest to escort loaded convoys home. The *Obsidian* and *Ravona* were to sail from Newhaven to Brest, and the *Arthur Wright* was sailed from Shoreham. The *Clan Ferguson, Margot, Governor* and *Teiresias* were sent from the Bristol Channel to St Nazaire.

Batory and *Sobieski* sailed from Brest on 15 June and anchored in St Nazaire Roads at 0830 on the following morning. By that time, the *Lady of Mann, Manxman* and *Canterbury* were loaded with 6,000 troops, but were held up by mines. The *Vienna*, which was in harbour under orders for Nantes, was to be loaded next. The *Georgic, Duchess of York* and *Sobieski* were to be loaded by dark and sailed. By the end of 16 June, 11,000 troops had been embarked at St Malo, leaving 5,000 there. Ten thousand five hundred had embarked at Brest, leaving 16,000 there. Seventeen thousand had embarked at St Nazaire, leaving 30,000 there, and the embarkation at Nantes was proceeding satisfactorily. An hour later a report was received from St Nazaire that the *Duchess of York* with 4,300 personnel and the *Georgic* with 3,982 were sailing for Plymouth; they were subsequently diverted to Liverpool.

The *Batory* embarked a total of 2,303, including British infantry, Red Cross and Salvation Army personnel, plus a few Polish troops, for Plymouth, and the *Sobeiski*, with 2,890, sailed for Falmouth. They were escorted by the *Whirlwind* and *Beagle*. The ships had been attacked by German bombers while in St Nazaire. The *Lady of Mann* arrived at Plymouth from Brest at 0450, and the *Canterbury* and *Manxmaid* arrived at 0521. The *Franconia* was temporarily out of action due to near miss by bombs; the main shaft and gearing were out of line. The *Bactria* and *Vienna* arrived at Plymouth that morning. The Captain of the *Wolverine*, having reported that a convoy of nineteen loaded ships would be ready by noon, was instructed to escort them, taking the trawlers *Agate* and *Cambridgeshire* with him. C in C WA ordered the *Westcott* to direct all ships due for Brest into the harbour. At 0900 the *Britanny*, *Trewal*, *Trelawny* and *City of Evansville* sailed from Avonmouth for the Loire via Quiberon Bay. The *Strathaird* and *Ormonde* reached Brest an hour before noon. By then there were sufficient ships at Brest.

Shortly after noon, the *Wolverine* reported that the convoy of nineteen had grown to twenty-six ships and had sailed from Quiberon Bay for the Bristol Channel at 4 knots (!). SNO Brest reported at 0317 that French troops from Narvik, who had been landed at Brest on Monday (17 June) from the *Royal Scotsman*, did not wish to be evacuated to the United Kingdom. Four hundred Polish troops in the *Ulster Monarch* were allowed to remain in ship.

At the outbreak of war, the *City of Derby* had been taken up as a MT ship. By June 1940, she was tasked with landing a replacement W/T (Wireless Telegraphy) Section of about twenty-five men, and their equipment, for Sedan, in Northern France. The Germans overran the area so quickly that the change-over could not take place. The group in Sedan were unable to reach Dunkirk, so the *City of Derby* made her way to St Valery to pick up the signallers who were attempting to reach Abbeville. When this too proved to be impossible, the ship followed the group to Cherbourg and then on to Brest, where the rescue was finally carried out.

The ship was ordered to go to a neutral Spanish port, a destination that filled both the signallers and the ship's crew with foreboding. The signallers asked if they could swim to cool off and enjoy what might be their last taste of freedom. The master anchored the ship off the lighthouse of Penfret on the Iles de Glénan; three of the signallers swam ashore to the surprise of the lighthouse keepers who were expecting the Germans. The keepers maintained that their radio was too weak to send a message to London, so one of the party swam back to the ship and returned in the jolly boat. In the boat they brought their own wireless set and a loaded revolver! After being reprimanded by London for breaking shipboard radio silence, which they hadn't, they were given permission to return to Liverpool.

As supplies were running very low, the master decided to first call into Brest. When they reached Brest Roads, they were forbidden to land as the Germans were 'knocking at the door'. At the time, those on the *City of Derby* were unaware of all the other ships rescuing troops from ports in the Bay of Biscay. When making for St George's Channel, they sighted a submarine periscope, so they diverted west of Ireland, finally reaching Belfast on 27 June. They were told to say that they were from Liverpool.

The *Ormonde*, *Otranto* and *Arandora Star* sailed from Quiberon Bay in the afternoon of 17 June with orders to report to *Wolverine*. SNO Brest reported that 30,000 had been embarked by the evening of 17 June and that the *Arandora Star* was not required and was being sent to United Kingdom. The SNO St Nazaire reported that the holds of all MT and store ships were crammed to capacity and the men were short of food and water. At 1445 on 17 June, the SNO St Nazaire reported that the *Havelock* had one engine out of action and was returning with the *Lancastria* to the UK. He asked for more destroyers as embarkation was badly delayed by lack of shipping. *Prinses Josephine Charlotte* sailed from Falmouth for Brest at 1628 on 17 June. On that day the *Guinean* sailed from Brest; an IWM photograph in the picture section shows her arriving off Falmouth, her foredeck crowded with troops.

The *Lancastria* and *Oronsay* had arrived at daybreak on 17 June. Early in the afternoon the air raids began, and at 1348 the *Oronsay* was hit with several killed on board. Captain Sharp, the Master of the *Lancastria*, had been ordered by two naval officers to take as many troops as possible, without regard to regulations and the availability of life saving appliances. The ship was said to have 2,000 life jackets aboard. By this time there were '7,000 to 8,000' weary men on board the *Lancastria*, an unknown number of women and children, and two pet dogs. Many of the soldiers stripped off and enjoyed baths and showers, while others headed to the bar.

Captain Sharp said that he had requested a destroyer escort, but received no response to his signals. He and Chief Officer Grattidge decided that they would wait until the *Oronsay* was loaded and sail with her. Afterwards, Captain Stevens of the *Havelock* said that the signal from the *Lancastria* had said that they were out of drinking water and it was Stevens' opinion that Sharp had 'not obeyed the order to sail'. That morning the *Havelock* had reported starboard propeller and tail shaft damage, with possible damage to the port propeller. Stevens had blamed the damage on his first lieutenant, who was handling the ship while the captain rested!

The attack on the *Oronsay* ended at 1540, but it was then the *Lancastria*'s turn, the first attack having missed. Had Sharp immediately given the order to sail it is doubtful that the anchor would have been raised by the time of the attack – even if it had, the liner would have still been in the area and would have most likely been attacked.

The *Lancastria* was only armed with a 4-inch gun and a few Bren guns that the soldiers had brought aboard. Six planes made the second raid and the ship was hit by four explosive bombs. Within two minutes she started to list and within twenty minutes the *Lancastria* had sunk, leaving the survivors to save themselves in a layer of fuel oil that kept increasing in size.

Rescue ships of all types converged on the area. Some naval reports seemed to suggest that the *Cambridgeshire* was the only rescue vessel, probably because the trawler, with a low freeboard, was able to rescue survivors directly from the water, while most other ships needed to use their boats. Boats from the merchant ships were loading survivors and taking them back to their ships. For this sort of work the chief and second officers of the small Union Castle cargo ship *Dundrum Castle* were awarded the OBE and the MBE respectively. The citation reads:

> They rescued over 120 men. Oil on the surface of the water made rescue work very dangerous, but these two officers made repeated trips with survivors of the *Lancastria* to ferry boats which were standing by. After these gallant and successful efforts the *Dundrum Castle*'s boats were the last to leave the scene.

The even smaller *John Holt* reported having 829 on board, many without clothing; the destroyers *Beagle* and *Havelock* had 600 and 460 respectively; while the Naval Yacht *Oracle* had 44. The liner *Oronsay* reported 1,557 passengers. It is not clear how many of these were survivors from the *Lancastria*, but this figure seems to include those who boarded before the casualty. The tanker *Cymbula*, which was returning from the Loire, carried 252 back to Plymouth. The Master of the *Cymbula* reported at 2355 that he had on board '250 army ranks, short of kit and two women survivors from *Lancastria*'. In all between 2,500 and 3,700 were saved. Estimates of those lost vary between 3,000 and 5,000, making this Britain's worst maritime disaster. The American researcher Don Kindell, who is usually most reliable, says that there were a total of 5,310 on the *Lancastria*, sixty-six crew and 2,833 passengers died.

Those who boarded the *Oronsay* were 'made comfortable' and the liner sailed at 2000. It was a long night for all. When they arrived off the British coast a call went out for a signalman to semaphore a message ashore. This mystified those who had missed the earlier briefing given by one of the ship's officers. They could not understand why the ship could not radio or send a signal on the Morse lamp. They were then told that when the *Oronsay* had been attacked the bridge deck had been seriously damaged, putting the wheelhouse and radio room out of action, and breaking the master's leg. The liner, listing and taking water, had been brought home using her emergency steering, without charts or radio. One soldier wrote some years later that the master was ordered to take the damaged ship to Oban, but he refused. The Plymouth Journal simply states 'June 18th – *Oransay* [sic] with wounded and other survivors from *Lancastria* and troops arrived Plymouth

1547.' By this time the list was so bad that the ship could not go alongside, so the survivors were ferried ashore.

Holt's *Teiresias*, which had arrived from Avonmouth, became the other casualty at St Nazaire. Hit by three bombs, one of which flooded her stokehold, she listed to starboard, split abaft No. 3 hatch, and sank at anchor. The cargo ship *Holmside* rescued the crew, with the exception of the bosun, who was killed in the attack.

By 1752 on 17 June, troops from St Nazaire had been evacuated and the town was presumed to be in enemy hands. *Ettrick* was told not to proceed there, but on 19 June at 0012 the *Oracle* signalled that she had sailed with rescued merchant crews, a few soldiers and refugees – 250 in all –and that the Germans were close to St Nazaire. The *Trelawny* had been heavily bombed, suffering slight damage; the *Floristan* was also bombed and had engine room damage. Understandably there is a great deal of confusion over times and dates.

Air attacks continued at St Nazaire. At 1851 the Commander in Chief, Western Approaches, informed the senior naval officers at Brest and St Nazaire and all ships in Western Approaches of the decision to withdraw the whole of the British Expeditionary Force immediately, and detailed the vessels that would be arriving at the various ports. The *Mackay* was informed that they were to be embarked on any ship for the UK.

The work went on. Writing about another Holt ship – the *Glenaffric*, under Captain Walter Harrison at St Nazaire – a Brigadier Cole said:

> On an ebb tide and without pilot or tugs the ship was skilfully and safely brought onto the quay, where the embarkation of the remaining troops was quickly carried out and with 4,000 rescued soldiers aboard she sailed after a trying night ... the ship was brought out of harbour under the most adverse conditions and, the convoy having already departed, the Master proceeded unescorted to a British port. Our men pay glowing tribute to the cheerful manner and quiet confidence displayed....

The Aerial log records the *Glenaffric* as being in convoy OLIVE when it sailed from the Loire at 1630 on the 17 June.

A troop convoy of the *Royal Ulsterman, City of Lancaster, Beltoy, Maurice Rose, Glanlea (Glenlea), Harpathian, Glendenning, Pollux, Lechistan* sailed at 1100. The ships, with their passenger numbers, were reported as: *Royal Ulsterman* 2,800; *Ulster Prince* 2,800; *Floristan* 2,000; *Baharistan* 2,000; *Clan Macpherson (Ferguson)* 2,000; *Dundrum Castle* 2,000; *David Livingstone* 2,000; *Fabian* 2,000; *City of Mobile* 2,000; and *Glen Affaric* 4,000 *(Glenaffric)*. The convoy escorts were the *Vanoc* and the *Beagle*.

At 0830 on 18 June, the *Beagle* reported that she had sailed from St Nazaire for Plymouth with the *Ulster Prince, Clan Ferguson* and *Baharistan*, each carrying approximately 3,000 troops, the *David Livingstone* with 800, and the *Beagle* herself with 600, all short of provisions. On 19 June at 1412, *Vanoc* reported different loading figures for some of the ships: '*City of Mobile* 3,000 troops with five stretcher cases; *Floristan* 3,500; *Essex Druid* 1,500 and five stretcher cases' – this was probably the *Fabian* GBWS, as the *Essex Druid* GBWQ was sold in 1938 – '*Dundrum Castle* 500; *Floristan* damaged in engine room by bombing.' Between 1700 and 1720 on 19 June, the *Royal Sovereign, Floristan, City of Mobile, Farrian, St Briac, Dundrum Castle* and French *Prestin* arrived at Plymouth; the *Beagle* sailed again at 1710! Also on 18 June, the Polish cargo ship *Lechistan*, with most of her outward cargo of coal on board, sailed from St Nazaire with 245 refugees and twenty-three soldiers; she reached Plymouth on 20 June.

The *Bellerophon* arrived at Plymouth at 0745 on 18 June. At 0845, the *Acheron* reported meeting *Lycaon* at 51° 00' N, 06° 00' W en route for the Bristol Channel with 800 troops on board and no rations. At 1914, the C in C ordered the *Vienna, St Julien, St Andrew, Cyclops* and *Bellerophon* to Dartmouth, the *Prince Albert* to Southampton and the *Bactria* to Barry. The *Arethusa* told the *Whirlwind* to intercept and escort the *Madura* out from Le Verdun to Falmouth and the *Nariva* to the Bristol Channel; both were carrying refugees.

The rescue tugs *Salvonia* (British), *Zwarte Zee* (Dutch) and *Marauder* (British) were ordered to return to Falmouth. At 0950 the *Wren* reported that she was in company with the *Thistleglen* and *Phillippa (Phillip M?)* carrying 2,500 troops for Falmouth. The *Clan Ferguson* and *Baharistan* arrived at Plymouth. The French ss *Meknes* arrived from Brest with about 3,000 French troops, eleven civilians, a French Admiral and a French General.

At 1041, the *Mackay* reported that the La Pallice gate was shut and she was endeavouring to have it opened; the *Alderpool* and *Lady of Mann* were outside. At about that time there were 25,000 Polish troops in ports between Brest, Vannes and La Rochelle; 5,000 between Bordeaux and Bayonne; and 30,000 fighting elsewhere. It was thought that the last group might eventually reach Marseilles or Bordeaux. An instruction was issued that every effort should be made to bring them to the UK.

The *Punjabi* and *Harvester* joined convoy Stable 2 at 1226; at 1035 this convoy had been reported in 47° 52'N, 06° 21'W, with 1,200 troops who were without food and water. The *Wincheslea* was instructed by C in C WA that the two to three thousand from Stable 2 were to be landed at Falmouth, and that the ships were to be diverted accordingly. The *Whirlwind* reported at 2025 that the *Madura* would arrive at Falmouth at 1030 on 20 June with 1,370 refugees. *Nariva*, with 265 on board, was sent to the Bristol Channel.

On 19 June at 2301, the C in C WA instructed the *Glen Holt* camp, *RMB, Impregnable, Raleigh* and *Gdynia* that all French, Polish, Belgian and other nationals, service or civilian, landed from France were to be identified as early as possible. The *Batory* was ordered back to France after offloading in Plymouth, but her crew refused unless her AA guns were augmented. At that time her total armament consisted of only two Lewis guns. The Navy sent a Polish armed guard aboard, under a Polish Lieutenant Commander, who took command of the vessel, though the master remained to navigate her. Thus the Navy could send arms to subdue the crew, but not to defend them against the enemy!

At 0144 on 20 June, the *Sturdy* was ordered to Southampton with the *Dundrum Castle*, *Mckares (Meknes)* and *City of Mobile*. All these ships had 6,500 troops on board; this convoy sailed two hours later. At 0600, the *Mackay* reported that she had 'sailed the cargo ship *Alderpool* with 4,000 Polish troops on board and the *Empire Industry* with forty'. On 22 June, the HM yacht *Maid Marion* arrived at Plymouth at 0333 with twenty-eight refugees. She was with the *Alderpool* who was carrying approximately 3,000 Polish troops and 528 civilian refugees, also mostly Poles, with no food and water on board. The *Mackay* and *Maid Marion* had made previous appeals on behalf of the *Alderpool*. Despite the dire situation, the Admiralty had ordered *Maid Marion* to escort the *Alderpool* to Liverpool, a day and a half away. It was only when the Captain of the *Maid Marion,* a retired Captain RN, expressed his intention to go to Falmouth that the Admiralty relented and allowed the ship to go to Plymouth instead.

Two British ships were abandoned in Brest. They were the *Dido*, 3,554 grt, and the *Luffworth*, 279 grt. The *Arandora Star* was chased by a U-boat but managed to escape. British accounts have tended to ignore, or at least gloss over, French losses at the time. The French ship *Champlain* (28,000 tons gross) was reported mined off La Pallice on the morning of 17 June, but it was not believed that the port was blocked. On 18 June, the *Capitaine Maurice Eugene* of 4,499 tons sank because of a magnetic mine; the tug *Provençal* and the naval vessel *Vauquois* sank for the same reason. The following day a SNCF steamer was sunk by German artillery.

Several of the merchant ships would have had particular difficulty in accommodating the survivors. As the tanker *Cymbula* had recently discharged she would not have been 'gas free', so any spark may have caused an explosion; this would have meant that survivors could have only been sheltered in the accommodation. All would have to be searched for cigarette lighters and even the nails in soldier's boots may have constituted a danger.

Some of the tramp ships lacked a tween deck – see the drawing of the *Derrycunihy* in the picture section which had a tween deck. To get down into the lower holds, passengers would have had to climb 30 feet or more, down a vertical ladder to the hold bottom. Fortunately the weather was reasonable so most could have stayed on deck, where they would have been cold, even in summer. The *John Holt* and other West African traders had additional accommodation forward. This was fitted to house 'Kroo boys', and while it was very simple it would have given some protection from the elements, with basic lavatories and washing spaces. In these days, 'Kroo boys' is probably not an acceptable term, but then it referred to members of the Kroo tribe who joined the ship at Freetown. The Kroo, not crew as some think, though that may have been its origins, were a tribe who were skilled as stevedores, particularly loading the heavy logs that were a feature of that trade.

Operation Aerial – Bordeaux to St Jean de Luz

The French Government had moved to Bordeaux on 10 June. On 21 June they rejected Churchill's offer of a union with Britain and sought an Armistice; this came into force on 25 June. The bulk of the civilian escapees who arrived in Bordeaux had come via Paris; some brought items that would be of great value to the soon-to-be-isolated British. Much of the British Expeditionary Force's equipment had been abandoned at or before Dunkirk; this could not have been avoided as the troops were embarked from the beaches or the mole. Some of the equipment abandoned during Dynamo was still being used by the Germans in 1944/5. By the time Operation Aerial was underway, every effort was made to save as much as possible through the western French ports. By now, most of the military personnel were Polish and Czech; they had marched there in good order and some had to march on to St Jean de Luz before they could be embarked.

Shortly after midnight on 17 June, the *Arethusa* reported that fourteen ships were sailing from Le Verdon for Falmouth, with about 1,200 British refugees, and also *Madure* (*Madura* with 1,370?) with 180 Embassy Staff and 8,000 (total?) refugees, bound for the Bristol Channel.

The small Polish cargo ship *Chorzow* (845 grt) had carried tar from London to Bordeaux, where she arrived on 13 June. On 18 June she 'embarked 193 Polish refugees and Polish National Treasure – the King's crown and valuables from King's castle'. She sailed from Le Verdon Roads on 19 June and arrived at Falmouth on 21 June, where she delivered her passengers and valuable cargo. The treasure was later shipped to Canada on the *Batory*. The *Arethusa* requisitioned a number of ships that had arrived from Casablanca with convoy 1K; they included the Dutch ships *Alcor, Bennekom* and *Stad Haarlem*, who took to Falmouth sixty-nine, 400 and 296 civilians respectively. Another requisitioned ship was the Polish *Robur III / Kmcic*; she carried about around 300 Polish troops to safety.

Just before noon on 20 June, the following ships sailed from Le Verdon for Falmouth: the *Kasongo* with 100 British passengers; the *Nigerstroom* with 600 British passengers; the *Ville de Liège* with 200-300 Polish and Czech troops; and the *Broompark* with 'an unknown number of British nationals and machine tools'.

The reference to the *Broompark* hides a most interesting story. Charles 'Wild Jack' Howard was the 20th Earl of Suffolk and 13th Earl of Berkshire. His mother Margaret was the daughter of the American businessman Levi Leiter. When his father was killed on active service in 1917, eleven-year-old Charles Howard acceded to the title. He entered the Royal Naval College, Osborne, and then Radley College, but left to sign on the merchant windjammer *Mount Stewart*. In one article the young Earl is described as an apprentice and in the other a cadet – the terms are interchangeable. The Mount Stewart's Articles are at the Memorial University of Newfoundland.

When Suffolk returned, his family bought him a commission in the Scots Guards, but he resigned. He then worked his passage to Australia on a steamship and found work as a farmhand; before becoming co-owner, with Captain McColm, formerly Master of the *Mount Stewart,* of a farm in Queensland. In 1934 he married the actress Mimi Forde-Pigott, stage name Mimi Crawford.

In June 1935, Suffolk was admitted to the Westminster hospital with a serious illness. This may have been when he contracted rheumatoid arthritis; he suffered from the after effects for the rest of his life and walked with a stick. His new wife encouraged him to study pharmacology at Edinburgh University, where he gained a first-class honours degree in 1937 and was elected a fellow of the Royal Society of Edinburgh.

At the outbreak of war he was classed as 'medically unfit' because of his arthritis, so he remained as a civilian. He was that rare combination of an academic, practical man and leader. Those who knew him remarked on his willingness to work hard and his ability to mix with all classes. Most found him to be a delightful man *'c'était un très chic type'* – Ansiaux, but to the old guard in the French Government, he was the personification of Perfidious Albion.

At the beginning of February 1940, the Earl went to Paris as a liaison officer for the British Department of Scientific and Industrial Research. He had volunteered to save items and people of value to the war effort. He took with him Eileen Beryl Morden, who had been a secretary with the Ministry of Supply. Major Ardale Vautier Golding, with his secretary Marguerite Nicolle, also went to France as part of the same mission. The Earl's colourful exploits become the talk of Paris and the Germans were aware of his activities. The major, nominally an officer in the Royal Tank Regiment, but in fact a member of the security services, kept a lower profile; he and Miss Nicolle escaped from Paris about an hour before the arrival of the Germans. Miss Nicolle's diary can be seen at www.ww2talk.com/forum,

Major Golding had studied mechanical engineering at the University of London, and from 1929-31 he attended the Military College of Science at Woolwich. After spending 1938/9 in Berlin, he was sent to Paris at the outbreak of war, where he was appointed liaison officer to the French Ministry of Defence. Once Lord Suffolk arrived in Paris, the two kept in close touch.

Major Golding got to Bordeaux in the early hours of Sunday 16 June, and Lord Suffolk arrived a few hours later in a lorry that Golding had procured for him when his car was taken. The city was in uproar, the population had trebled and many of the incomers were desperate to get out of France. With help from the consular staff of the British Embassy in Bordeaux, they requisitioned Denholm's coal fired tramp ship *Broompark*, under Captain Olaf Paulsen.

As a young man, Paulsen landed in Leith from Norway; he spoke little English, but he eventually gained his Master's certificate. 'He was a quaint mixture of showman and clown, but he had intense drive was ruthlessly efficient.' He retired when in his sixties, but was recalled in 1939 to command the newly built *Broompark*. Captain Paulsen was a large man who spoke both English and French with a strong accent. His Glaswegian and Arab crew would have been no easier to understand.

Suffolk knew that a M. Paul Timbal, the manager of the Antwerp Diamond Bank, was making his way across France with diamonds. On 8 June, Timbal had flown to London to meet with Sir Ernest Oppenheimer, the Chairman of De Beers, when it was agreed that the Belgian diamonds should be brought to the UK, with the diamond cutters and their families, if at all possible. M. Timbal and others travelled in his car, followed by an old lorry that he had bought for the purpose; it carried two crates of diamonds worth £3 million. The diamonds were in sealed packets, each labelled with the customer's name.

By this time, many of the diamantaires and their families were sheltering in Le Verdon or Royan. The French authorities wanted to keep the diamantaires in France; in the event few made it to the UK, and most later went on to New York or Havana. Timbal was also sent to the *Broompark* and was introduced to the Earl, who was the centre of attention. One account tells of him working stripped to the waist, displaying his tattoos and carrying two pistols, Oscar and Genevieve. He agreed that the diamonds should be loaded on the *Broompark* with Paul Timbal, Hubert Jacques, Nicholas Ansiaux and André Van Campenhout. M. Ansiaux was accompanied by his wife and her parents; he carried a brief case with a million Belgian francs for a stockbroker called Dewaay.

Later, Colonel Golding, as he had become, recalled:

> Quite by chance we discovered about 700 tons of recently delivered American heavy machine tools on railway wagons on the quay area. By arrangement with the Embassy, and helped by the French, we had them loaded on board, this took three days ... an employee of the Ministry of Aircraft Production arrived with two light lorries containing a few light machine tools.

Just after midnight on 18 June, the scientists Hans Halban and Lew Kowarski arrived with their families and a consignment of 'heavy water' that had originated in Norway. At that time, the Norsk Hydro Ryukan plant was the only place where heavy water (deuterium oxide) could be isolated. In early March 1940, Lieutenant Jacques Allier managed to fly all the remaining 187.5 litres in twenty-six cans to France via Scotland. The nuclear scientist Jean Frédéric Joliot-Curie took charge of the material. Joliot-Curie and his wife Irène (Marie Skłodowska Curie's daughter) shared the 1935 Nobel prize for chemistry; by the outbreak of the Second World War, Joliot-Curie was a professor at the Collège de France. When France was invaded, he and his colleagues loaded the cans and their research papers into cars. Each man was married with an infant daughter, who went with them. They first hid their cargo in a Banque de France vault and then in a women's prison, before moving it to Bordeaux, where it was loaded onto the *Broompark*. The ship was bombed, possibly because the Fifth Column were aware of her presence. After this they moved berth, which meant that Joliot-Curie could not find the ship; had he done so it was likely that the Earl would have made him stay.

By now there were 101 extra people on board. The women and children were put in the officers' cabins, while wooden platforms were fitted in the cargo hold for the men. The photograph of the *Broompark* in the picture section also shows two structures on deck, probably temporary lavatories (see *Calumet*). The *Broompark* sailed from Bordeaux shortly after 0600 on 19 June. Also aboard were a 'British Army Major and four troops'. A French reserve officer supervised the placing of an anti-submarine gun on the stern and provided a gun crew of four hand-picked from the French Navy. These facts are from Paul Timbal's account, provided by Bruno Comer. Suffolk and Golding's report states:

> We also succeeded in extracting from the Naval Authorities in Bordeaux two anti-aircraft 75mm guns one 'under and over' 9mm pair of Hotchkiss machine guns and one single barrelled Hotchkiss anti-aircraft machine gun of the same calibre.

Yet another Major was in Bordeaux at this time; Frank Foley who had saved so many Jews while in Berlin. One account says: 'While briefly in Bordeaux in June 1940 ... he continued to issue visas for Britain.'

On the way down the Gironde, the ship ahead was mined and sunk (*Mexique?*). Miss Nicolle records in her diary that 'more than a thousand passengers were saved'. Some secondary sources say that the ships sailed without pilots (this is possible – see the photograph of the *Broompark*); if so, this 60-mile river journey would have been hazardous. The ship stopped at Le Verdon to load ammunition for the guns. When the Germans became aware that the heavy water had left, Joliot-Curie convinced them that it was in the sunken ship.

A raft was built to house both the diamonds and the heavy water; the idea of this 'ark' was that it would float if the ship sank. Suffolk and Golding dictated a document – in English and French – setting out the precautions that had been taken to ensure the survival of the most precious items. Only the French version seems to be in the National Archives files. This was also signed by those in charge of the heavy water and the diamonds. The *Broompark* arrived at Falmouth at 0600 on 21 June. The master was as economical with words as he was with everything else; he does not record loading the cargo, or the passengers, but does say in an Official

Log entry that with 101 souls on board he decided to ignore a distress call from *ONVJ* (*Ville de Namur* with a cargo of 900 horses), 90 miles away. He had issued all available life jackets before leaving Bordeaux, but there were only sufficient for the women and children; the men had inner tubes taken from cars that had been loaded. An entry in the Official Log records that a lifeboat drill was held and the boats were swung out.

Nineteen vessels sailed from the Gironde between 17 and 23 June; two warships and several cargo liners. No reports explain the choice of the *Broompark*, who nevertheless did her job well.

Suffolk seems to have acquired a supply of champagne and is described as limping around the ship dispensing it to those who were sea-sick; telling them that it was the best cure for their affliction. Kowarski later described the Earl as being in keeping with his vision of the British aristocracy, garnered from novels by P. G. Woodhouse. This was probably unfair to Lord Suffolk, who was no Bertie Wooster and certainly not in need of a Jeeves to guide him through life.

The food that had been brought aboard by the passengers was pooled. Kowarski says that the ladies organised the meals, which Ansiaux describes as 'very unappealing'. In their report, Suffolk and Golding credit Mr Barton of the International Chamber of Commerce in Paris with organising the catering.

The *Broompark* arrived at Falmouth at 0600 on 21 June. Kowarski was taken with the beauty of the harbour, but noted that masts could be seen showing where ships had recently been sunk; as they approached the coast they saw a number of German aircraft. The passengers were weary and covered in coal dust, but most were put in nearby hotels were they were able to bathe and then eat before enjoying a sleep. The Earl and his companions' task would only be complete when they delivered their treasures in London.

The Earl sent a telegram to London:

OHMS PRIORITY = TRAINLOAD LEAVING SPECIAL TRAIN FALMOUTH 2300 APPROX STOP WILL TELEPHONE DEPARTMENT ON ARRIVAL = SUFFOLK AND BERKSHIRE

The train arrived at London's Paddington station at 0900 on 22 June, where they breakfasted at the G.W.R. Hotel. On the previous day, the Director of Scientific Research, Dr H. J. Gough, had briefed the Minister (Herbert Morrison or Harold Macmillan) who authorised the Admiralty to send a signal to Bayonne regarding the transport to the UK of uranium ore and the 'technicians'. When the Dr Gough went to the Admiralty he found that the First Sea Lord was 'at a conference ... and (he) waited till 7.0 p.m.' The second secretary at the Admiralty got in touch with the director of operations and was told that, 'as there were a number of merchant ships in Bayonne, the Admiralty did not consider it necessary to send a special destroyer.'

Lord Suffolk and Major Golding made a three page report, which concluded:

We should like to make this the occasion of expressing our warmest thanks to the following people:—

Captain Bichelonne and Colonel Raguet of the Ministere de l'Armament, without whose devoted help, without whose unparalleled efficiency and without whose heartfelt sympathies our mission could not even have started.

To the members of the British Embassy who were at that time in Bordeaux, with especial reference to the Commercial Attache, Mr Irving, and the Minister, Mr Harvey, who in the case of Mr Irving secured us our ship, and in the case of Mr Harvey secured us an omnibus passport and clearance through the Customs, without which our task would have been made immeasurably more arduous and difficult.

To Captain Paulsen, the Officers and members of the ship's crew of the s.s. *Broompark*, who afforded the most loyal, painstaking and hardworking assistance to us and who, in circumstances which might have been of extreme discomfort, did all they could to make us and our personnel as comfortable as circumstances would allow.

Thanks are also due to Mr Barton, who was a Director of the International Chamber of Commerce in Paris, and whom the Embassy asked us to transport as a passenger. Mr Barton took endless trouble to organise the catering department of our journey on the ship and did this very successfully.

Also our thanks are due to Monsieur Berthiez, who when we were faced with the removal of our dock foreman and dockers organised a scratch crew from the Port and with the aid of the 1st Mate of the ship and Colonel Liebessart, superintended the extremely difficult matter of loading these machine tools himself.

We should also like to comment most favourably upon the efficiency, courtesy and diligence shown to us by Lt. Commdr. Mills, R.N.V.R., of the Falmouth Contraband Control. This Officer did everything within his power to facilitate the landing and despatch of our personnel and valuables and was of the very greatest possible assistance to us.

Finally, we should like to cite in the very warmest manner possible the conduct of our two secretaries, Miss Morden and Miss Nicolle. Faced with the most uncomfortable possible conditions, faced with hours of work which frequently amounted to some twenty per day, faced at times with the greatest possible danger, they conducted themselves coolly, calmly and extremely efficiently and did what they could to render the operation a success.

An undated covering note, which is only initialled, says:

As we are in secret session I am able to tell the House of a piece of work by two officers of the Ministry who were in Paris as Liaison Officers with the Ministry of Armament. These officers, with the co-operation of certain patriotic Frenchmen and the British Embassy, succeeded in obtaining a ship and arming it against attack from the air. This ship was loaded with, among other things, machine tools and large quantities of valuable and secret stores, some of them of almost incalculable scientific importance. There were also embarked on this ship, owing to the efforts that were made, a considerable party of key personnel consisting of eminent scientists and armament experts.

In spite of an attempt to bomb it, this ship arrived safely in England and arrangements are being made for the personnel to continue their work in the service of the Allied cause and the stores have been safely disposed of.

Although I cannot do so publicly I should like to pay tribute to the highly successful efforts of the representatives of the ministry and also to the members of the British Embassy and to the officers and crew of the ship.

A considerable service has been rendered to the Allied cause by the safe arrival of this shipload.

This may well have been Herbert Morrison's or Harold Macmillan's report to the House. The heavy water was distributed between the prison at Wormwood Scrubs, the Cavendish Laboratory and the library at Windsor Castle, the royal residence to the west of London. The next occasion that the House of Commons sat in secret session was on the 27 June. Presumably because the mission was top secret, no awards are recorded, nor is it pointed out that the ship was a merchant ship.

On 22 June there were ninety-seven ships in Falmouth, so *Broompark* was instructed to sail for Swansea. In fact she sailed for British Columbia on 25 June, back under MOWT control. In Canada she loaded ore and lumber (sawn timber). On the return voyage in convoy HX 72 she was torpedoed and almost thrown on her beam ends. Most of the crew were saved by a corvette, though one fireman drowned. Captain Paulsen and seven of his deck and engineer officers remained on board and began the delicate business of righting the ship using water ballast. Then the balance of the crew re-boarded and the *Broompark* resumed her homeward voyage. Though she was bombed and machine gunned while approaching the UK, Paulsen brought his ship safely home. For this he was awarded the OBE and Lloyd's Medal for Gallantry at Sea. Shortly after that he joined the Denholm Superintendent's Department, where he remained for the rest of the War.

The scientists went on to have distinguished careers and played themselves in a post-war film about the epic escape to Britain. M. Timbal and M. Ansiaux – Baron Ansiaux as he became – continued to be important figures in the Belgian banking industry after the War. Despite Lord Suffolk's best efforts, Captaine Bichelonne and the others who had greatly helped the mission were refused permission to leave France because of the Armistice. Bichelonne died in hospital in Germany in 1944 in mysterious circumstances; had he survived he would have been put in trial by the French as a collaborator. There is no record of the 8 tons of uranium ore and 80 tons of tolite (as spelt in signal from First Sea Lord's private office – possibly pectolite, a mineral) being saved from France.

The Earl formed a three-person bomb disposal team that he called 'The Holy Trinity'. In 1941, the Earl, his chauffeur Fred Hards, Miss Morden, four sappers and one other person were killed on Erith Marshes while the Earl was attempting to defuse the thirty-fifth bomb. They may have been the first UXB team to encounter the booby-trapped /Y fuse. The Earl was awarded the George Cross. In the same supplement to *The London Gazette* (35220 15 July 1941) there were Commendations for 'brave conduct in Civil Defence' for 'Frederick William Hards (deceased), Van Driver, and Miss Eileen Beryl Morden (deceased), Shorthand-Typist – both from the Experimental Unit, Ministry of Supply.' Miss Morden died in the ambulance and is buried in a council grave with two others. When the grave was traced by Chris Ranstead, her name was misspelt as Norden – Mr Ranstead believes that this may have been corrected, but there is no mention of the Commendation for Brave Conduct. It may have been that only the George Cross and a Commendation can be awarded posthumously, which would account for what appears to be a rather niggardly treatment of this brave woman and of Mr Fred Hards.

Major Golding became a Colonel and retired in 1956; he died in Nantucket in 1992. No information has been found on Miss Nicolle, who writes in her diary that she 'left for Wye' at 2 p.m. on 26 June for '9 ½ days leave'; perhaps she also had a security clearance. However, Mr Ian Golding has pointed out that a Miss Marguerite Nicolle died on 17 July 1998.

Secondary sources have made the story somewhat Suffolk-centric, possibly because Lord Suffolk was such a colourful character. As Major Golding said in a letter to the *Sunday Times* 'I am sure Lord Suffolk, if he were alive today, would wish me to say that the task, though interesting and unusual, was not "fantastic" and was no more dangerous than any routine evacuation under the conditions.' It would also seem that he would have wished the important part played by his three colleagues to be recognised.

At 1312 on 20 June, the *Berkeley* was ordered by the Admiralty to get in touch with Feller & Co., 1, Espirit de Lois, Bordeaux, and arrange shipment of vital goods ex. Goth Co., Switzerland. These included Oerlikon guns, spares (and drawings?). One file states that 'valuable stores' had been shipped on *Swift* (a General Steam ship) on 17 June. On 22 June, B.N.L.O. Bordeaux was informed by the Admiralty that s.s. *Formedine* (*Fort Medine?*), with a valuable cargo of copper and machine tools, should be sailed without delay. The French ship *Le Trait* was included in the series of messages, but she was diverted to North Africa, with the goods ex Goth Co. The French Admiralty had already moved a large quantity of Belgian gold to a 'safe destination' outside France. Admiral Darlan was not willing to tell the British (or the Belgians) where this was. *Le Trait* remained under the French flag throughout the War, while the *Fort Medine* was seized by the British on arrival in Falmouth. Also during the night of 22 June, the French ship *Louis L D*, with a general cargo, 'deserted' convoy HX 50; she had been destined for Belfast, this act of barratry deprived the British of 7,000 tons of valuable cargo.

At 1730, the *Imogen* reported numbers evacuated as: *Witch*, 340, *Viscount*, 500, and herself with 466, including three British and fourteen Belgian soldiers. At 2130, the master of the French ship *Gravelinnes* asked for food for the 500 people on board. At 2258, the following were sent to the Gironde with orders to report to any British warship on arrival: the *Delius, Glenaffric, Clan Ferguson, Blairnevis, Cyclops, Beckenham, Clan Ross, Balfe, Kyno, Kuffra, Kelso, Maplewood, Calumet* and *Baron Nairn*. The signal said that the *Royal Scotsman* should have already arrived there. Another signal added that the *Ormonde*, with a capacity of 5,000, was also due at the Gironde, and the *Batory*, with a capacity of 3,000, had been ordered to Bayonne. These, and other ships, had their destination ports changed, sometimes several times.

On the *Calumet*, Thomson wrote in his diary:

> ... under the Admiralty as a transport, just returned from Norway. We were sent post-haste to Bordeaux to try to rescue some troops retreating from the Germans. But when we got within sight of the land, a lighthouse at the mouth of the Gironde called us up by Morse lamp, to say that the Germans were in the town, and it was too late. So the ship was put about for England, and we arrived back in Falmouth on 25 June.

The *Ettrick* reported that she was off the entrance to Bayonne and had been informed by the signal station that she was too large to enter. She requested further instructions and was told to stay under way in the vicinity and await orders.

At 1930, the *Berkeley* informed *Vanquisher* that she was with the *Clan Ferguson* and *Royal Scotsman* (also *Blairnevis*) with 4,000 Polish troops, leaving Le Verdon at 2115 for Liverpool, and that the *Delius* would follow on 23 June with another 2,000. The embarkation of 6,000 Poles was completed and *Delius* sailed at 0915, unescorted. By this time the *Beagle* was short of fuel. The French refused to permit further embarkation 'without British assistance'. Polish officers were remaining to divert the Poles to Bayonne; it was suggested that *Beckenham* 'be diverted thither'. When they were approaching the River Gironde, HMCS *Fraser* was cut in half when she was rammed by the Cruiser *Calcutta*, the fore part sank. HMCS *Restigouche* was ordered to sink the after part, after recovering survivors. On 24 June, when en route to St Jean de Luz, the cargo ship *Kufra* was rammed and sunk by the French ship *San Diego*.

It was decided that the small port of St Jean de Luz, near Bayonne, offered better loading prospects, so it was from there that the senior naval officer reported that 'no less than 9,000 Poles' sailed in the *Sobeiski* and *Batory* on 21 June. These ships were not escorted, but arrived safely at Plymouth on 24 June. It was also reported that British refugees embarking in the *Ettrick* would require close examination as there were some 'doubtful cases among them'. Poles continued to arrive and it was intended that the next embarkation would be on the *Arandora Star*. The SNO enquired when the *Arandora Star* might be expected and stated that *Fraser* had been 'withdrawn'. At 1000 on 23 June, he signalled that the *Ettrick* had been loaded with 1,000 refugees and another 3,000 had arrived. At noon he added, 'am now filling *Ettrick* to capacity by embarking 300 Poles ... when may we expect another ship?' When *Ettrick* sailed she was said to be 'full to capacity' with 2,000 troops. One passenger was King Zog of Albania.

At 1523 C in C WA informed Admiralty that it was understood that 49,000 troops still required evacuation so *Belgravian*, *Baron Nairn*, *Baron Kinnard* and *Kerma* were sent to Bayonne. At 2100 on 23 June, all embarkation ceased at St Jean de Luz, owing to the heavy swell. It was restarted at 0700 the next morning with the *Arandora Star* inside the breakwater being filled with Polish Army and Air Force. The signal added that Polish forces would require close scrutiny. At 1430, 2,600 Poles remained at St Jean de Luz. The cargo ship *Clan Ross* was attacked by aircraft at 1344 when she was 30 miles NNW of St Jean de Luz. *Clan Ross*, and the empty *Cyclops*, *Kerma*, *Glenaffric*, *Belgravian* and *Beckenham*, were escorted back to the UK by the *Mackay* and *Viva II*.

On 23 June, the Polish drifters *Delfin II*, *Korab I* and *Korab II* had arrived at Barry Dock with Polish soldiers from La Rochelle. That evening, SNO sent a signal pointing out that C in C's signal of 2356 on 22 June, refusing permission to embark wives and families, was 'causing difficulties and heart rending scenes'. He asked if he could promise embarkation after priority commitments had been fulfilled, saying that it was impossible to be sure of the identity of any of those who wished to board. At 0731 on 25 June, the C in C signalled that the wives and families of Polish soldiers could be embarked 'if accommodation available', and approximately 2,000 womenfolk embarked in the *Batory* and *Sobieski*. These were presumably included in the 9,000 total that these Polish liners had on board. Because of the earlier crew trouble, Captain Pacewicz was relieved on arrival at Plymouth and Captain Deyczakowski took command; at the same time the armed guard disembarked.

The small cargo ship *Kelso* replaced the *Arandora Star* at the loading berth and only when enemy aircraft were sighted, and with the Armistice in force, did she and the *Baron Kinnard* sail for Liverpool with a total of 2,000 troops. The *Baron Nairn* also sailed for Falmouth for the same reason, with 1,200 Polish troops and British refugees aboard. Food must have been a problem because even in peacetime, the Baron ship's owners were known throughout the service as 'Hungry Hogarth's.' They reached their destination four days later. Just over a week later, the *Arandora Star* was torpedoed; of the 1,673 on board, 470 Italian and 243 German POWs died, plus thirty-seven guards. Captain Moulton, twelve officers and forty-two crew also lost their lives. At 1721 on 25 June, the C in C informed the Admiralty that it was intended to release merchant ships reserved for Aerial as no further requirement could be foreseen: the Armistice had come into force.

On 28 June, the trawlers *St Malante* and *Bervie Braes* arrived at Plymouth at 0724, and the *Baron Nairn* arrived at 0735 with refugees from St Jean de Luz and anchored in Cawsand Bay. A small French fishing boat with twelve male refugees also arrived at Cawsand at 0750, and one minute later the *Glenaffric* passed the signal station at Plymouth.

Operation Aerial was over, though refugees continued to arrive. At 0825, the French fishing vessel *Dom Michel Nobletz* arrived from Ushant with one British and seven French refugees, thirty-three sailors and seven soldiers. She was also without food and water.

Winser says:

> No reliable figures have been found of the number of civilians who crossed from France but, without any doubt, no fewer than 211,000 servicemen and evacuees embarked ... during the ten days of Operation Aerial.

Official figures for those (troops?) landed in the UK during Operation Aerial were: British 139,812, French 17,062, Poles 24,352, Czechs 4,938, Belgians 163; Total 186,377. All but a few thousand were carried in about 180 merchant ships. In all, fifty-three merchant ships were lost during the evacuation of France. Less people were saved during this operation than Dunkirk. For that reason those who learn about it regard it as less successful than Operation Dynamo; but the distances were much greater and those saved had to be fed and sheltered for one to three days, rather than a few hours. It could therefore be said that this was a more difficult task, and in terms of man/miles, the larger of the two.

> Decorations: The KING has been pleased to grant unrestricted permission for the wearing (or for the acceptance by the next-of-kin) of the Cross of Valour (Krzyz Walecznych) which has been conferred by the President of the Polish Republic upon the under-mentioned Officers and Men of the Merchant Navy in recognition of their gallant conduct during the withdrawal of Polish troops from France in June, 1940:—

The Late Captain Edgar Wallace Moulton, Master, S.S. *Arandora Star*. The Late Joseph Brindley, Bosun's Mate, S.S. *Arandora Star*. Captain John William Cromarty, Master, S.S. *Glendinning*. Captain Duncan Darroch, Master, M.V. *Royal Scotsman*. Captain Lachlan Dewar, Master, S.S. *Baron Kinnaird*. Captain Tom Valentine Frank, Master, S.S. *Alderpool*. Captain Alfred Hinchcliff, Master, S.S. *Kelso*. Captain John Murray Legg, Master, M.V. *Ettrick*. Captain Richard William Stanley Marshall, Master, S.S. *Glenlea*. Captain Duncan McCall, Master, S.S. *Blairnevis*. Captain David Frederick Owens, Master, M.V. *Ulster Monarch*. Captain Henry Edward Geves Scott-Smith, Master, S.S. *Clan Ferguson*. Captain William Warriner Watson**, Master, S.S. *Delius*. Mr George Smith Anderton, Chief Officer, S.S. *Kelso*. Mr Arthur William Craib, Chief Officer, S.S. *Baron Kinnaird*. Mr Alexander Miller, Chief Officer, S.S. *Glenlea*.* Mr William Ritchie Pitkeathly, Second Officer, M.V. *Royal Scotsman*. Mr Wroth Thomas Coull Lethbridge, Troop Officer, M.V. *Ettrick*. Mr Hall Wilson, Chief Steward, S.S.

Blairnevis. Mr Albert John Toy, Chief Steward, S.S. *Delius*. Mr John Whyte, Steward, S.S. *Glendinning*. Mr Joseph Lois, Able Seaman, S.S. *Alderpool*.

The Czechoslovak War Cross 1939 -1945 was awarded to: Jean Monamicq, Master *Forbin* (French merchant ship). The award to the Master of the *Ville de Liège* was cancelled as the vessel had moved to the US Flag and the officers concerned were no longer on the vessel. Three naval officers were also recommended for awards – for organising the disembarkation at Falmouth! (For other Czech awards see next chapter). Others from these ships, and other merchant vessels, received British decorations as well.

---

*   Master's comments: 'not long returned from his experiences on the *Graf Spee*' and 'was very cool under a difficult situation'.

** Award made to Captain A. W. Gough, who was in command at the time; Captain W. W. Watson's award was upheld for his work in evacuating Polish troops from Norway. Mr Watson, chief officer, suggested that he was the Watson concerned; this was not accepted as the authorities 'did not like the tone of his letter'!

Evacuations from the South of France through, and from, Gibraltar

On 1 June 1940, the Orient Line passenger vessel *Orford* was bombed and set on fire off Toulon. The vessel was abandoned and fourteen of her crew were killed. *Orford* appears to have been the only passenger ship that was available to perform an evacuation from the South of France. It was known that British, Czech and Polish forces and civilians were making their way south.

Early in the War, the British Expeditionary Force had established a base at Marseilles, from where troops were to be embarked for the East; it was felt that this was preferable to the longer sea voyage from Southampton. In May 1940, the local commander asked what arrangements were made for evacuation in the event that Italy entered the War; he does not appear to have received a reply. When the military command realised the gravity of the situation, they began to arrange evacuation by train. The port chosen was La Pallice , right across the country. As we have seen, events moved quickly and the 700 or so troops embarked on three ships on 18 June. The cargo ship *Finland* sailed with the *Alma Dawson*, *Coultarn* and *Toussika*; of these the *Toussika* is named in the signals as being the only vessel that could load MT stores.

The destroyer *Keppel* left Port Vendres for Sète to organise the evacuation of Czech and Polish troops, arriving at 0740 on 23 June. *Velox* was sent to Port Vendres from Gibraltar, arriving at 0600 on the same day. During the afternoon of 24 June, the British steamers *Oakcrest*, *Britannic* and *Lord Cochrane* reached Sète. They were also involved in the evacuation of Port Vendres, as were the British ships *Apapa*, *Coultarn*, *Gartbrattan*, *Viceroy of India*, *Northmoor* and *Neuralia*, and the Egyptian steamers *Mohamed Ali el Kebir* and *Rod el Farag*. *Keppel* left Sète with the *Mohamed Ali el Kebir* and joined the destroyer *Velox* which sailed from Port Vendres at 0300 on 26 June with the *Apapa*. The ships travelled in company to Gibraltar, where they arrived on the same day.

The British expatriates living on the Riviera expected 'a cruiser' to evacuate them in the style that they felt was their due; in the event, they had to embark on two 'overcrowded filthy ships' that had recently discharged their coal cargoes in Toulon. One of these ships had 'only two lavatories'. Several vessels picked up at more than one port and then sailed independently from France, arriving at Gibraltar between 26 and 30 June. One woman, who remained behind, said that her friends had written that they had to suffer these conditions all the way to Liverpool.

Ashcrest and *Saltersgate* had discharged their coal cargoes in Toulon, and after two days, during which their crews did their best to clean the ships, boarded a total of 1,300 refugees, mostly civilians. From Cannes they sailed first to Marseilles, where the refugees were forbidden to land, then were instructed to join a French convoy bound for Oran. Other evacuees, including some Poles, went to Oran in French ships.

The author W. Somerset Maugham was on the *Saltersgate*. He wrote about the voyage in these small tramp steamers in *Strictly Personal*, published by William Heinemann in 1941. Some of his recollections, written soon after the event, are comic, while others are tragic. He says 'One lady, when she came aboard, told an officer that of course she wanted to go first class, and another called the steward (there was only one) and asked him to show her where the games deck was. "It's all over the ship, madam," he replied.'

Somerset Maugham then goes on to say that, after some initial disorder, 'Wardens were chosen for each hatch to keep order, see that nobody smoked below or after dark and that the hold was kept reasonably clean.' He comments, as others did, on the shortage of water. Those that boarded had been told to bring food for three days; others who had brought nothing were fed from the ships stores. After the three days everyone joined the food queue. One can only imagine the problem of feeding 500 people (800 on the *Ashcrest*) especially as a few of the less considerate joined the line twice. Eventually the ship could only supply a small piece of bully beef and a few sweet biscuits to each person.

Ashcrest developed engine trouble and put back. This meant that she was able to load extra food, but it also meant that she made the rest of the trip unescorted. When they were attacked by an Italian submarine, the sole gunner returned fire and the ship made a smoke screen enabling her to escape. Those aboard thought that *Ashcrest* was on fire, though 'everyone remained calm'. On *Saltersgate*, four people 'went out of their minds' and at least two died.

After five days at sea they were told that they would be landed in Oran, to await instructions from Gibraltar. On the day of arrival, conditions were worsening; most were in high spirits but bad news was to come. France had capitulated and the French colonial authorities expected to receive instructions to detain the ship and those on board. After heated, but fruitless, discussions between the master, the Nice vice-consul and the shore authorities, the master managed to contact Gibraltar by radio. The instructions were to obtain as much food as possible and sail for Gibraltar. As it was a Sunday, many of the shops were shut. However, the master and the ship's chandler went round in a taxi and bought 500 lbs of bread, as much fruit as they could get, plus the all-important cigarettes and matches.

They again set sail, arriving in Gibraltar on Tuesday morning, 'This time we thought our troubles were really over.' But they were again told that they would not be allowed to land; at this news many broke down. After much discussion, the children, the sick and elderly were taken off, and presumably, transferred to the troopers and passenger ships. The remaining 280 passengers were allowed ashore in batches to do shopping, and in many cases, to bathe.

The ships then set off in convoy, arriving in Liverpool after an eleven-day voyage. Somerset Maugham writes: 'I should not like to end this part of my narrative without paying a tribute to the crew who worked like dogs to make our lot tolerable, to the officers who gave up their cabins to the old and the sick, and, to the skipper, Captain Stubbs, to whose courage, skill and firmness we owed it that we were brought safely home.' When talking about the optimism of the British seamen he says of those on the *Saltersgate* 'The crew were rough Glasgow boys.... They were friendly and willing and they bubbled over with high spirits.'

The numbers are not known, but Roskill says that 'some 10,000 passed through Gibraltar from French Mediterranean ports.' When the rescue ended on 14 July-thirty nine ships had been employed and 12,832 troops were evacuated from Sète, Port Vendres and Marseilles. Mr R. A. Butler, speaking in the House of Commons on 17 July said that it 'was not in the public interest to disclose what steps had been taken [to evacuate British citizens from the South of France]'. On 15 June, he had talked of 'the difficulty of providing British shipping for purposes of this kind at the moment when very heavy calls were being made on it for the evacuation of the British Expeditionary Force and Allied Armies from France.' This was rather a strange statement when the Prime Minister had said that the evacuation of the BEF had been completed by the 4 June 1940 at Dunkirk.

A group of Czech civilians had also travelled south where they hoped to board a ship; they included a young woman called Marianne Adler, who had arrived in Sète. The Czech military prevented them from boarding as they were 'neither dependants of soldiers, nor embassy employees'. The French took pity on them and left them a camion to sleep in. The following morning the master of a British cargo ship heard of their plight and took them aboard (*Northmoor?*). 'He declared that his orders were to pick up refugees, army or no army, and so we entered the ship.' 'Being considered by the Czech burocrats [sic] as the "illegals" getting the worst sleeping places and being the last ones in the queues for food.'

The ship then set sail for Gibraltar. Miss Adler says:

When I say 'ship', you must not expect a nice steamer with cabins etc. It was in fact a coal freighter, which had unloaded its coal in Marseilles and was ordered to pick us up. It was correspondingly dirty, and we were just spread out on the floor of a big bunker under the deck. What made it worse, there was a shortage of water, and we often had to weigh up whether we should use our ration for drinking or washing. In Gibraltar the ship did not land, but waited for three days in midwater for a larger ship to arrive and take us over. The water shortage became more acute during that time, and we were relieved when the ship at last arrived. It was a large troop ship, *Neuralia*, which had just come from India and had a mixed English and Indian crew. On it were loaded Czech and Polish troops. This ship was a different proposition from our previous freighter. Very spacious, cabins for one or two people, a large laundry room where at last we could wash our clothes. The weather was warm and we spent a good part of the day on the deck.

We had turned into the Atlantic and went straight on, as if heading for America.... We tried to guess: United States, Africa, I thought already of camping out in the open in a tropical climate.... Some of the few older people on ship were worried and depressed, one young woman jumped into the sea with her baby in a fit of despair – a tragedy of which I only learned later. But for young people like me, who had no ties, it was like a big adventure. Eventually the news seeped through: Great Britain was to be our aim. The big roundabout way we had taken, was mainly to avoid the sea mines. My heart sank when I heard this. It was an anti-climax to my tropical fantasies; also I imagined England as a country where the rain and fog never stop and the sun never comes out through the clouds. Our first impressions of Liverpool, where we landed after having been three weeks at sea, were apt to confirm the prejudice. The sky was dark and it poured with rain. Yet, this was to prove one of the loveliest summers, to correct my ideas about England. From the start, officials we had met in England were civil and friendly, something we had not experienced in Belgium or France.

Miss Adler seems to have married and settled in Britain.

A Czech soldier retells his own experiences on the same voyage:

A convoy of some 3,000 Czechs eventually sailed for England in two large ships.... At that time, a boat was sailing along the French Riviera picking up British and American civilians who were also being evacuated from France. The Captain was given strict orders that he could not carry army personnel. The commander of the Czech Forces decided to formally dissolve the Czech army so we then became *de facto* civilian refugees. The Captain permitted us to board his boat which was heading for Oran in Morocco.... During the journey the Captain received orders to sail to Gibraltar from where we would be taken to England. Once at Gibraltar, we were anchored in the bay and not permitted to enter harbour. We had to wait for the assembly of a convoy to protect us on our journey across the Atlantic because of the risk of attack from German U-boats.... After a few days of being anchored in the Bay, a convoy was assembled and we sailed into the Atlantic, travelling westwards about three-quarters of the way to America before turning eastwards and sailing around Ireland.... We landed at Liverpool after nearly 14 days at sea.

A Shetland Islander called Tommy Thomson was at that time an AB in the Merchant Service and he kept a diary through much of the War. This was contrary to instructions, but these diaries have proved an excellent source of information. Writing about his time on the cargo ship *Calumet* he says:

On Sunday 30th June we shifted into Devonport. Here the *Calumet*, was hastily fitted out for carrying troops. Wooden stairways were fitted for access to the tween decks, and provision made for slinging hammocks, there were six hatches. Against the bulwark on the port side of the after deck, three coal burning cooking ranges were set. On the starboard side, at the fore end of the after deck, a primitive structure of wood and canvas equipped with buckets served for toilets.' [See *Broompark* photograph in the picture section].

On Tuesday 2nd July, tenders came alongside, full of French Matelots. They loaded 1,100 of them on board of us, and we immediately hove up the anchor and sailed from Plymouth. We were bound for Casablanca in French Morocco, this we only found out after we had sailed and joined a convoy. It was important that destinations should be kept secret. There were ten ships in the convoy all similarly loaded with French navy men who had escaped across the Channel on the fall of France to the German army, and had no wish to continue the fight. They were all in uniform and were being repatriated to French Morocco. We had an escort of destroyers, and we were the Commodore Ship, which meant we carried the Naval Officer in charge of the convoy.

The weather was good being summertime. During the passage to Casablanca, the British Navy sank the French warships in Oran harbour, and somehow or other our French sailors got to hear of it, and there was a change in the attitude, as if they didn't like us anymore. Our accommodation was right forward and in the night the French were sleeping everywhere all over the decks. Catering was a problem as the coal-burning stoves on the open deck were only allowed to be lit at dawn and at dusk. The convoy arrived off Casablanca on Tuesday 9th of July. Our ship lay at anchor until Thursday 11th, when we were shifted into the harbour. On Friday the 12th we got alongside and disembarked the sailors. The shore authorities were distinctly hostile towards us. After the fall of France, Italy came into the war on the side of Germany, and Italian war planes started dropping bombs on Gibraltar, a great many women and children were evacuated down to French Morocco. Now with this drastic change in circumstances they came to be in hostile territory, and the ships that brought the French sailors here had to take the refugees back out again.

As the sailors disembarked so the ship's crew had to turn to and clean the holds, so as to re-embark the women and children. The shore authorities allowed us a minimal amount of time alongside the quay, just long enough for one lot to get ashore, and the other to get aboard. In all we embarked 605 women and children, and we sailed from Casablanca at 8 pm. We arrived at Gibraltar at 4 pm the next day on Saturday 15th July, and anchored in the bay. All the women and children were taken ashore by tender. I have no figures of how many refugees were on board the other ships.

In Weymouth, the attitude to the French was unchanged. The *Meknes* (Commander Dubroc) had been repatriating 1,180 French seamen. She had been granted safe passage under the terms of the Armistice and was sailing fully lit.

On the 25th July 1940, at about 9.15 am, intimation was received that about 1,000 French Naval Ratings were expected to be landed at Weymouth shortly, their ship, the *Meknes*, having been torpedoed in the Channel on her passage to France where the men were to have been repatriated. At noon 842 survivors arrived at the Alexandra Gardens Theatre, Weymouth, and were immediately fed with soup, bread, biscuits, cheese etc., for which they expressed their gratitude. The men were in a pitiable state, many of them having lost nearly all their clothes and footwear. After the meal they dried their clothes, shaved and washed and at about 3.45 pm, a second meal was served. Chars-a-banc [A type of early open top motor coach with bench seats, each seat having its own door on both sides – a term for a coach that was still in use in Dorset] arrived at five o'clock to take the men to the Railway Station for despatch to another Centre.

Thomson says:

We lay at anchor in the bay from then until the 30th July, nobody allowed ashore, a very strict lookout was kept at night time, as the Italians were using frogmen from a Spanish base to plant limpet mines on ships anchored in the bay. At night there were frequent air raids on the rock. Carpenters from Gibraltar came off and worked at improving the facilities, for access to the holds and for cooking, and toilet arrangements. They built a temporary deck house over the stoves on the after deck, and fixed the toilets so that they could flush.

On Thursday the 30th July, we embarked 270 people mostly women and children, with their personal belongings. Among them the Chief of Police from Gibraltar and his family. Two other policemen, and eleven Italian internees. There was no segregation of the internees, indeed they were most useful, as they took over the catering for the refugees, and looked after that for the whole of the voyage home. They also had piano accordions and often entertained the refugees in the evenings. There were only six ships in the convoy this time, all carrying refugees, and bound for Avonmouth. We were 15 days on the passage from Gibraltar to Avonmouth, as we had to steam a long way to the westward to keep clear of the German scout planes. A great stack of loaves of bread was put on board at Gibraltar, and there was nowhere to store it, so it was built on top of No 4 hatch, and covered with a tarpaulin. After four days it started to go mouldy. Fresh water was a problem, and it had to be rationed.

All of the refugees were Spanish speaking. On Saturday the 10th a German plane was sighted, but he went away and nothing came of it. On Wednesday 14th August we arrived at Avonmouth and disembarked our evacuees to the tune of wailing air raid sirens. We were in Avonmouth until Sat 17th August, on which date we shifted across to Barry in South Wales.

An article in the *Jamaican Gleaner* newspaper says that 'the first set of 1,104 Gibraltarians (185 men, 673 women and 246 children) arrived on the *Neuralia* in October, 1940. A second group of 393 (the last set of Gibraltarians to be evacuated) arrived in November.'

Mr Thomson then joined the *Wallsend*. He was torpedoed and landed at Cape Verde island of San Antonio, after a boat trip of more than a week. The Portuguese brought him and others back to Lisbon, from where Mr Thomson and some of his colleagues volunteered to join the *Takoradian*, which had been released by the Vichy authorities in Dakar.

> The Vichy French puppet Government in West Africa had captured a great many British Merchant Seamen, some from captured ships and others from torpedoed ships which had managed to land on the coast. The French had a large prison camp at Timbuktu on the Niger River, and the captured seamen were confined in this prison. Two British merchant seamen died in this camp and are buried in what must be the smallest CWGC cemetery. With the fall of Dakar and the collapse of the Vichy regime, the seamen got liberated, and some of them were sent to Freetown, to stay at the Grammar School (where Thomson and the other crews were billeted) while awaiting repatriation. They had gone through great privation. One chap told of being torpedoed on the coast of Africa, and after several days in a lifeboat they landed on the coast where they were found by the natives, who took them to their village and treated the well, until the French authorities got to hear of them and came and collected them. They were put on a train and were four days on it and then for eleven days in canoes down the Niger River to the prison camp at Timbuctoo. When they arrived at the Grammar School they were in a half starved condition, skin and bone.

The *Ringulv*'s crew, who had helped in the evacuation of Le Havre, were moved from camp to camp by the Vichy French, being imprisoned in nine in all. They met other merchant seamen, and Jews, Spaniards and Poles in the camps. 'The condition of the Jews was particularly pitiful; they were being used as slave labour building a railway in the desert.' They were described as being 'starved, sick, with only a few dirty rags as clothes.' *Ringulv*'s crew were understandably bitter about the treatment they received from the compatriots of those that they had so recently saved.

The story of the evacuations that were carried out after Dunkirk has received very little attention. Many want to cling to the idea of the 'Miracle of Dunkirk', when the Navy and the little ships alone saved 'every last man' of the BEF. Possibly the idea that civilian merchantmen had to 'finish the job', did not make for the right sort of story. The retreat from Singapore in 1942 was a replay of the chaotic events in France and elsewhere in Europe. Churchill prevented the news of the loss of the *Lancastria* getting more than very limited coverage at the time. Writing later, he said that he did this because the public had enough bad news. He then says that he 'forgot' to allow the release, but the papers will not be released until 2040!

Writing about the Army in his book *The Last Act – The Story of the British Forces in France After Dunkirk*, Basil Karslake says: 'there were many people who thought it better that the story should remain untold.' He confirms that 'whole files and certain important documents were missing' when documents from the post Dunkirk operations were released for study at the PRO. He goes on to say that 'it is possible that some people may not care to learn that their idols had, during this part of their careers, feet of clay.' Elsewhere there are references to officers 'disappearing to look after themselves'.

The Czechoslovak War Cross 1939-45 was awarded to the following MN personnel: Chief Officer Lancelot Hill of the *Mohamed Ali el Kebir*; the master lost his life before the award. Francis Nesbit, Master of the *Northmoor* 'showed great zeal and energy' rescuing 1,563 from Sète. Herbert Wilson, Master of the *Gibel Dersa*; Edward Davies, Master of the *Apapa*; and Thomas Muckle, Master of the *Rod el Farag*. The masters of the merchant ships had been asked to recommend one of their crew, but most were unwilling to single one out.

Children's Overseas Reception Board and Other Civilian Evacuations

There were voluntary civilian evacuations from Britain during 1939 and 1940, though many who might have wanted to go could not afford the cost. Sea transport was the only option, as at that time few passenger aircraft existed that were able to cross the Atlantic Ocean; some that could were German and had been converted to long-range Kondor bombers that were to become the scourge of the Merchant Navy. There seems to have been no appreciation of how risky it had become to cross the Atlantic in merchant ships. This becomes most obvious when considering the work of the Children's Overseas Reception Board (CORB) and the American Committee for the Evacuation of British Children, both of which were set up in 1940 to evacuate British children.

The children were exposed to the perils of the sea at a time when the merchant fleet was losing an average of three ships a day. Those who conceived and operated the schemes must have been unaware of the risks involved, or they chose to ignore them. The first CORB sailing to Canada on the *Anselm* was on 21 July 1940, but there were earlier sailings, possibly under the American scheme.

The masters of all merchant ships bore heavy responsibilities and carrying children in a war zone was an additional one that they would surely have declined to accept, had they been given a chance. To add to their problems, some fare paying passengers objected to the presence of the children on the ship. Captain Power of the *Nestor* was among those who had this problem. He solved it by inviting the passengers and the CORB escorts to a cocktail party, 'where he told the private passengers in no uncertain terms that the children were "evacuees, not refugees"; that they were his "main concern"; and that, if anyone was not satisfied, the ship was calling at Capetown and they knew what they could do about it.' But the U-boat problem was one that even the masters could not solve. Up to that time ships carrying children had not been hit, though several ships in their convoys were. Some children on one ship recalled sailing past survivors in the water – at this time ships were told not to stop to rescue survivors. Several other groups remembered hearing depth charges.

The Dutch liner *Volendam*, with a total of 320 children and thirty-one escorts and medical personnel on board, sailed from Liverpool on 28 August 1940. The ship joined convoy OB 205; another ship in the convoy was the *Rangitata*, which was also carrying a party of CORB children. Captain Holland, of the *Rangitata*, insisted that the children slept on the floor of the first-class lounge. They were not permitted to go below for any reason. When the alarm was sounded aboard the *Rangitata*, the children went to their boat stations, from where they saw the *Volendam* 'all lit up in the mist'.

The *Volendam* was acting as Commodore ship, and the commodore, Admiral G. H. Knowles RNR, had been made aware that a U-boat was operating near the route of the convoy. The thirty-four merchant ships were escorted by a destroyer and two sloops. At 11 p.m., only 50 minutes after the warning about the U-boat had been received, *U-60* torpedoed the *Volendam*. Two torpedoes blew an enormous hole in the bows of the ship, causing an explosion and fire: it was amazing that no-one was killed. The children assembled in the ship's library, where the master, Captain J. P. Wepster, spoke to them. He had radioed for a rescue tug, but by midnight the weather was worsening and it was this, rather than the fire, that caused the master to give the order to abandon ship.

There had been a number of lifeboat drills so the children abandoned ship in good order, and without panic. The Naval escort ships went off to hunt for the U-boat. All eighteen lifeboats were launched safely and only the ship's purser was lost – he was struck on the head with the block of the lifeboat fall (tackle). Three merchant ships dropped back to pick up survivors; this was at considerable risk to themselves and contrary to their standing orders. They were the tankers *Bassethound*, 1,174 grt, and the *Valldemosa*, 7,220 grt, and the Norwegian banana carrier *Olaf Fostenes*, 2,994 grt. The low freeboard of the tankers, particularly the tiny *Bassethound*, helped in the recovery. The *Olaf Fostenes* had a higher freeboard so the master arranged for the baskets that the ship normally used to load its banana cargo to be used to recover survivors.

Every covered space on the rescue ships was full to capacity with salt-soaked humanity. The galley staff on all three ships served hot drinks, bread and butter and boiled eggs continuously, as they put back to land their precious cargoes. The *Volendam* was saved by the Admiralty Salvage Tug *Salvonia* (also RNR and T124 manned). This calamity did not seem to bring home the gravity of the situation to any of the parties involved. The Ministry of Information made propaganda out of the affair, which the newspapers copied, and the British then seemed to make the mistake of believing their own propaganda. The presence of the three ships willing to save the passengers from the *Volendam* was a matter of luck. The authorities decided that any further rescue would be as successful, but the next one wasn't.

The liner *City of Benares* sailed on Friday 13 September 1940, also from Liverpool, joining convoy OB 213 as Commodore ship, en route for Canada. The Admiralty had recommended the suspension of the scheme as there was no hope of adequately protecting the CORB ships; in fact they were unable to provide adequate protection for any merchant ships. The naval escort left the convoy at 16° west, less than 200 nautical miles west of the Irish coast. The Admiralty were aware that U-boats were operating at least 400 miles further out in the Atlantic. Before he left the convoy, the senior officer escort warned the commodore that a U-boat was operating beyond 20° west. This was reaffirmed in a further message from the Admiralty. For some inexplicable reason, the commodore kept the convoy in formation at a speed of 7.5 knots, though the *City of Benares* could make twice that speed. It was said that the master had wanted to proceed alone at full speed, but he was overruled by the commodore. The same mistake was made on at least one other occasion – in convoy OB 288, the details of which are in the next chapter. The weather was deteriorating with gusts of gale force, and a heavy confused sea.

The first two torpedoes fired by the *U-48* missed their two-funnelled target, but the third hit, and another hit the cargo ship *Marina*. The *City of Benares'* chief officer – Mr Hetherington – reported to Captain Landles Nicholl that the engine room was flooding, and as the ship was listing to port and settling by the stern, the master gave the order to abandon ship. According to one report, thirty of the children were killed by the explosion. The CORB escorts pulled the children from their cabins and ushered them up to the boat deck. Because of the weather and the ship's list, only the lifeboats on the portside could be launched. To add to the problems, several of these tipped or flooded on launching.

Mr Hetherington helped Majorie Day to board his boat, together with a seriously injured girl that she was tending, but the girl was one of the first to die. The children showed great bravery during their ordeal, one boy cradled a dying woman's head, while stroking her hair and talking of rescue. In the middle of that dreadful night, those in the lifeboat heard the sound of singing and found two CORB girls clinging to the keel of an upturned lifeboat – they were dragged aboard. Bess Walder and Beth Cummings were the only survivors of more than twenty people who had clung to the keel of the boat. Twenty hours later, these survivors were picked up by HMS *Hurricane*, one of the escorts from OB 214 who had been sent to help. They were the last that *Hurricane* found. The destroyer had passed many small dead bodies and several empty waterlogged lifeboats. In all, *Hurricane's* commanding officer, Lieutenant Commander Hugh Simms RN, rescued 105 survivors from eleven boats and five floats; it was a brilliant feat of seamanship. Three of the children could not be revived.

CORB escort Mary Cornish, an accomplished pianist and a music teacher, had mustered evacuees from D deck, but in the confusion she became separated from her charges, who were taken to a lifeboat by Mrs Towns, another escort. Miss Cornish joined one of the last lifeboats to leave the ship, with five CORB boys; the twenty-two-year-old Fourth Officer Cooper was in charge. Shortly afterwards, Fr O'Sullivan, a Catholic priest, arrived with another boy. Mr Cooper told Assistant Steward Purvis to make a further search to ascertain if there were any more children in their cabins. Mr Cooper held on for about a quarter of an hour in case there were stragglers. The other portside boats had been launched when he gave the order to lower his boat. The boat 'was launched in an orderly manner' – with four lascar crewmen standing by the falls; they, and the assistant steward, were then embarked. Mr Cooper made yet another search round the deck, before pulling the boat clear of the casualty. The boat put back alongside to embark four more crew who had appeared. The boat again lay off until around 11 p.m., when the ship sank by the stern. Another nine survivors, including a cadet, were then rescued from rafts.

In all the boat contained forty-six people, six CORB boys, five British and thirty-two Indian crew members, one passenger, Miss Cornish and the priest. Theirs was the most horrendous voyage of all – it was to be eight days before they were rescued. They made their way slowly homeward, taking turns to operate the levers of the Fleming propulsion gear. Mr Purvis rigged an awning in the bows to shelter the boys, who were in their pyjamas. It was said that they had only one coat and one blanket between them, but there seem to have been a good supply of blankets in the boats. Miss Cornish kept their spirits up and tried to divert their attention from their hunger and massaged their feet.

There was no sign of the other boats, but they fell in with a boat from the *Marina*, with whom they stayed until dawn when the other boat set sail. Cooper decided not to set sail as the weather was heavy, and his boat was crowded. On Thursday in moderating weather, sail was set, but only until Friday afternoon when the wind increased to gale force and the boat rode to a sea anchor and the oil bag was used. At 4 a.m. on Saturday, they again set sail, on an easterly course, and at 4 p.m. a ship was sighted. Miss Cornish's petticoat was hoisted to the masthead to attract attention. The ship appeared to be preparing to pick them up, when it suddenly sheared off and steamed away. Mr Cooper was of the opinion that the ship was zigzagging and may not have seen them. That evening they were again forced to heave to, and it was not until Monday that they could safely hoist the sail again: they continued under sail, and at 1 p.m. on Wednesday one of the boys sighted a Sunderland flying boat. Miss Cornish's petticoat was again hoisted and the alert Australian crew of the Sunderland flying boat saw them.

The aircraft signalled with an Aldis lamp and a naval signalman, who was a member of the boat's crew, replied by semaphore and the plane dropped a smoke float. The Sunderland, or another one, returned, dropping a parcel of food. Mr Cooper decided to lower the sail and heave to until help arrived, which it did at 4.30 p.m. in the welcome sight of the destroyer HMS *Anthony*. The boys were lifted from the boat by the navy sailors and the other survivors were helped aboard. One Lascar seaman, who was very ill, was first tended in the boat by the destroyer's medical officer, but he died after being taken aboard the destroyer.

Mr Cooper reported:

All the children were in good form, having, I think, looked on the whole thing as a picnic, and only one child was suffering from trench feet. We were all attended to by the Officers and men of the destroyer from whom we received every consideration and kindness. I hadn't at any time any anxiety regarding the food supplies in the boat.

He goes on to list those who helped by steering the boat and praises Miss Cornish for her efforts. He ends:

> Everyone behaved very well, and spirit of loyalty to orders and comparative cheerfulness prevailed throughout the entire 7 days and 19 hours.

Only when 'her' boys were safely tucked up in officer's bunks did Mary Cornish accept the offer of tea and bread and butter, but before she could start her simple meal, she collapsed.

Mr Cooper was awarded an MBE, and Miss Cornish and George Purvis each received the BEM. Miss Annie Ryan, stewardess, and Mr Edward Richardson, passenger, were commended. Seventy-seven CORB children, fifty-six other passengers and 121 crew members died in the sinking of the *City of Benares*. The most important questions were unanswered:

> Why were the children put in such a hazardous position?
> Why did the escort vessels leave so early?
> Why did the Commodore keep the vessels together, as a convoy, at 7.5 knots or less?
> And why did it take eighteen hours before any kind of help was at hand?

Within weeks of this calamity the CORB scheme was 'suspended' and was never resumed.

Merchant ships continued to transport British citizens who wished to go to other parts of the Commonwealth or America and their citizens who wished to return to their own country. The American Committee for the Evacuation of British Children took on the responsibility for children who were evacuated to the United States. Between June and October 1940, they safely moved 836. Sailings continued into early 1941 (e.g. *Warwick Castle* January 1941).

As the USA was still a neutral country, the early evacuees were first landed in Canada and then transported overland. Their records are at the Borthwick Institute of Historical Research, York University.

> [This archive holds forty-two boxes of records of the] English Branch of the American Committee from its inauguration in June 1940, and its Northern Branch Office in York and research on the papers by Doctor Ian Whitaker, Reader in Sociology at the University of York 1969. The role of the English Committee was to select children and to organise their evacuation to America. Between June and October 1940, 836 children were evacuated. This collection includes administration files 1940-1947; evacuation schemes by commercial firms and other groups 1940-1946; details of evacuation, lists of children and other details; correspondence 1940-1946; papers relating to the children's return to Britain 1943-1948; papers regarding publicity 1940-1946; miscellaneous

papers, including files on individual children 1940-1947; Northern Branch Office files, including files on individual children 1940; research papers of Ian Whitaker 1969.

There was a steady exodus of people whose countries were now occupied. Understandably, Jewish people were keenest to get as far away from the advancing Germans as possible and many crossed the Atlantic completing journeys that had often begun in Eastern Europe.

When their country was overrun in 1939, a large group of Poles were deported to forced labour camps in Russia where they remained until after July 1941. Seventy-seven thousand soldiers and 43,000 civilians, including about 20,000 children, then trekked from Russia to Persia and elsewhere in the Middle East. From there, the soldiers went on to fight in North Africa and Italy. Their dependants, and the many children who had been orphaned on the way, were to be relocated to other parts of the British Empire. Several countries offered sanctuary, including New Zealand which offered to take 733 children and ten guardians. A group left Korramshah on the *Sontay*, a ship that the British had seized as a war prize. Conditions on board were grim, but improved when they were transferred to an American troop ship in Bombay on 10 October 1944. This ship took them to New Zealand, where they at last found a safe haven. Some Polish citizens still live in Iran.

First Low Water, 1941

In May 1940, the British and Allied merchant fleets lost a total of eighty ships, up from the previous high of seventy. With the evacuation from France in June, the figure leapt to 134. In that month, Grand Admiral Dönitz made his first journey to Brittany, the fall of France having handed him the prize of an Atlantic base. He moved his headquarters to the château at Kernével in October, and the construction of submarine pens at Lorient was begun. The U-boats had been using bases in St Nazaire and Brest a few weeks after the fall of France, while the Italian submarines worked from Betasom in the Gironde.

After the fall of France, the merchant fleet was largely able to concentrate on its primary task of sustaining Britain, though the introduction of the WS troop convoys, popularly known as 'Winston's Specials', tied up a number of the fast passenger and cargo liners. Allied merchant ship losses remained close to 100 per month for the rest of 1940, and about 60 per cent of the ships lost were British. The principal convoy routes were to and from North America and to the Mediterranean and Africa and onward to the East. Outward convoys were generally escorted to about 20° west – about 600 miles west of Eire. From there they were sometimes joined by the Armed Merchant Cruiser that had handed over her inward convoy to the warships from the UK. The Canadians met convoys on the far side of the Atlantic. Until early in 1941, the British escort groups were assembled on a trip by trip basis. Warships concentrated on hunting U-boats away from the convoys, while the U-boats sought the convoys. In the second half of 1940, only nine U-boats were lost: the Royal Navy did not sink one in the four months from 3 November 1940. In his book *Hitler's U-Boat War*, Clay Blair says ' In all of 1940 British forces had positively destroyed only twelve ocean-going German submarines.' Several Italian submarines were sunk.

Many convoys and independent ships crossed the Atlantic safely, mainly because Dönitz had only a fraction of the 300 U-boats that he needed to bring Britain to its knees. But the few boats that he had were able to wreak havoc when they discovered the merchant ships.

February 1941 was typical of the disastrous months of that winter; even during the first week of that month the enemy sank twenty vessels. The first convoy to be attacked was HG 53, bound from Gibraltar to the UK. It was sighted by *U-37* (Clausen) when he was on passage towards Freetown. Of the twenty-one merchant ships in the convoy, only three were less than ten years old, the two oldest having been built at the beginning of the century.

The escort was provided by the sloop *Deptford* and the destroyer *Velox*. The attack began at 0400 on Sunday 9 February, just after the moon had set. The *Courland* and the *Estrellano* were the first to be sunk. The master, twenty-seven crew and two DEMS gunners went down with the *Courland*. The 1910-built *Brandenburg* stopped to recover the master and twenty of the crew of the second casualty, and six were lost. Clausen remained in contact and vectored in a group of Condors. They seriously damaged the *Varna*, but she was able to continue. Then, in quick succession they sank the *Britannic, Jura, Dagmar 1* and the Norwegian *Tejo*. *U-37* then sank the *Brandenburg*; only one person out of the two crews on board the *Brandenburg* survived the sinking. In all, eighty-six seafarers died, including seventy-three British merchant seamen. As the convoy commodore was among the casualties, the Master of the *Egyptian Prince* took charge of the convoy. The *Velox* returned to Gibraltar to re-fuel and land survivors. This left Lieutenant Commander Thring's sloop *Deptford* as the only escort. He was also charged with meeting up with the unescorted SLS 64, so a single sloop was supposed to provide an escort for two convoys. Thring was aware that the *Admiral Hipper* was at sea. Clausen directed the heavy cruiser to the convoy, where she sank the *Iceland*.

On the night of 13 February, the damaged *Varna* sank in what Lieutenant Commander Thring described as: 'the most monumental gale ... the sea running was the heaviest I have ever seen.' All of her crew were rescued by the *Empire Tern*, a 2,600 grt cargo ship, completed in the USA in 1919. Thring said: 'How *Empire Tern* managed such a feat will always be a mystery to me; it must have been one of the finest bits of seamanship ever carried out.'

By 30 January 1941, sufficient ships had assembled at Freetown, Sierra Leone, to make up another convoy in the SL series [Sierra Leone for Liverpool] – this was to be SL 64. Nineteen of the merchant ships could not even maintain the convoy speed of 9 knots and the Navy could not spare ships to escort both convoys. Once at sea, the slower ships were left behind, while a single Armed Merchant Cruiser stayed with the twenty-eight ships of SL 64. The slower ships were to remain together, as convoy SLS 64 or SL 64S with the Master of the *Warlaby* as Commodore.

On 12 February, the *Hipper* found SLS 64. Early in the morning, one of the convoy, the *Margot*, sighted a strange Man-o-War. At 0625 *Hipper* opened fire on *Shrewsbury* and the commodore signalled all ships to alter course. *Hipper* then attacked in order: *Warlaby, Derrynane, Westbury, Perseus, Borgestad, Lornaston* and *Oswestry Grange*. *Derrynane, Borgestad* and *Lornaston* had opened fire on the enemy and received 'very heavy punishment'. The first two sank with all hands and *Lornaston* was badly damaged. *Borgestad* appeared to hit the control tower of the attacker. *Hipper* then attacked *Margot*. *Blairathol* rescued a total of eighty-six from four ships, and the *Polyktor* rescued twenty-one from the *Perseus*. Other ships involved were the *Ainderbury*, which, with survivors, made Funchal, escorting the *Lornaston*. *Clunepark* was damaged, abandoned and re-boarded, and with her rescuer, *Blairathol* (also damaged), she also made Madeira for repairs. There is a photographic museum in Funchal, but only the 'more interesting' negatives have been catalogued, so it has not been possible to check the existence of photographs of these ships. The picture of *Empire Flag* in the section was probably taken by the same photographer whose work is in the museum.

The *Gairsoppa* (from SL 64), whose cargo included 3 million ounces of silver, was sunk in mid-February (half of this cargo was recovered in July 2012); of a crew of eighty-five, only the second officer survived. The *Nailsea Lass* was sunk on the 24 February. Five of her crew did not survive and her master was taken prisoner.

Almost 250 seamen from convoy SLS 64 lost their lives – sufficient to crew five ships. The Admiralty regarded these ships as independents and did not count them in convoy loss statistics. The commodore, the Master of *Warlaby*, was killed in action as was his second officer. The chief officer survived and made the report. George Medals were awarded to Captain D. A. MacDonald of the *Blairathol* and Captain I. L. Price OBE, *Margot*.

The outward bound convoys to North America were the OA and OB series. The OB 285 had sailed from the UK on 1 February and had dispersed on 17 February. On 22 February when the ships were nearing Newfoundland they were set upon by the battleships *Gneisnau* and *Scharnhorst*. *Gneisnau* sank the *Trelawney*, the tanker *Harlesden* and the cargo ship *Kantara*, plus the steamer *A D Huff* which had been in convoy OB 286. The *Scharnhorst* sank the tanker *Lustrous*. The ships were together in position 47° 12'N, 40° 13'W, with the exception of the *Harlesden*, who was reported to have been sunk less than 3 miles away. It would appear that they were together as a 'group,' even though the Navy avoids saying that they were in convoy. Normally they would have at least had an AMC as an escort. Ten crew members were lost in the attack and the rest were taken prisoner and sent to Milag Nord.

Convoy OB 288 had originated in Liverpool, with other ships joining via Loch Ewe. The *Empire Fusilier*, *Empire Steelhead* and *Kasongo* turned back with mechanical problems. The *Keila* and the *Kingston Hill* were bombed and were escorted back by the corvette HMS *Picotee* and the Smit tug *Thames*. Captain Walter Niven, the Master of the *Kingston Hill*, was killed in this attack. By now the convoy was reduced to forty-one ships. The other escorts were the destroyers *Achates*, *Antelope*, *Georgetown* (senior officer escort), the corvette *Heather* and the trawler *Ayrshire*. An 'Ocean Boarding Vessel', the HMS *Manistee*, was also with the convoy. Both the *Ayrshire* and the *Manistee* were merchant vessels that had been requisitioned by the Admiralty.

The C in C Western Approaches signalled OB 288 to 'disperse at dark 23rd when last escort leaves.' At 1900 on 22 February the convoy was plotted as being in 59°20'N, 14° 32' W. Despite the fact that the convoy had been attacked by aircraft and that the C in C WA probably knew that it was being shadowed by one or more U-boats, the escorts left the convoy on the next morning. The commodore, in the *Sirikishna*, kept the convoy in formation on a north-westerly course until well after sunset on 23 February. He may have been expecting to be met by an AMC. It was tracked all day by a U-boat and by then at least six submarines were converging to form a patrol line lying north-west/south-east through 59°N, 21°W.

When the commodore ordered the convoy to disperse, he told them to maintain convoy speed for a further 30 minutes. The vessels fanned out on predetermined courses between north, through west, to south-south-east. At this time the weather was fair with a light wind and a moderate north-westerly swell. There was no moon, but visibility was recorded as being about 7 miles as the Northern Lights were exceptionally bright. Then the U-boats attacked.

The *Anglo Peruvian* reported that 'When the attack took place we had no escorts with us for 12 hours and it is noticeable that it is always during a period when we are alone that the U-boat attacks occur. The danger spot seems to be [between?] 18° W and 25° W. [It] would be so much better if the Ocean Escorts could meet a convoy when the other escorts leave.' *Marslew* reported '2245/23 torpedoed 59°18' N 21° 30' W 291° [from] Rockall.' *Manistee* was 'Torpedoed 2145/23, 58° 13' N 21° 33' W at 0618/24, course 093° speed 7.5 knots, torpedoed again and sunk in 58° 55' N 20° 50' W.' Nine merchant ships were lost in this encounter, plus the *Manistee*. Two hundred and forty-six seafarers lost their lives, including 192 British merchant seamen. Most were from the UK, but others came from as far afield as Canada and Aden.

Four merchantmen from the convoy were more fortunate. Three had been overhauled by the, almost new, British cargo ship *La Pampa*, which sighted the U-69 as it was preparing to fire a torpedo. She increased to full speed and fired at the submarine with her 20-mm guns. The U-boat managed to crash dive before the *La Pampa* rammed, but by the time *U-69* resurfaced, the merchant ships were below the horizon. *La Pampa* had saved herself and those who were with her. The British authorities did not accept the master's version of events, but many years later, when the log of the *U-69* became available it confirmed the encounter.

Convoy OB 290 left Liverpool on 23 February, with a six-ship escort. The convoy was not detected until Kapitänleutnant Prien, in *U-47*, chanced on it on 25 February. Prien called in six FW 200 bombers who attacked repeatedly. Aircraft sank the *Beursplein* (Dutch), *Llanwern*, *Mahanada* and *Swinburne*. The *Amstelland* (Dutch) was taken in tow, but sank on 28 February; they damaged the *Leeds City, Blankaholm* (Swedish), *Suriname* (Dutch) and *Melmore Head*. U-47 sank the *Borgland* (Norwegian) and *Kasongo* (Belgian). Her third victim, the *Rydbolholm* (Swedish), sank on 28 February and *U-47* also damaged the *Diala*. The Italian submarine *Bianchi* sank the *Baltistan*. There were fifty-two deaths, with lost cargoes including locomotives, aircraft and military stores and vehicles.

Over one hundred Allied merchant ships were sunk during February. Two enemy submarines failed to return and there has never been a satisfactory explanation for the loss of the U-boat ace Günter Prien in the *U-47*. The British credited the sinking of the Italian submarine *Marcello* to various aircraft and ships, before finally concluding that she had been sunk by the ex-American 'four stacker' *Montgomery*. That ship's report says '1550/22 HMS *Montgomery* attacked firm contact with six depth charges. There was no evidence of destruction.'

The British, unaware of the full extent of the calamity, dismissed the German claim to have sunk a large tonnage of Allied ships during the last week in February. In fact their losses exceeded 200,000 gross tons of merchant shipping.

SS *Merchant* reported having just missed ramming a U-boat in the same area at 2330 on 1 March and to have fired sixty machine-gun bullets into the conning tower and hull. At the same time, ss *Negala* claims to have hit a U-boat with her fourth shell, which was not seen to explode; the U-boat remained on the surface for a quarter of an hour afterwards. Merchant ships were told not to enter any such incidents in their official logs, so information about such incidents is difficult to trace.

A merchant ship initiated the next known sinking of a submarine, the *U-70*, on 7 March. The Dutch tanker *Mijdrecht*, after being torpedoed and with an enormous hole in her side, swung and rammed the U-boat which was forced under the full length of the ship. When being questioned about the damage caused by the *Mijdrecht*'s attack, survivors of *U-70* said that the conning tower was badly dented aft, the bearing disk (Peilscheibe) was carried away, both periscopes were put out of action, and everything on the bridge was smashed; nevertheless, no internal damage was caused, but a stream of water, over 2 in. in diameter, entered the boat through the broken off rod of the bearing disk; the lighting system was not affected. The crew described the U-boat as having rolled over on one side, as though struck by a huge wave. *U-70* went down slightly by the stern, and submerged to a depth stated to have been 20 metres (53.6 ft). Three Royal Navy ships claimed the credit, as the submarine had 'only been lightly damaged by the *Mijdrecht*'.

In a telegram entitled 'Report on military situation', dated 2 March 1941, the British told the Americans: 'Since commencement of hostilities 54,693 ships have been convoyed, out of which 192 British ships and 31 Allied ships and 19 neutral have been lost.' The Americans must have wondered why the Limeys were bleating about only having a few weeks' food and fuel left, when they said they had lost so few ships in convoy. For the Germans this was the first 'Happy Time'.

In February, the Western Approaches Command, under Admiral Sir Percy Noble, had been moved to Derby House, Liverpool. Admiral Noble had appointed Vice-Admiral Sir Gilbert Stephenson to train the escorts at a base on the island of Mull. Admiral Stephenson became known as the 'Terror of Tobermory', but the rigorous training he organised, weeding out the incompetent, meant that the escort groups at last began to reach the standard needed.

On 6 March, Prime Minister Winston Churchill declared the start of the Battle of the Atlantic (really the Atlantic War). In doing so he was admitting that the hunting groups that he had keenly supported were ineffective. As Minister of Defence, he chaired the Battle of the Atlantic Committee. He presented a thirteen-point action plan to the committee, in order to achieve a successful outcome in this desperate fight.

Immediately after the SLS 64 disaster, the convoys SL 65 and SLS 65 were combined; the escort included a light cruiser, seven destroyers, a sloop and two corvettes. The much needed improvement in standards took longer to take effect, and Allied merchant ship losses continued to mount: March, 139; April, 155, and May, 124. The improvement, when it came, was dramatic. In July, only forty-four ships were lost, and numbers continued at this sort of rate until December, when losses increased sharply when Japan entered the War. In the ten months from March 1941, the Kriegsmarine lost a total of thirty-five U-boats.

Unlike the Battle of Britain, which spanned the autumn of 1940, this new battle was to last for most of the War. As it was fought far from the seas and skies of Britain, civilians generally had little idea of how their fate depended on a successful outcome, nor did they have regard for the civilian casualties of the war at sea. Exhausted and traumatised, and sometimes penniless, in clothes given to them by their rescuers, seamen were often harangued and insulted on trains and buses as they made their way home on survivors' leave. They were asked 'why aren't you overseas, fighting with our brave lads'.

In an effort to counter this, merchant seamen were issued with a silver (actually aluminium) lapel badge with the letters MN, surrounded by a rope and surmounted by a Tudor crown. Some seamen wore this upside down, when they said that the letters meant NW, not wanted.

Until 1942, a merchant seaman's pay was stopped on the day his ship sank, though the better companies did not enforce this rule. A seaman's wife would sometimes learn that she had been widowed when a letter arrived from the shipowner; paragraph two could say something like 'please return the last monthly allotment, as your husband's ship sank before it was paid'.

Questions asked in the House of Lords and letters in *The Times* did lead to an improvement in pay and rations, though British merchant seamen still earned considerably less than other Allied crews. However, they did earn more than their Royal Naval counterparts, who were often bitter, forgetting that their terms were 'all found' and they had a non-contributory pension scheme that also provided a widows pension.

From May 1941, a pool was set up and seamen were put on continuous pay, many for the first time. In the autumn of 1941, a case was put for a Royal Commission on the future of the Merchant Navy. The National Maritime Board fought against the proposal, contending that the officers' and seamen's representatives on the board opposed it, as did the shipowners. No doubt this was the view of some in the latter group.

Under the pension scheme that had been set up for officers in 1938, a payment, made up of the officers' contributions plus 2½ per cent, would be paid on death. Few of the widows of those officers killed in 1941 would have received as much as £100. Ratings and petty officers were only eligible for the State Pension, though the NMB letter mentions a Royal Seaman's Pension Scheme, saying that there was 'a dearth of applicants' – probably because they knew nothing about it. It was to the credit of the Admiralty and some senior naval officers that they supported many of the suggestions of reform.

A letter in *The Times* on 8 November acknowledged that 'we depend on our Merchant Navy to bring us food, without which we could not exist for two months, and the oil without which the Fighting Services could not operate.' And 'lacking the Merchant Navy we should have no need of warships to repel an invasion, since the enemy could starve us into submission.'

Shipowners and Members of Parliament (some wore both hats) worried whether the merchant crews would turn to communism, but mostly they did not. The average merchant seaman is not a political animal, and those who made the hazardous trip to Russia would have lost any 'Red' tendencies. It is true that the Merchant Navy had its own version of the communist song 'The Red Flag'. The first verse was: 'The working class, can kiss my ass, I've got a chief mate's job at last / The apprentices, may laugh and jeer, but I'm the second engineer.' The Red Flag that they promised to 'keep flying high', was the Red Ensign, affectionately known as 'The Red Duster'. But they had little to sing about as losses mounted during the first half of 1941.

Unknown to those at sea in either service, and to almost everyone else, the principal reason for the improvement in July was Bletchley Park's ability to break the U-boat code, or Enigma as the British called it. The British and French had been given a tremendous start when the Poles handed over the results of their work breaking the Enigma codes from 1930. The Germans were using a three-rotor machine, the rotors being chosen from a set of five. They thought that the system could not be broken, but three brilliant Polish mathematicians used an abstract branch of pure mathematics to do just that. They went on to discover the secret wiring of the rotors. In September 1938, the Germans began to use a new procedure to encipher their messages and the Poles were unable to decipher more until they developed an electro-mechanical machine that they called a Bomba to aid the search for the 'ring settings.' They smuggled the results of their work, and two Bombas, to Paris and London.

In January 1940, further work by an equally brilliant team at Bletchley Park (BP) enabled the Luftwaffe key 'Red' to be broken. In May 1940, the Germans again changed their method of working and the two Turing/Welshman Bombes, developed at BP, became the regular method for breaking the ciphers from August 1940 – just in time for the Battle of Britain. The German Navy used a similar machine, with the addition of a further two 'naval rotors' and a plug board, and this increased the possible combinations from sixty to 336. It could take four days to discover the settings, which meant that the resultant intelligence was of little practical use. A number of 'cribs' were needed to find the current settings.

In March 1941, the German naval trawler *Krebs* was captured off Norway, with two Enigma machines and the settings list for the previous month. With these, Bletchley were able to read the U-boat signal traffic for February. Then in

May 1941, the code books for June were captured on board the German weather ship *München*.

On 9 May 1941, Kapitänleutnant Fritz Julius Lemp on the *U-110* was attacking a convoy when his periscope was spotted by HMS *Aubretia*, who depth charged the U-boat. Two other escorts, the *Bulldog* and *Broadway*, joined in the hunt and Lemp was forced to the surface and abandoned ship. The crew left the U-boat believing that it would soon sink. When Lemp realised that this was not happening he started to swim back to the boat, but drowned. Lieutenant Commander A. J. B. Cresswell, RN, Captain of the *Bulldog*, had intended to ram the U-boat but broke off the attack when he realised that it might remain afloat long enough to board it. He sent Sub Lieutenant David Balme and a whaler crew to the damaged U-boat. They recovered the Enigma code machine, ciphers and code books, and the important *'Offizier Code'*. The operation was code-named Primrose and Admiral Sir Dudley Pound, the First Sea Lord, sent to *Bulldog* 'Hearty congratulations. The petals of your flower are of rare beauty.' This was probably the most important capture of the Second World War and the secret was even kept from the crew of *U-110*. The Hollywood film *U-571* was said to be 'a thrilling story about an American crew on a top-secret mission to capture an Enigma Cipher Machine from the German U-Boat.' It is a work of fiction, in no way were the Americans involved – they were not even in the War at the time!

In June 1941, Germany invaded the Soviet Union. That August, Britain and the Soviet Union invaded and occupied Iran and forced Reza Shah to abdicate in favour of his son Mohammad Reza Pahlavi. The invasion was brought about by the Shah's refusal to permit the Allies to use the Persian Corridor to ship supplies to Russia and to protect Britain's oil supplies. The Allies also claimed that Reza Shah's unwillingness to expel German nationals was a factor, though there were only between one and two thousand Germans in the country. Churchill later called this operation 'The Bridge of Victory'.

The Allies took control of the Trans-Iranian Railway in September and shipments from the UK began: British Army Royal Engineers (RE), commanded by Brigadier Godfrey D. Rhodes, took over the Southern Division between Tehran and the port of Bandar Shahpur on the Persian Gulf. The Soviet Army operated the Northern Division between Tehran and the port of Bandar Shah on the Caspian Sea. At first, at the British-operated section of the railway it was only able to move one freight train per day. The engineers built new railway yards at Bandar Shahpur, Ahvaz and Andimeshk and a junction at Ahvaz for a new line to Khorramshahr on the Shatt al-Arab, substantially expanding the freight capacity. The Southern Division locomotive depot at Ahvaz had two German 2-10-0s, seven German 2-8-0s, two class 41.01 2-8-0s built by Beyer, Peacock & Co. in 1934, two class 80.14 0-10-0s from an Austrian locomotive builder, and seven smaller locomotives. All except the 2-10-0s were in poor condition, as was some of the freight rolling stock.

The REs built a yard at Abadan to transfer locomotives from merchant ships to barges to take them up the River Karun, and a derrick on a jetty on the Karun at

Ahwaz to unload them from the barges onto the railway. Stanier 8F 2-8-0 steam locomotives from the London Midland and Scottish Railway (LMS) fleet started to arrive in December, after a three-month voyage round the Cape of Good Hope. Because of their size, most merchant ships had to carry the locomotives on-deck. Twenty-seven coal-burning 2-8-0s were in service by February 1942, and many 20-ton wagons that had also made the long voyage from the UK also started to arrive. In all, 143 of the Eight Freights were shipped to Iran, with 840 wagons. Over 200 of these locomotives were loaded for the Middle East, of which twenty-three were lost in transit.

Through the efforts of several locomotive preservation societies, a number of these locomotives have been repatriated. One, LMS No. 8233, was among the first to be requisitioned by the WD, who gave her the number WD307. She was one of a group of six loaded at Cardiff. The cargo ship *La Pampa* was in the port loading locomotives in September, but it is not known if she loaded all six – this ship could have stowed that number of locomotives under-deck. In Persia, WD307 became ISR No. 41.109 and joined her sisters in the epic task of supplying Russia 'by the back door'. In 1944, No. 41.109 was converted to burn oil, and in 1946 she was transferred overland to the Suez Canal Zone. She is now back in the UK, and owned by the Stanier 8F Locomotive Society. *La Pampa* spent the next fifteen months ferrying locomotives, rolling stock, barges and supplies between India and the Persian Gulf. Though far easier than the northern route, crews suffered without air conditioning; the ship's cook died of heat exhaustion.

Once enough LMS 2-8-0s were in service, some of the German locomotives were released to increase the fleet on the Northern Division that the Soviets were operating. Between February and August 1942, ninety-six oil-burning LMS 2-8-0s entered service on the Southern Division, and by December 1942, when control was handed to the Americans, another nineteen coal-burners had joined them. In that year, the United States delivered twenty-four diesel-mechanical 0-4-0 shunter locomotives that Iran had ordered before the Allied invasion.

During the first quarter of 1942, the railway carried 978 tons a day. Performance progressively improved and by September 1943 they were moving 5,400 tons per day. Double-headed 700-ton trains battled up 1 in 65 gradients, through many tunnels (the British locomotives were without headlamps, much to the amazement of their American colleagues), in temperatures of over 90°F. A far cry from hauling coal trains across Copy Pit summit in the Pennines. Eight million tons of cargo were moved through the Persian Corridor, which represented 75 per cent of the material supplied to Russia, while the Arctic convoys delivered 23 per cent and 2 per cent went via Vladivostok (this last route had to be abandoned once the Japanese entered the War).

Several of these locomotives survived and have been brought back to their homeland by enthusiasts; had their shipping counterparts been equally keen; we would now have a cargo ship on the Mersey as a permanent memorial to our merchant seamen.

Guinean, Falmouth 18 June 1940. (*IWM F4824*)

The crew of the Canadian-built *Fort Dease Lake*. (*Illustrated London News Ltd/Mary Evans Picture Library*)

Broompark sailing from the Gironde, June 1940. (*Dr Don Cody and J & J Denholm*)

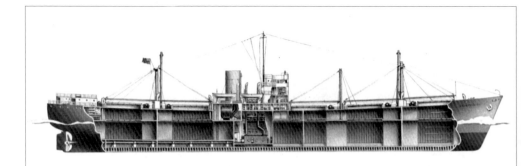

M.V. "DERRYCUNIHY." Built for **McCowen & Gross Ltd., London.** Shelter Deck—Coal, Grain and General Cargo. Length b.p. 425'-0". Breadth 57'-0". Depth mld. 37'-9" to shelter deck. Deadweight—10,200 Tons. Draft—27'-4¼". Engines—Doxford opposed piston two cycle Diesel. Auxiliaries—Steam driven. Boilers—Two, oil-fired. B.H.P.—2550. Speed—12 Knots.

The *Derrycunihy*, an open shelter decker. (*http://www.burntisland.net/derrycunihy.htm*)

La Pampa on trials, 1938. (*Gotaverken*)

La Pampa sails for home. (*Gotaverken*)

Alt disembarking at Southampton. (*IWM H1839*)

Alt arriving at Southampton with 2,000 troops. (*BRB (Residuary) Ltd.*)

Alderpool with 3,528 Polish troops and civilians. (*Polish Institute & Sikorski Museum, London & Mrs Halina Macdonald*)

Empire Flag, a 'B' type standard cargo ship at Funchal, Madeira. (*Captain John Donaldson*)

Saltersgate – Czech Soldiers evacuated from the South of France. Courtesy of Mr John Schaffa, whose father is in the bottom left of the group photograph.

Right: Bayano children. Courtesy of 'the wee guy in the front right wearing the home made jumper!' (*http://www.mercantilemarine. org/showthread.php?6379-SS-Bayano-11*)

Below: Empire Macalpine. (*IWM A 27324*)

Left: Some of the gravestones of the unfortunate *Chumleigh* crew. (*Billy McGee*)

Below: Merchant Ships from KMF 1, off Algiers (*IWM A 12746*)

Troops on the *Lady of Mann* waiting to leave Brest, June 1940. (*IWM C1751*)

Beached coasters discharging at Normandy. British flag, US built, 'Jeeps', one is *Waldo Hill*. (*IWM 24363*)

Above: Tugs and others at the Eastern Solent; the liner on the right is *Aorangi*. (*IWM A 23836*)

Left: Survivors boarding the *John Holt*. (*www.lancastria.org.uk*)

Below: Empire Lance, Merchant LSI(L). (*IWM A 23095*)

Troops on the *Bellerophon*, June 1940. (*Captain Peter Jackson*)

Saminver, British Flag Liberty ship. (*IWM A 23033*)

A Malta-bound convoy under attack, photographed by Sgt Bill Lazell. (*Paul Lazell*)

The *Ohio* discharges the oil that saved Malta. (*IWM A 11498*)

Ships discharging in Grand Harbour, photographed by Sgt Bill Lazell. (*Paul Lazell*)

The first of the few: *Rochester Castle* enters Grand Harbour, photographed by Sgt Bill Lazell. (*Paul Lazell*)

Port Chalmers enters Grand Harbour. (*IWM GM 1426*)

Port Chalmers safely in Grand Harbour, photographed by Sgt Bill Lazell. (*Paul Lazell*)

A band greets the *Melbourne Star*. (*IWM GM 1429*)

The *Brisbane Star*'s shattered bow. (*IWM GM 1457*)

Greece and Crete

From 4 March 1941, Operation Lustre involved landing 58,000 soldiers and their mechanical transport in Greece. The Suez Canal had been mined by the enemy, so the merchant troopers could not transit the canal northbound to help in the operation; so much of the task fell to the Navy.

The convoys with the landing force were attacked. Losses were: *Marie Maersk* (Danish), *Nicholas Embiricos* (Greek) and *Solheim*, HMS *Bonaventure*, *Koulandis Xenos* (Greek) and *Homefield, Devis, Northern Prince*, and the tanker *British Scientist*; the last four were British. Several other ships were damaged and withdrawn.

During an air raid on Piraeus on 6 April, the *Clan Fraser* was hit. Her cargo included 350 tons of ammunition, which detonated, devastating the harbour. The ships that sank as a result were the *Syrian Prince, City of Roubaix* and *Patris*, and the Greek *Agalliani, Acropolis, Artemis Pitta, Constantinos Louloudis, Styliani, Evoikos, Petalli, Milos, Pont Clear, Nitsa* and *Kira Panagia II*. Twenty-five caiques and three British auxiliary ships, the rescue ship *Viking*, the auxiliary caique *Halcyon* and the armed yacht *Surf* were lost.

On Friday 18 April, 'large numbers of the British colony were evacuated in two ships which sailed after dark,' while about 1,500 still remained on shore. Many were evacuated later by Greek steamers sailing to Crete after dark.

On 24 April, orders were given to begin Operation Demon to evacuate the army, but the shortage of small landing craft delayed this. The first evacuation took place on the night of 24 April at Port Raphtis and Nauplia, but it was complicated when HMS *Ulster Prince* ran aground and blocked Nauplion, the harbour. The next night, 25 April, an evacuation took place at Megara, and on the night of 26 April the evacuation was planned for Nauplion, Tolon, Port Raphtis, Raphina and Kalamata. In all, about 50,172 troops were evacuated, approximately 43,000 by merchant ships. The *Pennland* (Dutch?) and *Ulster Prince* were lost.

The most significant loss was the Dutch ship *Slamat*, which had sailed from Nauplion on 27 April with about 600 troops. Shortly after sailing, she sank following a merciless bombing raid. A rescue was carried out by the *Diamond* and the *Wryneck*, but these two destroyers were sunk several hours later. Only fifty survived out of a total of 1,000. Some later reports said that the master had hazarded his ship by remaining to load extra troops. This was probably unfair; had he sailed earlier he would have not been far enough away to escape, as the loss of the much faster destroyers show. The *Khedive Ismail* sailed without troops, mainly because landing craft were unavailable; this caused some in the Navy to suggest that merchant ships were unsuitable for evacuations.

On the night 26/27 April, 8,000 people, including the majority of the Australian troops, were evacuated in the transports *Dilwarra*, *City of London* and *Costa Rica*. They were escorted by the destroyers *Pheobe*, *Flamingo*, *Hero*, *Hereward* and *Defender*; the last taking 250 men and the Yugoslavian crown jewels. The ships became part of convoy GA 14 to Alexandria.

Convoy GA 15 sailed from Suda at 1100 on 29 April, reaching Alexandria on 1 May. It comprised: the *Delane* (Commodore), with 625 Italian officers, 700 Distressed British Seamen, 585 troops and 120 Fleet Air Arm; the *Thurland Castle*, with 2,640 mostly New Zealanders; the *Comliebank*, with 1,450 troops; the *Corinthia*, with 330 consular staff and British subjects and 332 troops; the *Itria*, with 1,775 RAF and 237 troops; and the *Ionia*, with 450 walking wounded, 237 nurses and 157 troops. A total of 5,558 people were transported.

The *Thurland Castle*, on which were the nurses, most of the 2/11th battalion, and others, was dive-bombed several times on the way to Crete, but was not hit, though several men were wounded by splinters. When the *Thurland Castle* visited New Zealand in 1944, still under the command of Captain John J. Knight, the master and the crew were fêted by the people on shore, as a reward for saving so many Kiwis.

The next port to be evacuated was Suda Bay on Crete, where the evacuation was ordered on 27 May and completed on 1 June. Here the largest casualty was the Dutch passenger ship *Costa Rica*, but all 2,600 troops that she carried were rescued. Other casualties included the *Dalesman*, on which Cadet J. Dobson was awarded the BEM (Civ), *Logician* and *Araybank*. All three were sunk during air raids, and were salvaged later by the Germans.

Despite being clearly marked, the hospital ship *Aba*, with 630 patients on board, was damaged, first by Italian aircraft and then during two German raids. The cruisers *Coventry* and *Dido* attempted to drive off the German bombers and Petty Officer Alfred Sephton RN was awarded a posthumous Victoria Cross for his part in the defence. Other losses included the *Eleonora Maersk* (ex-Danish), the RFA tanker *Olna*, the minesweeper *Widnes* (also salvaged by the Germans), and the destroyers *Juno* and *Greyhound*. The cruisers *Fiji* and *Gloucester* were sunk when they went to pick up survivors from the *Greyhound*. Over 500 survived from the *Fiji*, but 693 of the *Gloucester*'s complement died. On 23 June, the destroyers *Kelly* and *Kashmir* were sunk by dive-bombers and the whaler *Kos XXIII* was scuttled. The aircraft carrier *Formidable* was seriously damaged and the destroyers *Imperial* and *Hotspur* were so badly damaged that they had to be sunk.

Night (April)	Kalamata	Monemvasia	Tolos Navplionl	Rafina & Porto Rafti	Megara	Kithira	Milos
24–25			6,685	5,700			
25–26					5,900		
26–27	8,650		4,527	8,223			
27–28				4,640			
28–29	332	4,320				760	
29–30	33						
30–1 May	202						700
	9,217	4,320	11,212	18,563	5,900	760	700
		Total embarked			50,672		
		Lost in Slamat			-500		
					50,172		

The embarkation figures in the naval reports do not always agree with these totals, but the differences are understandable if it is remembered that the embarkations took place at night and in great haste and that among those evacuated there were Greeks and refugees.

As the records of the campaign are incomplete, it is now impossible to state exactly how many British, Australian or New Zealand troops took part. Nor is it known for certain just how many were evacuated or how many were casualties and prisoners of war. So far as can be determined by the Historical Section of the United Kingdom Cabinet Office, the strengths and casualties of the forces were:

	Strength	Killed	Wounded	Prisoners
British Army	21,880	146	87	6,480
Palestinians and Cypriots	4,670	36	25	3,806
RAF	2,217	110	45	28
Australian	17,125	320	494	2,030
New Zealand	16,720	291	599	1,614
Totals	62,612	903	1,250	13,958

Some historians regard the German campaign in Greece as decisive in determining the course of the Second World War, maintaining that it fatally delayed the Axis invasion of the Soviet Union. Others hold that the campaign had no influence on the launching of Operation Barbarossa and that British intervention in Greece was a hopeless undertaking, a 'political and sentimental decision' or even a 'definite strategic blunder'. Whatever the rights and wrongs of the British Army's intervention, it had, for the third time, resulted in disastrous losses among its shipping, in this case particularly naval vessels. Another commitment that tied up naval and merchant ships for the rest of the year was supplying the besieged garrison at Tobruk. By the time that siege was lifted in December, Hong Kong had fallen and the Japanese had landed in Malaya, leading to Britain's 'Second Low Water'.

Second Low Water, 1942

The Japanese landing at Kota Bharu in Malaya coincided with their attack on the United States naval base at Pearl Harbor, Hawaii. This brought the United States into the War on the side of the British, but for various reasons it was many months before this had a positive effect on what was now a fight not only with the Germans and the Japanese, but also the Italians, the Vichy French and the Thais. The intervention of the Thais and inaction by the French in Indo-China, aided the Japanese advance, both down the Malay Peninsula and into Burma. From April 1941, the Ultra keys used by the U-boats in the Atlantic began to differ from those used by the surface ships of the German Navy (Dolphin). Bletchley Park (BP) realised that a new Enigma machine would soon be brought into use.

In January 1942, the Germans introduced a new version of the 'Short Signal Weather Code' which BP had used for their 'cribs', and on 1 February 1942, they brought the four-rotor Enigma machine into use, and with it a new 'Shark' key. If BP had had any cribs, they had no four-rotor Bombes, an electro-mechanical device based on the Bomba developed by the Poles, to test them on. In March 1942, the Germans broke the British Naval Cipher No. 3, which they called the Convoy Code. It was five months before the Admiralty learned of this set back, and not until June 1943 that they replaced the code. The Admiralty's tardiness caused unnecessary losses of Allied ships and men, but not all of the losses can be blamed on this single failure. Instructions for convoys and stragglers were handed to masters in sealed envelopes, so the amount of radio traffic was less than that generated by the U-boats. The U-boats' task was made somewhat easier when those at Kernével realised that the Admiralty were routing convoy after convoy close to the Great Circle route. A Great Circle is the shortest distance between two points on a sphere. A ship that fell behind the convoy was a 'straggler', the opposite being a 'romper.'

The U-boats' 'Second Happy Time', was off the American coast and lasted from January 1942 to late summer. Admiral Ernest King USN was well known as an Anglophobe; he was also preoccupied with the war in the Pacific. Rear Admiral Adolphus Andrews had responsibility for the Atlantic Seaboard, but the equipment he had was out-dated and unsuitable for anti-submarine work. The long range

aircraft that could have plugged the gap were controlled by the Army Air Force
(USAAF). There was bad blood between the two services and the USAAF was not
trained or equipped for anti-submarine work. What could not be excused was
the refusal to set up some sort of convoy system. There was no blackout, even
coastal neon signs were left on; ships continued to ply their peacetime routes and
the Germans were able to sit offshore and torpedo the ships silhouetted against
the lights, some within sight of New York. Rodger Winn's Submarine Tracking
Room in London had been able to follow the progress of the U-boats across the
Atlantic and cable an early warning to the Royal Canadian Navy. Winn correctly
deduced the target area and passed a message to Admiral King warning of a 'heavy
concentration of U-boats off the North American seaboard'. The area commanders
were informed, but little or nothing was done, and submarines sank 609 ships,
totalling 3.1 million tons for the loss of only twenty-two U-boats.

Mercifully, the British Merchant Navy annual death toll never again reached
the one in twenty mark that it had in 1941. One of several improvements that
aided this was the introduction of dedicated convoy rescue ships in 1941. The
number increased through 1942 and 1943. Nonetheless, deaths increased again
in 1943. Until the 1944 introduction of Red Ensign Corvettes, modified for this
work, the rescue duty fell mainly on the coastal packets, the class of vessel that
had performed well during the evacuation of France. Their bigger sisters had been
allocated to act as Infantry Landing Ships LSI (L); later chapters describe some of
the work carried out by these vessels. Most of the British LSIs remained under the
Red Ensign, though some of the purpose-built ones were transferred to the Navy
in late 1944 and 1945. Only one of the packets employed as rescue ships was over
2,000 tons; these ships had been built to make short passages to off-lying islands
and to the near continent.

Improvements in the number and quality of the escorts and better equipment
were cancelled out by the ever increasing number of U-boats and the failure to close
the North Atlantic Air Gap, known by the seamen as 'The Black Pit'. Aircraft were
flown from bases in the UK, Newfoundland and Iceland, but Bomber Command
refused to allocate enough long range aircraft for the task, which meant that
convoys were especially vulnerable in the days it took to transit the gap. Air Chief
Marshall 'Bomber Harris' insisted that 'his' aircraft be used to attack Germany
and to bomb the submarine pens in north-west France rather than protect the
essential convoys. Churchill supported Harris. The attacks on the submarine pens
came too late and were therefore useless. The failure to close the gap meant that
several times in that year Britain had only enough oil to last only a few weeks.

In *The War at Sea 1939-1945*, Captain Stephen Roskill says:

In the early spring of 1943 we had a very narrow escape from defeat in the
Atlantic ... had we suffered such a defeat, history would have judged that the
main cause had been the lack of two more squadrons of very long range aircraft
for convoy escort duties.

It was incredible that the comparatively small number of long range Liberators that Coastal Command required could not be met when they were needed the most. Yet instead of protecting trade, so as to ensure that they would not lose the war, the British implemented an offensive bombing campaign in a fruitless effort to win the war. In so doing, the British continued to neglect their defensive forces and, sadly, it took until a near-disaster in terms of devastating shipping losses in the autumn of 1942 for the British leadership to re-evaluate the strategic situation and begin allocating proper resources to close the air gap.

Churchill had accepted the idea of equipping merchant ships with a single fighter – a modified Hurricane – as a stop gap measure until suitable escort carriers became available. The first of these Catapult Armed Merchantmen (CAM), the *Michael E*, came into operation in May 1941, but she was torpedoed a month later before her aircraft could be launched. In all, thirty-five were converted and twelve of these had been lost by 1943, when they were superseded by the MAC ships. Under the Lend-Lease Agreement, six American escort carriers had been transferred to Britain between October 1941 and March 1942, 'but the Admiralty saw fit to send them to shipyards for ... modification'. During the long period that these vessels were in the shipyards, three classes of Merchant Aircraft Carriers (MAC) were built using standard merchant ship hull designs, but with diesels of one third more horse power, giving them a service speed of 12 knots. Tankers and grain ships were chosen, as neither needed their own cargo handling gear. The vessels were commanded and manned by merchant men. Flight crews, maintenance teams and medical staff came from the Fleet Air Arm. These ships are often wrongly prefixed HMS, but they always wore the Red Ensign of the Merchant Navy. As normal, the MOWT put the management of the ships into the hands of shipowners.

The grain ships were of about 8,000 grt, 440 feet long and with a beam of 57 feet. Each carried four Fairey Swordfish aircraft and a total crew of 107. They were equipped with hangar and lift. The six grain ships were the *Empire Macalpine*, *Empire Macandrew*, *Empire MacKendrick*, *Empire MacDermott*, *Empire Macrae* and *Empire MacCallum*. The Empire oil tankers were slightly larger, at just over 9,000 grt. They were 460-485 feet long and of about 60 feet beam. This class carried three Swordfish aircraft and had a crew of about 110. As they had no hangar or lift, the aircraft had to be stored and maintained on deck. These ships were the *Empire MacCabe*, *Empire MacColl*, *Empire Mackay* and *Empire MacMahon*. All four were managed by the British Tanker Company (British Petroleum).

The Rapana class oil tankers were conversions of existing Shell tankers and remained under Shell management; they were of about 8,000 grt. This class also carried three Swordfish aircraft and had a crew of about 100. Again they had no hangar and lift and the aircraft had to be stored and maintained on deck. They were the *Acavus*, *Adula*, *Alexia*, *Amastra*, *Ancyclus*, *Gadila* (Dutch), *Macoma* (Dutch) *Miralda* and *Rapana*. North Atlantic convoys each had one or two of these vessels. None were lost in service, nor were any ships lost from convoys that included a MAC ship equipped with aircraft. During the build-up for the D-Day landings, some acted as aircraft transports.

One of the more unusual operations involving merchant crews during the War was the transport of ball bearings through enemy controlled waters from neutral Sweden to the UK. The scheme was the brainchild of Frederick George Binney, who in 1939 had been recruited by Iron and Steel Control, Ministry of Supply. As their representative in Sweden, his job was to purchase steel, machine tools and ball-bearings essential to the British armament industries. Sir George Binney DSO as he became, was something of a gentleman adventurer. He was educated at Summer Fields, Eton and Merton College, Oxford. He had organised various Arctic expeditions and had worked for the Hudson Bay Company and United Steel Companies.

With the occupation of Denmark and Norway, the British found it nigh on impossible to ship sufficient amounts of the materials that Binney had bought, so he conceived a series of daring runs to carry the badly needed cargoes to Britain. The first of these, Operation Rubble, took place in January 1941, using five of the Norwegian ships that were detained in Sweden. Binney had contacted the masters of the British steamers *Romanby*, *Blythmoor*, *Mersington Court* and *Riverton*, who were interned north of Stockholm, asking for volunteers to man the Norwegian ships *Elisabeth Bakke, John Bakke, Tai Shan, Taurus* and *Ranja*. Some of their crews were, understandably, not keen to make the trip. None of the British masters were willing to go either, but their chief officers and various crew members were. The British officers were put in command of the vessels, though the Norwegian masters remained aboard as representatives of the owners, Nortraship. Many of the crew also remained. The crews were supplemented by Britons from the four ships that had been sunk at Narvik, and seamen of other nationalities, including some Swedes.

The news of the breakout leaked when the master of one of the Norwegian ships asked his owners in Norway for instructions. The message fell into the hands of the Gestapo, and as a result the *Ranja* was substituted for the *Dicto*. Once the fleet was at sea the battle cruisers *Scharnhorst* and *Gneisenau* passed them, but neither party became aware of the other. *Ranja* was attacked by aircraft and her Swedish first mate, Nils Ryderg, was shot and later died. He was awarded a posthumous OBE. The ships arrived safely in Kirkwall.

A total of 146 men and one woman (the wife of Hans Hansen, chief engineer on *John Bakke*) reached Orkney; fifty-eight were British, fifty-seven Norwegian, thirty-one were Swedish and one was Latvian.

Buoyed up by the success of Operation Rubble, Binney set to organising a much bigger project that was to become Operation Performance. This time the British chartered ten of the Norwegian ships that remained in Sweden and loaded them with more valuable material. The British masters who had declined to join the first breakout volunteered this time. It was decided that they would take charge of the vessels until the limits of Swedish territorial waters were reached, when their regular masters would resume command. Strangely, the Norwegian masters were excluded from the pre-sailing conference.

The ships, in the order that they sailed from the partly frozen Gothenburg harbour were: *Charente*, with a crew of twenty-three British, five Norwegians, one Polish and two Dutch; *Buccaneer*, with five British and forty-one Norwegians; *Lionel*, with forty-one Norwegians and one British; *Stirsten*, with forty-eight Norwegians and one British; *Dicto* (flag ship, with Binney on board), with thirty-one British and twelve Norwegians; *Gudvang*, with twelve British and thirteen Norwegians; *Rigmor*, with four British, one Swedish and thirty-five Norwegians; *Skytteren*, with fifteen British and ninety-six Norwegians; *Lind*, with two British and eleven Norwegians; and *B P Newton*, with five British and sixty-six Norwegians.

This time the Germans were waiting. Only two ships, together with the crew of a third, reached the UK, and two made it back to Sweden. The others were sunk or scuttled by their crews to prevent the ships and cargoes falling into German hands. Mrs Lawson of www.warsailors.com has calculated that of the 471 people involved, 234 were taken prisoner, including eight women and children. Of those taken prisoner, forty-three died; most of those were executed. At sea, nineteen people died, including seventeen missing in a lifeboat from the *Stirsten*. The ships that returned to Gothenburg, with their cargoes, were the *Dicto* and *Lionel*. An effort was made to get them out during the winter darkness on 17 January 1943, but again the Germans were waiting and the ships turned back. Another attempt in February was abandoned for the same reason.

The British continued to fly small cargoes out, but it was obvious to Binney that the only way to obtain enough ball bearings was to transport them by sea. His new plan involved using modified fast Motor Launches. After some deliberation the Admiralty made five diesel-powered gun boats available for the work. These had been part of an order of eight destined for the Turkish Navy. Three were handed over to Camper and Nicholson for conversion and the other two went to the yard of Amos and Smith in Hull. Everything forward of the engine room was stripped out to make a hold in which 40 tons of ball bearings could be stowed, and the bridge structure and accommodation were substantially altered. The boats had a maximum cruise speed of 20 knots, with a range of 1,200 miles at 17 knots. The Hull-based liner company, Ellerman Wilson, managed the boats, which they manned with trawler men and volunteers from among their crews. These ships could not be under the White Ensign of the Royal Navy as warships are only permitted to remain in a neutral port for 24 hours. In accordance with usual Merchant Service practice, the Radio Officers were supplied by Marconi or IMR (International Marine Radio?).

All five vessels first sailed on 26 October 1943, but four were forced to turn back because of a combination of engine problems and bad weather. The fifth was the *Gay Viking*, who reached the UK with 40 tons of ball bearings. Over the next five months, another eight successful trips were completed and cargoes totalled

347.5 tons out of a planned 400 tons. The Germans captured the *Master Standfast* in November. The *Nonsuch* only completed one trip, because of engine problems, which plagued all of the vessels. *Hopewell* completed two trips and *Gay Viking* and *Gay Corsair* did three. Later they were used to carry supplies for the Danish Resistance, but that was a failure.

Stalin's requirements meant that the PQ convoys, on the northern route, had to be sailed in the summer during unbroken daylight. Losses from the winter convoys had been comparatively light, but PQ 16 lost seven ships at the end of May, while two more ships were wrecked after arrival. PQ 17, initially of thirty-nine ships, sailed from Reykjavik on 27 June with 30 per cent British, 60 per cent American, two Russians and a Dutch ship. The convoy had the rescue ships *Rathlin*, *Zaafaran* and *Zamelek* and a close escort of eight, plus two anti-aircraft ships, the ex-MacAndrews Line *Palomares* and *Pozarica*. On 30 June, they were joined by six destroyers and four corvettes. From 1 July, British and American cruisers, screened by destroyers, provided close escort, while the British Home Fleet and two USN ships of Task Force 39 formed the distant cover. Commodore J. C. K. Dowding was in the *River Afton* with Captain H. W. Charlton as master. The vice-commodore was Captain G. W. Stephenson of the *Hartlebury* and the rear commodore was the Master of the *Empire Byron*. The senior officer escort was Captain Broome, Captain of the *Keppel*. Heavy surface units of the Kriegsmarine were in Norwegian waters, as were U-boats and the Luftwaffe.

The American ship *West Gotomska* was damaged and she put back, and after refuelling the warships at sea, the RFA *Gray Ranger* returned with the destroyer *Douglas*. The convoy was detected on 1 July and was attacked, mainly from the air. Two ships were sunk on the morning of 4 July, and a third was so badly damaged that it was sunk by the British submarine P 614 later in the day. The convoy was, however, still in good order that evening when a series of signals were received from the Admiral of the Fleet, Sir Dudley Pound.

At 2111, 4 July: 'MOST IMMEDIATE. CRUISER FORCE WITHDRAW WESTWARD AT HIGH SPEED'. This was followed at 2123 by: 'IMMEDIATE. OWING TO THREAT OF SURFACE SHIPS, CONVOY IS TO DISPERSE AND PROCEED TO RUSSIAN PORTS' and at 2136 by, 'MOST IMMEDIATE. MY 2123. CONVOY IS TO SCATTER'.

On the bridge of HMS *Keppel*, Broome was described as being extremely angry. He wrote later:

I was angry at being forced to break up, disintegrate such a formation and to tear up the protective fence we had wrapped around it, to order each of these splendid merchantmen to sail on by her naked defenceless self; for once that signal reached the masthead it triggered off an irrevocable measure. Convoy PQ17 would cease to exist.

The signal was received in the convoy with disbelief, ship after ship replying that the message from *Keppel* was 'not understood', so Broome took his ship around the convoy repeating the Admiralty orders. He closed the *River Afton* and put the commodore 'in the picture'. Writing later he said: 'When I sheered *Keppel* away from *River Afton* I left an angry, and I still believe, unconvinced Commodore.' Commander Broome was correct; the convoy ceased to exist and so did two thirds of the ships that had been part of it. Of the initial thirty-four ships, only eleven reached their destination, delivering only 70,000 out of 200,000 tons of cargo. A furious Admiral King re-assigned US Task Force 39 to the Pacific, though it has to be said that his ships had also obeyed the instruction to leave the convoy.

Lieutenant Commander Hill on the *Ledbury* wrote later:

There were twenty three (sunk) in that PQ 17, one-hundred-ninety seamen killed, four-hundred or five-hundred aircraft were lost, about three-hundred tanks and a hundred thousand tons of war material. That's what resulted from that Admiralty signal. It was really terrible, even now I have never got over it, because for the Navy to leave the Merchant Navy like that was simply terrible. American(s) just said 'The Limeys are yellow' ... the Tirpitz was not within three or four hundred miles of the convoy. She came out eventually ... the following day. She was sighted by a submarine which made a signal; the Germans intercepted that signal and called her straight back to harbour. There was no threat to the convoy at all except from the air and all these poor merchant ships. One merchant ship signalled: 'I can see seven submarines approaching me on the surface' and there was continual air attack. It was simply awful.

Within the year, Captain Stephenson of the *Hartlebury* (vice commodore) died at his home in Hull of illness thought to have been brought on by his experiences. There is no record of how many others died after the event.

Vice Admiral O'Brien, then serving on HMS *Offa* said:

I have never been able to rejoice with my American friends on Independence Day. July 4 is, to me, a day to hang my head in grief for all the men who lost their lives on convoy PQ17 and in shame at one of the bleakest episodes in Royal Navy history, when the warships deserted the merchant ships and left them to their fate. For that in simple terms is what we were obliged to do.

One more convoy went to Russia that summer. It was numbered PQ 18 and was destined to be the last of that series. The escorts that would have been with a subsequent convoy were drafted to Operation Torch, which is dealt with in the next chapter.

When the convoys to Russia resumed in December 1942, they were prefixed JW and the return series RA, with the numbering starting each way at fifty-one. PQ 18 included forty-four merchant ships, half were American (including Panamanian), fifteen British and the rest were Russian. Despite being heavily escorted, thirteen of the merchantmen were lost, ten of them in air attacks.

In another attempt to placate Stalin, a decision was made to sail a dozen unescorted merchant ships to Murmansk and Archangel in an operation codenamed FB. Seven of the ships were British and five were American. A Russian ship was added at the last moment, making an unlucky thirteen. Several armed trawlers and two submarines were stationed along the route. The ships that made this lonely trip were designated as 'independents' with 'volunteer crews'. They sailed from Iceland at 12-hour intervals.

The accounts of all of their voyages are harrowing, but none more so than that of the tramp ship *Chumleigh*. Owned by Tatem of Cardiff, she was a typical British tramp, run by a company whose feeding standards were, at best, average for the day, though she was reported to have good accommodation. The ship did not appear to have a gyrocompass, necessary for any voyage to high latitudes; having this equipment might have prevented her loss. She was well armed and had twenty-two DEMS gunners, and as usual these servicemen had signed on as 'sailors'. *Chumleigh* was commanded by thirty-five-year-old Captain Daniel Williams, who had been chief officer on her previous trip to Russia. *Chumleigh* again sailed for Russia after a month in London. In Iceland the crew were 'asked' to volunteer; if they did they would receive a special payment for the run of £100 per officer or £50 per rating.

The voyage took the ship to the north of Iceland, past the unseen island of Jan Mayen and onward to pass south of Spitsbergen (Svalbard). The ship's radio officers brought in distress messages from four other independent ships, and one from a ship in a homeward convoy. On 5 November they received a message from the Admiralty instructing them to go to 77° north, before steering to pass Spitsbergen. A ship's articles only permit her to go to 72° north. This instruction meant going more than 300 miles north of that.

By this time the ship had been on dead reckoning for several days, with wandering compasses and in snow storms. Dead reckoning is an estimate of a ship's position based on her course and speed, plus any known current; as one approaches the magnetic pole the compass wants to point downwards, towards the pole. During a brief break in the cloud, the *Chumleigh* had been located by an enemy reconnaissance aircraft. At 2330 on 5 November 1942, she struck a reef off the South Cape. The ship partly rode over the reef and was in danger of breaking her back, so the master ordered the crew to abandon ship.

Captain Williams remained aboard with Chief Officer Fenn and Second Engineer Middlemiss in an unsuccessful attempt to re-float the vessel. The first death occurred when two men were thrown in the water while abandoning the ship. At about 0300 on 6 Novemeber, a radio distress message was sent. Some writers have assumed that this was only monitored by the enemy, but a website about the minesweeper HMS *Gleaner* includes the following: 'Information was exchanged with the Russian staff. Among that supplied to them was ... (b) distress message from *Chulmleigh* read on 78 k/cs at 0708/6th.' Time zones can differ within a few hundred miles in these latitudes. Admiralty monitoring stations also received the message and there are reports of the message being received by other British stations and ships.

The beginning of the brief Arctic twilight showed the men that they were in a horseshoe shaped lagoon, surrounded by breakers. With a little more light, Captain Williams and his officers on the other boats were able to make out an opening in the reef, which they rowed through. Five Ju 88 bombers arrived and began to circle them and the crews prepared for a machine gun attack, but the aircraft bombed the ship instead. The ship was later torpedoed as well. The smallest of the boats was abandoned and its crew shared between the other two.

By the morning of 9 November, Captain Williams' boat was out of sight of land and they had lost sight of the other boat. The master decided to start his boat's engine (as was usual the other boat had no engine), and with this they regained sight of land and found the chief officer's boat. Williams and Fenn decided that the motor boat should go on ahead to Barentsburg, which they believed to be about 80 miles to the north. Williams drove his crew on, with the boat shipping water, the gunwales covered with ice and the sails frozen hard.

At first light the engine was restarted and a few hours later in fading light they sighted the entrance to the fjord in which lay Barentsburg, but at that point the engine failed. Not long after this the master also lapsed into unconsciousness.

Chumleigh's twenty-two-year-old third officer, David Clark, was now in charge of a waterlogged boat, containing twenty-seven men, one of them delirious and the master apparently dying. Clark already had frostbitten hands and feet, as did many of his crew. Just before noon, the sky lightened and he found that they had lost sight of land again. He urged his failing men on to make sail and within an hour they saw land once more. He realised that if he did not find shelter soon they would all die, so he gave up any thoughts of making Barentsburg. He could see only a continuous line of breakers, so he steered south along the reef, but the wind again reached gale force. When it was again dark they saw lights on the shore and the weary third mate took the boat back towards the reef several times, hoping to find an opening. It was not until 0200 on 12 November that a huge ground swell picked up the boat, carried it across the reef and threw it and its occupants onto the beach.

To his amazement, Clark saw that there were a group of wooden huts only 20 yards away. But even crawling that distance was too much for many of the crew: three died where they lay. Clark, and the few others who were able, managed to bully and cajole or drag the rest to one of the huts where they all fell into an exhausted sleep. When they woke they explored the other huts and found that one contained a wood burning stove, matches and a supply of tinned food. Later visits to the other huts in the group yielded other food, and this, together with the remaining stores from the lifeboat, meant that they now had food and warmth.

After a few days members of the party improved, including Captain Williams who was again able to take charge of the team. They were in a very poor condition, with most suffering from "immersion foot' – the brave third officer being particularly badly affected. Only the four Army DEMS gunners seemed in reasonable shape. In the next four days, thirteen died from gangrene, and the gunners helped the two officers by burying the dead and foraging for food.

Twice Mr Clark and Lance Sergeant Peyer attempted to hike to Barentsburg, but were forced to give up. Three of the gunners then made another unsuccessful attempt to seek help. They did find a small hut with more food, which was opportune as their stores were running low. In mid-December, when there was no light at all, Captain Williams and Gunner Whiteside set out once more, but they were again forced to return. On Christmas Eve another member of the party died and Williams again set out in the darkness, taking with him the tough gunners Peyer and Whiteside. This time Whiteside collapsed and again they returned. Unknown to them all the time they were 'only' 6 miles from Barentsburg.

On the morning of 2 January, Whiteside threw open the door of the hut and started to babble incoherently. Williams went outside where he saw two figures in white winter camouflage skiing towards the hut. They were Norwegian soldiers on patrol: the crew's fifty-eight day ordeal was over. The nine survivors were gaunt and hollow eyed, their clothes in rags with stinking pus soaking through home-made bandages. The Norwegian soldiers left all the food and cigarettes that they had with them and set off back to Barentsburg. With them went Gunners Whiteside and Burnett. The next day two sledge parties and a doctor arrived and Mr Clark and AB Hardy, the two most seriously ill, were taken back to Barentsburg. The doctor stayed with Williams and the other four, who were collected the next day.

Over the next two months they were nursed back to health and two months later they were collected by two warships and taken back to the UK. When they reached home, and were discharged as at 6 November and were sent on survivors' leave. Mr Clark received £27.10.7d and the others between £11 and £41.

This may have been because they had received the special payment for the run of £100 per officer or £50 per rating. Captain Williams was made an OBE, Mr Clark an MBE, but both were invalided out. The gunners Richard Peyer, Reginald Whiteside and James Burnett received the BEM. Other survivors were: Able Seaman A. T. Hardy, Chief Radio Officer R. B. Paterson, Gunner T. Burnett, Gunner F. Callan RN, Lieutenant Sergeant R. A. Peyer, Gunner J. Swainston and Gunner R. Whiteside. Those who died on Spitsbergen, including two sixteen-year-old apprentices, were re-buried at the Norwegian town of Tromso with other casualties from the Russian convoys. The graves are the most northerly marked by the Commonwealth War Graves Commission and are cared for by the people of the town. The most isolated are probably the two merchant seamen buried at Timbuctu. No more was heard of the Chief Officer Fenn's boat. Mr E. J. Fenn had been awarded an OBE and Lloyd's Medal for Gallantry at Sea for his part in saving crew and service personnel off Singapore while Chief Officer of the *Derrymore*.

The merchant ships involved in Operation FB were:

Briarwood, Daldorch and *John H B Latrobe* (US) – returned to Iceland.
Dekabrist (Russian), *Empire Gilbert, Empire Sky*, and *William Clark* (US)
   – *Dekabrist* was sunk by aircraft, the other three by U-boats. Plus *Chumleigh*.
Empire Galliard, Empire Scott, Hugh Williamson (US), *John Walker* (US),
   Richard H Alvey (US) – these five reached Russia.

Twenty-three Russian ships sailed independently to Russia; all but one arrived safely.

About 1,325 merchant seamen and DEMS gunners sailed on the ships; 332 of that number lost their lives. Each British ship carried about twenty gunners (two and a half times normal), so about one third of those lost would have been gunners. The gunners did not receive the bonus. Some seamen thought that FB meant 'Foolish B******'; had they known who was behind the project they might have assumed that the B meant Billmeir, and the F? On the Russian Run, 829 Merchant Navy men and more than 1,000 Royal Naval personnel lost their lives.

Another epic Arctic voyage was that of the tanker *Hopemount*, one of seven ships from convoy PQ 14 to reach Russia. The ship was sent east with an icebreaker; joining a Russian convoy near Port Dickson, she reached Tiksi at 134 ° east longitude. When the crew returned after six months they were all suffering from scurvy.

The island of Malta had been a British colony since 1800 and was an important naval base. After the loss of Singapore, maintaining a presence in Malta was essential, particularly as it was strategically placed to interfere with Axis convoys sent to General Rommel in North Africa. But the Axis dominated the Mediterranean. A series of small convoys had taken supplies to the Island with increasing difficulty. There were even operations to run single unescorted ships. The first such voyage was by the tramp steamer *Parracombe*. This ship had been built for the shipowners Pyman and sold in 1940, when they went out of business. The buyer was Jack Billmeir, who first owned ships in the early 1930s. He had made his fortune supplying the Republican side in the Spanish Civil War, and was happy to risk his ships, and their unfortunate crews, in such adventures.

Parracombe sailed from the UK on 17 April 1941 in convoy OG 59. She was loaded with twenty-one cased Hurricane fighters and their spares, sixty-eight rocket projectors, with their ammunition, and other military stores. She passed through the Straits of Gibraltar, where the escort left. The presence of the British escort, and the uninterrupted passage, would surely not have been missed by spies on the Spanish mainland. Her crew were kept busy over the side; while underway she changed her name, first to *Santa Marija* and then to *Sainte Marie*, and the ensigns were changed first to Spanish and then to French. Nothing more was heard from her after clearing the Straits. Later it was learnt that she had sunk on 2 May, after a series of explosions, and that only eighteen of her crew of forty-seven (elsewhere thirty-six) were saved. Among those who were lost were a catering boy and a mess boy who were 'just laddies of fourteen or fifteen'. After 28 hours in the water, the survivors were picked up by a French flying boat. Some were hospitalised, while others were sent straight to a prison camp.

Over the next twenty months, the prisoners were moved from camp to camp.

> [Then,] one morning we got up to a great shock ... there were no guards and there was a train outside. It took us to a place called Philip Tomas and next day we started to walk thirty miles to Gafsa, which had the biggest railway terminus in Tunisia. We heard the Yankees had taken over the aerodrome.... We took a train to the Port of Algiers and were brought home on a passenger ship called the *Orontes*, ending up at the Tail o' the Bank – Dunoon.

Jack Billmeir became a pillar of the community and was made a CBE in 1953, for "Services to Shipping."

In June 1942, with supplies running dangerously low, a decision was made to send two simultaneous convoys to relieve the island of Malta. Operation Vigorous was to sail from Alexandria and Operation Harpoon from Gibraltar. With the exception of the US tanker *Kentucky*, the merchant ships that were to make up the Harpoon convoy sailed from the Clyde on 5 June 1942, in convoy WS 19Z. They were *Burdwan*, *Chant* (American), *Orari*, *Tanimbar* (Dutch) and *Troilus*. The British had no fast tankers in their merchant fleet; for these they were reliant on the US and the Norwegians. The Royal Navy provided an escort of an anti-aircraft cruiser, nine destroyers, a fast mine layer and numerous smaller ships. Distant cover was provided by a battleship, two aircraft carriers, three cruisers and supporting destroyers.

The convoy passed Gibraltar on 12 June. The Italians attacked by air on 14 June, sinking the *Taminbar* and so damaging the *Liverpool* that the *Antelope* towed her back to Gibraltar, with the Italians attacking all the way. Later that day, the covering force returned to Gibraltar and the *Welshman* made a run for Malta with supplies, returning the next day. The now lightly defended convoy was subjected to a coordinated attack by the Italian navy and air force. Two British destroyers were disabled by gunfire and one Italian destroyer was set on fire before the engagement was broken off. The tanker *Kentucky*, the *Chant* and the *Burdwan*, were disabled and later sunk. On the evening of 15 June the remaining ships ran into a minefield off Malta. Two destroyers and the *Orari* were damaged, the last losing some of her cargo. The *Orari* and the *Troilus* made it to Malta, with their depleted escort, but without the desperately needed fuel that had gone down with the *Kentucky*, the RAF had only seven weeks' supply.

Operation Vigorous (convoy MW 11) sailed from the Eastern Mediterranean on 12 June. It was made up of *Aagtekerk* (Dutch), *Ajax*, *Bhutan*, *Bulkoil* (US Tanker), *City of Calcutta*, *City of Edinburgh*, *City of Lincoln*, *City of Pretoria*, *Elizabeth Bakke* (Norwegian), *Potaro* and *Rembrant* (Dutch). The very strong escort under Admiral Vian included eight cruisers and twenty-six destroyers, four of which were Australian. Almost from the start the convoy came under bomb, torpedo and surface attack. On the evening of 14 June, two of the Royal Navy ships were lost and another two damaged. The next day, RAF aircraft from Malta attacked the Italian fleet, with some success. On 15 June, the Admiral received a signal confirming that the Harpoon convoy had reached Malta. That evening, with the warships short of fuel and ammunition and with a large Italian fleet at sea and repeated attacks by Axis aircraft from North Africa, the operation was abandoned. Losses were the cruiser *Hermione*, the destroyers *Airedale, Hasty* and HMAS *Nestor*, together with the merchant ships *Aagtekerk* and *Bhutan*.

Another convoy was needed to prevent the surrender of the island. Malta had, only a few months before, been awarded the George Cross, which is still on the upper hoist of its national flag. As the British had no fast tankers the Texas Oil Company was told to hand over their *Ohio* to the British. They would have been far from happy, as were the owners of the *Kentucky* that had been lost in the Harpoon convoy. The British crew who were sent to the *Ohio* couldn't believe their luck. The accommodation was far superior to anything they had seen, and American rations were still on board. They were told that they were on a dangerous mission and could leave if they wished, but no one did. The other two American ships, with American crews, and US Armed Guards manning the guns, were the *Almeria Lykes* and the *Santa Elisa*. The rest of the fleet were the fast British cargo liners: *Brisbane Star* and *Melbourne Star*, (Blue Star Line, sisters of the *Empire Star* – see the Fall of Singapore chapter), the *Waimarama, Wairangi* (both Shaw, Savill) and *Empire Hope* (MOWT, managers Shaw, Savill), the *Clan Ferguson* (Clan Line), the *Deucalion* (Holt) and the *Glenorchy* (Glen Line-Holt), the *Dorset* (Federal), the *Port Chalmers* (Port Line, Commodore ship), and the *Rochester Castle* (Union Castle). Petrol in drums was loaded on the cargo ships, so that the ships that made it would deliver at least some of the desperately needed fuel. That fuel was to lead to the loss of more than one ship in the convoy.

After the convoy conference, the Commodore A. G. Venables and the masters boarded Rear-Admiral Burrough's flagship HMS *Nigeria*, where the plan was explained in detail. Each master received personal messages from the First Sea Lord wishing them 'God speed' and an envelope marked 'Not to be opened until 0800 hours August 10.' To disguise the destination, the convoy was designated WS 21S when it left the Clyde on 2 August. The WS convoy series usually carried troops and equipment to the Middle East and South East Asia, via the Cape of Good Hope and were popularly known as 'Winston's Specials'. At least one young man knew where they were heading – Apprentice Frederick Treves saw it stencilled on a packing case that his ship was to load. The convoy was escorted by an enormous fleet of both close and distant warships, designated Force X and Z. One of the close escorts was the destroyer *Ledbury*, still commanded by Lieutenant Commander Roger Hill.

By the time the convoy passed Gibraltar on 10 August, the enemy were well aware of its existence, though they may have believed that it was intended to go through to Egypt. On 11 August the escorts refuelled from the two RFA oilers to ensure that they had enough fuel to return from Malta. On that day the aircraft carrier HMS *Eagle* was torpedoed by the *U-73*. She sank with the loss of 160 of her 927 crew. Another aircraft carrier, HMS *Furious*, succeeded in flying off thirty-seven Spitfires destined for Malta, but not all made it. With her task completed, *Furious* returned to Gibraltar. On 12 August, Axis planes wrecked the flight deck of *Indomitable*, setting the carrier on fire fore and aft. This left the escort with only one serviceable aircraft carrier, and meant that a number of *Indomitable*'s aircraft had to be dumped after they landed on the remaining carrier. Force Z was ordered back to Gibraltar. That, and losses among the other warships, meant that the escort had been reduced by half, so three more warships were sent to supplement it. That evening the attacks were stepped up. The first merchantmen to be sunk were the *Empire Hope* and the *Deucalion*. The *Brisbane Star* had her bow shattered during this attack. By this time the convoy was said by one RN commander to be 'chaotic', but all ships were steaming in the correct direction.

Until now the attacks had come from the under the sea and from the air, but by 13 August, the ships were passing through Axis minefields and torpedo boats made no less than fifteen attacks. The *Wairangi* was hit in the engine room and was permanently disabled and the *Almeria Lykes* was hit at in No. 1/2 hold bulkheads and was unable to continue. HMS *Manchester* was torpedoed, abandoned and had to be scuttled. The *Santa Elisa* and the *Glenorchy* were both torpedoed and abandoned, but most of the crew survived. *Rochester Castle* was also torpedoed, but managed to keep going. To add to their misery, British fighter aircraft from Malta fired on the convoy.

Then twelve Junkers 88s attacked the *Waimarama*, setting the deck cargo of aviation fuel on fire; the ship blew up with a tremendous explosion, leaving 'a great pylon of flame on the sea', and sank. Roger Hill DSO, DSC, RN, who was interviewed in 1996, said:

> You never saw anything like it. The flames were hundreds of feet in the air, black smoke. It was a terrible sight and she went down in about five minutes ... all its petrol was in five gallon drums on the upper deck and of course they all went off and then the heat exploded all the rest of it and the whole sea was covered in flames.... I had said to the lads that as long as there was a merchant ship afloat, we were going to stay with it – we weren't going to have any PQ 17 stuff on this convoy – and I reckoned, that by going into the flames, I was sort of redeeming myself for the terrible leaving of the merchant ships in PQ 17. So we dived into the flames. It was an extraordinary experience for the whole sea was on fire. What struck me so much was the heat – it was terrific. I was leaning over the side looking for survivors and I was holding on to my beard because I was frightened it would catch on fire. So we went in and started picking up survivors and the boys were absolutely marvellous. They put a rope around themselves and over the side they went ... we finally joined up with the convoy and the coxswain, who was steering the ship was one deck below me; he had a porthole in front and he said: 'There's a man over there in the flames Sir.'

I said: 'Coxswain, all I can see are flames and smoke, I didn't want to go back again.'

He said: 'No I saw him move his arm Sir.'

'Alright we will go and get him,' and this was John Jackson who was the Wireless Officer of the *Waimarama*, who was the only officer survivor of that ship. He couldn't swim and he was on a sort of large bit of wood, so I put the ship right alongside him and he came up the netting.

Third R/O Jackson owed his life to Frederick Treves who had managed to get the non-swimmer on a piece of board. For this Treves was awarded the BEM. When he was rescued by *Ledbury*, Treves found that the commanding officer was also an ex-Pangbourne boy. HMS *Pangbourne* was a training establishment on the Thames; its cadets went into either sea service. Frederick Treves, who became an actor, was the great nephew of Sir Frederick Treves, the Dorset-born surgeon.

Despite the heroic efforts of *Ledbury*, only twenty-seven of the crew of 107 were saved. *Ledbury* picked up more than that, but the others came from the *Melbourne Star*, which had been engulfed in the flames. Several of her crew jumped over the side thinking that their own ship was on fire. Sixty dive bombers then turned their attention to the already damaged *Ohio*. Two aircraft crashed into the tanker, and though she had avoided mines and torpedoes, two bombs wrecked her boilers, leaving her dead in the water. *Dorset* was disabled by three near misses, and with a flooded engine room on with the high octane fuel on fire, the cargo liner was abandoned.

Rochester Castle, *Port Chalmers* and *Melbourne Star* reached Grand Harbour at 1800 on 13 August. The next day the *Brisbane Star* came into harbour under her own steam.

The *Ohio* was still being attacked and eventually, with his ship's back broken, Captain Mason ordered his crew to abandon ship. But for the second time they re-boarded, and supplemented by naval personnel and Junior Third Officer F. A. Larsen Jr, and Cadet-Midshipman F. A. Dales from the sunken *Santa Eliza*, she entered Grand Harbour steered by a minesweeper with *Ledbury* and *Penn* supporting her. Roger Hill said:

The entry into Malta was really amazing. We stopped just outside the entrance to the main harbour and went and pushed the Ohio's bows. I pushed her right round 140 degrees and had her pointed for going into harbour. A tug came out from Malta and she went in and the whole of the battlements were black with people. There were bands playing everywhere, people cheering, children shouting 'We want food, not oil' and I think the most wonderful moment of my life was when we went into Malta with everybody cheering.

Ohio arrived on 15 August, the day of Santa Marija, the Feast of Assumption. The arrival of the Santa Marija convoy is still commemorated in churches across Malta.

Vice-Admiral Syfret was knighted for his 'bravery and dauntless resolution'. Captain Dudley Mason received the George Cross (the highest civilian award for gallantry); four of his officers received the Distinguished Service Cross and seven crew members the Distinguished Service Medal. The two young American officers from the *Santa Eliza* were awarded the Merchant Marine Distinguished Service Medal, for 'heroism beyond the call of duty'.

In paragraph fifty-seven of a report on Mediterranean convoy operations published in *The London Gazette* of 10 August 1948, Admiral Sir Edward Neville Syfret GCB, KBE wrote:

> Tribute has been paid to the personnel of HM Ships but both officers and men will desire to give first place to the conduct, courage and determination of the Masters, officers and men of the merchant ships. The steadfast manner in which these ships pressed on their way to Malta through all attacks, answering every manoeuvring order like a well-trained fleet unit, was a most inspiring sight. Many of these fine men and their ships were lost but the memory of their conduct will remain an inspiration to all who were privileged to sail with them.

Officers and men from both sea services were awarded military awards, including Roger Hill, Commanding Officer of the *Ledbury*.

The First of the Flood

Early in 1942, the British were having great difficulty sending sufficient material and reinforcements to their troops in North Africa via the Mediterranean. The only alternative route was the long haul around the Cape of Good Hope. This was also the supply route for troops in India and the Persian Gulf. Much of the heavy equipment, such as railway locomotives and army tanks went from there up to Russia. The island of Madagascar, which lies about halfway between the Cape and Aden, was controlled by the Vichy French.

The British feared that the French might allow the Japanese to establish a base on Madagascar, so in March they sailed the invasion force Ironclad from the UK to Durban. The convoy of nineteen merchant ships then sailed from Durban during the three days from 25 April 1942. It included a Royal Fleet Auxiliary (RFA) modified as a landing ship; a shallow draft tanker converted to be the first tank landing ship with bow doors, the first such vessel that the British had; two liners as HM infantry assault ships, and the *Royal Ulsterman*, which was also commissioned. The fleet was escorted by no less than three battleships, three aircraft carriers, six cruisers, eighteen destroyers and twelve smaller warships.

The objective was to land at Diego Suarez, on the north-east corner of Madagascar, to capture the French bases. Some of the warships were positioned to the east of the intended landing site, as protection against an attack by the Japanese. Over 13,000 soldiers, 321 vehicles and eighteen guns were landed. They were not only from the UK, but included substantial contributions from South Africa and Rhodesia (now Zimbabwe). Initially there was strong resistance, but within two and a half days this was overcome. Part of the Vichy force withdrew to the south.

The British lost the corvette *Auricula* when she struck a mine. Three Japanese submarines arrived at the end of May. A spotter plane launched by one found HMS *Ramillies* at anchor. Though *Ramillies* moved anchorage, she was badly damaged by two midget submarines that the Japanese launched. They also sank the tanker *British Loyalty*. *Ramillies* was later repaired and the *British Loyalty* was re-floated. British losses in the operations were 105 killed and 283 wounded; the Vichy lost about 150 with 500 wounded. The British had their first success, and as was to be the case in all subsequent landings, the merchant fleet was heavily involved, again including the Polish liner *Sobieski*.

In an effort to persuade the Vichy French to switch to the Allied cause, a consignment of gold was sent to the island. When this did not have the desired result, the British planned further landings in Madagascar in August. The first, codenamed Operation Stream, was to land on the west coast near the town of Majunga. The MT ships *Advisor, Charlton Hall, Gascony, Ocean Viking, Ross* and *Wanderer*, plus the *Kola* with cased petrol and the oiler *Easdale*, sailed from Mombasa on 3 September. Two days later they were followed by the troopers *Dilwara, Dunera, Empire Pride* and *Empire Trooper* and a day later still they were followed by the hospital ship *Vasna*.

On 7 September, another convoy sailed from Diego Suarez. They were the MT ships *Delius, Empire Squire* and *Ocean Vesper*, with the Personnel Ships *Abosso, Empire Woodlark, Khedive Ismail* and *Llandaff Castle*. Both convoys had a heavy naval escort, or as Winser describes them, 'Naval vessels in support'. The two convoys joined on 9 September and the landings took place early next morning, 8 miles north-west of Majunga, and shortly afterwards at the town itself. As a diversion, *Empire Pride* transferred her troops to the destroyer *Napier*, who landed them almost 400 miles south at Morondava.

After capturing Majunga, some of the troops moved on to the capital Antananarivo, which they occupied. Others re-boarded their transports and were taken to the east coast, with the objective of taking Tamatave. The troops on the *Khedive Ismail* were transferred to the destroyers *Active, Arrow* and *Blackmore*. They landed on 18 September, together with others that had been transported on the HMS *Inconstant*. The French at first refused to surrender, but a few minutes' bombardment by the Royal Navy ensured a change of mind. This was fortunate as several of the British landing craft had broached to while attempting the landing. The *Ocean Viking*, with vehicles, was grounded for two hours and grounded again while approaching the berth, remaining there until the following morning. The three Personnel Ships and the cargo vessel *Gascony* berthed without incident. The administration of the island was handed to the Free French, who were unhappy about the British landing on French territory without involving them.

In October 1942, Bletchley Park received a new edition of the 'short signal weather code book' and other documents from the captured *U-559*. Acquiring these valuable items cost the lives of Lieutenant Anthony Fasson and AB Colin Grazier from HMS *Petard*. The two men were each awarded a posthumous George Cross and Boy Seaman Thomas Brown, at only sixteen, was awarded a George Medal for the same operation. It was not until 13 December that the first decrypted and translated signals were passed to the Submarine Tracking Room. In those grim ten months, almost 1,400 Allied merchant ships were lost.

Stalin had pressed the leaders of the United States and Britain to open up a second front and so relieve the pressure on his beleaguered Russian defenders. The American generals favoured an early landing in occupied Europe, but the

British, with their unfortunate experience at Dieppe, believed that this should be delayed until sufficient resources could be built up. As an alternative, they proposed an invasion of North Africa. For the British, this had the advantage of aiding their Eighth Army at Tobruk and reducing the bases from which the enemy could attack their Mediterranean convoys. President Roosevelt supported Prime Minister Churchill in this, but Churchill had to allow the Americans to lead the land operation.

It was agreed that those countries under Vichy French control would be invaded; Morocco and Algeria first and then Tunisia. The first landings were to be at Casablanca (Western), Oran (Central) and Algiers (Eastern), followed by Bougie. The Western task force was to be shipped directly from the United States in a new series of UGF (fast) and UGS (slow) convoys. The troops and equipment for the other two beaches were provided jointly and were supplied via the UK in a series of KM convoys, also a new series and again both fast and slow.

The convoys from the UK were scheduled to transit the Straits of Gibraltar between the evening of 5 November and early morning 7 November, to arrive at Oran and Algiers on 8 November. The American force was to land at the Moroccan ports of Port Lyautey, Fedala, Casablanca and Safi on 7 November.

Some historians have suggested that the sailing of convoy SL 125 from Freetown was timed divert attention from the invasion convoys. Günter Hessler's account in *The U-boat War in the Atlantic 1939-1945* does not bear this out. He says:

'Operation Torch' involved the use of a vast quantity of shipping, yet the event took the German Supreme Command so much by surprise that it was incapable of mustering even the few military means at its disposal for repelling the invasion.

They did not expect an invasion in North Africa that autumn, though they thought that the Allies might try a landing in Spain (neutral, but sympathetic to the Axis). As soon as Dönitz was informed of the landings on 8 November, U-boats were sent to the Mediterranean, hence the sinkings from 11 November.

Convoy SL 125 of forty-two (elsewhere reported as thirty-seven) ships had left Freetown on 16 October 1942, with the Flower class corvettes *Petunia, Cowslip, Crocus* and *Woodruff* as escort. German cryptographers decoded messages with information about the convoy and sent the ten U-boats of wolf pack Streitaxt (Battle axe) to intercept it west of the Canary Islands. They found them on 27 October, about 200 miles west of the Canary Islands. The U-boats sank twelve ships: the *Anglo Maersk, Pacific Star, Stentor, Nagpore, Hopecastle, Brittany, Bullmouth, Corinaldo, Silverwillow, President Doumer, Baron Vernon* and *Tasmania.*

RAF Coastal Command long range bombers arrived over the convoy on 31 October and the U-boats abandoned the attack early on the next morning, when the remnants of the convoy were on the latitude of Lisbon. Minus their twelve companions and several ships that had gone their own way, the convoy reformed under a new commodore and reached Liverpool on 9 November. Over 400 seamen lost their lives, as did passengers from the *President Doumer*. This was the greatest loss of ships, men and cargoes from an SL convoy, even worse than SLS 64.

Convoy KMS 1G sailed from the River Clyde on 22 October 1942. It consisted of forty-nine merchant ships and seventeen escorts, the numbers vary slightly depending on the source of the information. KMF 1 left the Clyde on 26 October 1942, with forty merchant ships and thirty-six escorts. The ships from this convoy went both to Oran and Algiers. Those ships that were destined for Algiers arrived in the final hours of 7 November. At Algiers the force consisted of 20,000 British and American troops. These were under American command, as it was felt that this might be more acceptable to the French, who had not forgiven the British for sinking their fleet in 1940. Naval forces were commanded by a British Admiral. When the landing craft were launched towards midnight on 7 November, there was a moderate swell, a new moon and a brisk westward current. There was no French resistance at the first two sites, though some of the landings were complicated by the weather. The troops at the third sector had to contend with fog, but resistance was limited.

The only fighting took place within the port of Algiers itself, when two destroyers attempted to put ashore a party of American infantry to prevent the French from scuttling ships and sabotaging the dock installations. Heavy shells badly damaged the destroyer *Broke* but the second ship got through and disembarked her landing party. *Broke* sank on 9 November while under tow. From daylight on 8 November, four carriers provided air cover over the invasion area. By the end of the day the port was in Allied hands.

The bulk of the ships from KMF 1 went to Oran. The escorts *Walney* and *Hartland* forced their way into the harbour at Oran on 8 November, but both were set on fire by guns from the shore and blew up. Allied warships sank one Vichy-French destroyer and drove a second ashore. A third returned to harbour. Oran fell on 10 November. The only loss was the torpedoing of *Thomas Stone* at 0535 on 7 November; this ship was damaged beyond repair.

The invasion of Morocco was an American operation. Convoy UGF 1 left Hampton Roads on 24 October 1942 and arrived off the Moroccan coast on 8 November. It consisted of thirty-eight ships and no less than fifty-six escorts. Hague's records say thirty-six merchant ships and sixty-two escorts (the escorts were designated as Task Force 34). The American forces landed at Safi, which they captured within a few hours, Fedela, where they experienced weather problems and met resistance, and Mehedia and Port Lyautey, where they also met resistance.

On 10 November, Vichy-French forces in North Africa were ordered to surrender. But German U-boats and aircraft counter-attacked. *U-431* sank the destroyer *Martin*, while the sloop *Ibis* was sunk by aircraft. The cargo ship *Garlinge* was sunk by *U-81*. The next day, 11 November, *U-173* sank the transport USS *Joseph Hewe* and the tanker USS *Winoski* was damaged by a torpedo, as was the destroyer USS *Hambleton*. On that day, British forces were landed at Bougie. There were heavy losses among the transports then and later. In the afternoon, the MT ships *Urlana*, *Glenfinlas* and *Stanhill* entered Bougie, while in the Bay troops were being disembarked from the *Karanja*, *Cathay*, *Awatea* and *Marnix van St Aldegonde*.

In the evening, the last group was attacked, first by about thirty Ju 88s, followed by He 111 torpedo bombers. *Awatea* (Union ss Co. New Zealand) was hit by four bombs, causing a fire in number two hold and flooding the engine room. With the ship listing 40 degrees, fire fighting efforts were unsuccessful and the liner was abandoned. *The London Gazette* says that warships saved the crew, but a photograph on a website shows the crew on the *Marnix van St Aldegonde* and expresses their thanks for being saved by that ship. *Cathay* (P&O), with about 1,200 troops on board, was hit by a bomb and the troops were offloaded by all available landing craft before this ex-liner caught fire. *Cathay* burned all night. After discharging troops at Algiers, the transports *Viceroy of India* (P&O) and the Dutch *Nieuw Zeeland* were torpedoed by U-boats when off of Oran.

Early on 12 November, HMS *Tynwald* (ex-IOM ss Co.) suffered two violent explosions. The ship was abandoned and survivors were picked up by boats from *Roberts* and *Samphire*. At dawn, *Karanja* (BISN) was hit by at least two bombs; an oil fuel fire immediately broke out amidships and spread rapidly. The traumatised survivors from *Cathay* and some military personnel lowered the lifeboats without orders. On the same day the *Browning* was torpedoed off Oran. Off Fedala, Morocco, the US transports *Edward Routledge*, *Asker H Bliss* and *Hugh L Scott* were torpedoed by the *U-130*. After sailing from Algiers, Holt's *Maron* was torpedoed and at Bougie their *Glenfinlas* was sunk by aircraft, though she was later re-floated. On 14 November, the *Narkunda* (P&O), which had sailed from Bougie, sank following an air attack with the loss of thirty-one crew. Off Portugal, the *Warwick Castle* (Union Castle), returning in convoy MKF 1 from Algeria, was torpedoed and sank with the loss of sixty-two crew. The attack on the convoy continued on the next day. The escort carrier *Avenger* was torpedoed and blew up with the loss of over 600 lives. The trooper *Ettrick* was torpedoed and sank – yet another loss for P&O.

Ashore, things were at last going well for the British Eighth Army. The Battle of El Alamein had been won by 4 November and Rommel withdrew. The Eighth Army entered Tobruk on 12 November and Benghazi a week later, having advanced 600 miles in a fortnight.

Convoy KMS 2 left Loch Ewe on 25 October, arriving in Algeria without loss on 12 November 1942. There were fifty merchant ships and twenty-five escorts. They were mostly designated as mechanised transports. Cargoes included armoured fighting vehicles, guns, petrol and about 2,000 tons of stores each. Each ship carried a small number of troops. Six purpose-built Tank Landing Craft made their appearance for the first time during these landings, all under the White Ensign. There were a series of follow-up convoys which are not included in the tables.

With the safe arrival of all four ships of the STONEAGE convoy at Malta in November 1942, the siege was in effect lifted. While some later convoys were attacked, no merchant ships were lost. The Allies were beginning to wrest control of the Mediterranean from the Axis forces. In his report about Operation Torch, Admiral of the Fleet Sir Andrew B. Cunningham, GCB, DSO, Commander-in-Chief, Mediterranean paid tribute: 'To the courage, determination and adaptability of the Merchant Navy.'

The Landings in Sicily and Italy

At their meeting in Casablanca in January 1943, Churchill and Roosevelt agreed that the invasion of Northern France should be delayed until 1944, but that an Italian Campaign would begin in summer 1943. The first objective was to land on the Italian island of Sicily, giving the Allies control of the strait between Sicily and Tunisia. This would then allow them to advance onto the Italian mainland.

A fleet of 2,500 ships were assigned to the operation, including 180 purpose-built landing craft, with bow ramps, which could land troops and vehicles on the beaches. Eight adjoining landing sites were chosen: three were allocated to the Americans and five to the British. Merchant ships were loaded in the USA, in the UK, in North Africa and in the Middle East.

Convoy KMS 18 sailed in two sections. KMS 18AG, consisting of eight escorted naval landing craft, sailed on 20 June 1943. One of these, *LST 406*, was sent into Londonderry to load machinery parts and was then told to catch up convoy KMS 18B. The LCT convoys caused Admiral Cunningham a great deal of concern. Despite his misgivings, the inexperience of the crews and the unproven nature of the ships did not cause major problems and only one LCT was swamped and capsized. A shortcoming that could not be overcome, however, was the low speed of these vessels; convoys with LCTs could only maintain 5½ knots in good weather, with the result that some arrived late.

The second section of the convoy, with twenty merchant ships, sailed from the Clyde on 24 June and passed Gibraltar on 3 July. The next day it was attacked by U-375. In the evening she torpedoed the *City of Venice* and then the *St Essylt*; twelve died. These two ships had been members of a group of seven that were to transfer to the fast convoy KMF 18, and unload immediately on arrival at the beachhead. On 5 July the Commodore ship *Devis* was sunk by U-593 and fifty-two troops died. The remaining ships arrived at the invasion beaches on 10 July.

The faster ships of KMF 18 sailed from the Clyde on 28 June. All arrived at the Husky landing sites on 11 July. Three were the White Ensign LSTs *Boxer*, *Bruiser* and *Thruster*; other HM ships were the Headquarters ship *Hilary* (formerly Booth Line), the *Glengyle* and *Ulster Queen*. Fourteen merchant ships and one RFA carried more than 16,000 troops between them.

The other vessels from the UK had sailed as early as March 1943, making the long voyage via the Cape of Good Hope. When they reached Suez they exercised before embarking the troops and then transited the Suez Canal. In all, eighteen landing and personnel ships formed up in Port Said as convoy MWF 36. Five flew the White Ensign of the Royal Navy. The balance was made up of merchant ships from Britain, Holland, Norway and Poland. Many of the vessels were veterans of the landings in Africa. During the voyage the fast convoy caught up with the convoy MWS 36, which consisted of thirty-two cargo ships. These vessels were loaded with military stores and petrol, and most carried a few hundred troops. Only two had been built before the War. A few of the faster cargo vessels changed convoys. The sole casualty from this convoy was the MT ship *Shahjeha*, which was torpedoed by the *U-453* on 6 July. She sank the next day after being engulfed by fire. Her cargo had included vehicles, stores and cased petrol, and also four teams of service personnel who were to discharge ships on arrival. Because of this the ships' crews at the Normandy landings were required to discharge their own ships and be willing to transfer to other ships as required. Five more RN landing ships sailed from Sfax on 8 July.

Convoy NCF 1 was an American convoy of sixteen merchant ships that sailed from Oran on 5 July and arrived at the US Western Task Force Dime Beach on Saturday 10 July. There were also two former Belgian ships, the LSI(S) *Prince Charles* and *Prince Leopold*.

The landings began in the early hours of 10 July. The British Eastern Task Force achieved their objective within five hours. As soon as they had disembarked their troops, the large landing ships left the beachheads, with the exception of the Norwegian *Bergensfjord* who had a naval port party aboard. When a flight of German bombers arrived to attack the beaches they also attacked the *Bergensfjord*, the US Liberty ship *George Rogers Clark* and *LST 407*. All three suffered damage and incurred casualties. Later that day, the fully-lit hospital ship *Talamba* was bombed and sank 5 miles off the coast. The Dutch *Baarn* was attacked by a Ju 88 and set on fire on 10 July; the ship was scuttled because of the risk of her ammunition exploding. In the evening, the US Liberty *Joseph C Cannon* received a direct hit, which was said to have penetrated the ship's bottom, but she returned to Malta under her own power.

At 0500 on 12 July, the illuminated hospital ship *Dorsetshire* was attacked while taking off wounded, and sustained some structural damage. After this, hospital ships were kept unlit at the anchorages. At dawn that day, the *Ocean Peace* was also attacked; a near miss on her forepart ignited the petrol in her cargo. When the fire got out of control the ship was sunk to prevent a disaster. Just before noon on 13 July, the newly arrived US Liberty *Thomas Pickering* was attacked by two aircraft and became a total loss. The *Fort Pelly* was sunk in an air attack on Augusta on 20 July. The following day, also at Augusta, the *Empire Florizel* was sunk in another air attack. On 26 July, Ropner's *Fishpool* was attacked and sunk at Syracuse.

On 3 September, the British Eighth Army, veterans of the North African campaign, landed unopposed on the Italian mainland in 'Operation Baytown'.

They had been ferried across the narrow Straits of Messina by landing craft. They were then to go northwards to link up with American and British forces that were to land at Salerno in 'Operation Avalanche'. Salerno had been chosen because its beaches were suitable and it was as close to the important port of Naples as it was possible to get, without attempting a landing in the Bay of Naples itself.

The Salerno landing sites were divided, with the British X Corps taking the northern beaches, and the American Fifth Army the southern ones. The invasion was to take place on the morning of 9 September. On 24 August, some confusion was caused when the General of the Fifth Army advanced the time of H-Hour by 30 minutes. An added complication was the BBC's announcement on the evening before the landing that the Italians had capitulated. The Naval Commander-in-Chief, Admiral Cunningham, was concerned that the news would engender a sense of complacency, which to some extent it did. This was a problem, because the Salerno area was still strongly defended by German troops. Landings also took place in the southern ports of Calabria and Taranto.

The principal US convoy was NSF 1, which sailed from Oran on 5 September. There were several British landing ships in this convoy. The British convoys were the FSS 1 and FSS 2 from Bizerta, and the TSS 1 and TSF 1 from Tripoli. The first letter shows the sailing port, F = Bizerta, N = Oran and T = Tripoli. The second shows the destination, while the third indicates whether the convoy was 'fast' or 'slow'.

Of the forty one ships in the British convoys, just under one third sailed under the White Ensign, three under the American flag and six under other European flags. The rest, almost half, were under the Red Ensign. By this time, French ships were occasionally re-appearing in Allied convoys. Fifty-three purpose-built tank landing ships and 114 infantry landing craft played a very significant part in the operation. A number were lost. Even before the landings, four landing craft were put out of action at Tripoli when one LCT, with an ammunition cargo, was being loaded with smoke containers that spontaneously combusted.

On 6 September, the ships in Bizerta Bay were attacked by a large flight of German aircraft, but no damage was done. On the morning of 8 September, *LCT 624*, loaded with high octane fuel, was attacked; the vessel caught fire and sank. That afternoon, *LST 417* was hit by an aerial torpedo and had to be beached. There were other casualties among these ships.

Because of a minefield along the 100-fathom line, the deep draught LSI (L)s had to launch the landing craft 9-10 miles from shore. This meant that the troops had a 1½-hour journey to the beaches, so it was a worrying time for all. Jack Mount was watching the landings from behind enemy lines. He had advised that the beach was also mined and heavy artillery had been deployed by the Germans. He believes that Allied troops were not made aware of this. Despite fierce resistance, the Allies succeeded in taking Salerno. A number of landing craft were damaged. The Germans mounted a strong counter attack which was repulsed.

On 13 September, the hospital ship *Newfoundland* was attacked by dive-bombers. She was ordered to put to sea for the night, joining two other hospital ships. Again all were illuminated. The next morning she received serious bomb damage and was set on fire. Nurses and patients were evacuated to the *St Andrew, Tairea* and *Lienster*, the last named having also been attacked. The master and seventeen volunteers remained aboard the *Newfoundland*. Though the fire-fighting equipment had been put out of action, they, with the help of two US destroyers, brought the fire under control. The ship survived, but had to be scuttled on the following day as she was a danger to navigation. Captain John Wilson was awarded the OBE and his injured second officer, Robert Walton, was awarded the MBE.

The *Empire Charmian*, a heavy lift ship, being used as a landing ship carrier, was attacked when returning to Messina and the master was killed. The Admiralty's *RFA Derwentdale*, similarly fitted, was also attacked and was towed to Malta for repairs.

Because the Allies were unable to progress north from Naples, they planned to land on the flat beaches near the fishing port of Anzio, 40 miles south of Rome. This area was sparsely populated as the beaches were backed by the Pontine Marshes. Shipping and troops were in short supply as preference was already being given to the intended landing in northern Europe.

In all, 243 ships sailed from Naples on 21 January. Of these, only fourteen were merchant ships, including five LSI(L)s, five hospital carriers and four Liberty store ships. There were also six LSI(L)s, now under the White Ensign. The rest of the fleet were warships and landing craft of many types. The overall commander of land forces was Major General Lucas of the US Army. Despite being poorly resourced, the troops achieved almost complete surprise and the build-up of troops and equipment proceeded quickly. Under continuous German artillery and air harassment, the Allies off-loaded twenty-one of the follow-up cargo ships and landed 6,350 tons of material on 29 January alone. Ninety-seven attacking Luftwaffe aircraft were shot down by 1 February. The Germans succeeded in sinking one destroyer and a hospital ship, as well as destroying significant stocks of supplies piled on the crowded beaches. Lucas ordered the rest of the troops ashore, so that a total of 61,332 Allied soldiers landed in the beachhead. By the end of January, 237 tanks, 508 artillery guns and 27,000 tons of stores and equipment had been landed. But General Lucas had allowed the advantage to slip away. He was relieved and sent back to the United States in February. The Germans, having been told by Hitler to defend Anzio 'to the death', counter attacked from the surrounding mountains and pinned the Allies down until the spring. It was not until June that the Allies entered Rome, four months later than they had intended.

No British ships were lost on the day of the landings, but on the following day three of the hospital carriers were attacked. *St Andrew* was undamaged, but her sister *St David* sank in five minutes. *Leinster* also suffered bomb damage, but she and *St Andrew* rescued 160 survivors between them. The Liberties *Hilary A Herbert* and *Samuel Huntingdon* were seriously damaged. The second ship was from a follow-up convoy. The greatest loss of life was suffered when the cruiser *Spartan* was hit by a glider bomb and sank little over an hour later.

The Normandy Landings – Operation Neptune

The British began planning their return to Europe soon after their hurried retreat in June 1940. When the Americans came into the War they were keen to invade in 1943, but Churchill preferred to first attack Italy, the 'soft under belly' of Europe as he called it. The landings were scheduled for May 1944, but postponed until June to allow an increase from three to five Army divisions. The operation was codenamed Overlord, with the marine side being Operation Neptune. The Americans took overall charge while the British retained the naval command. To decode high-level teleprinter traffic between Berlin and major command centres, the British developed the world's first electronic computer. The machine, called Colossus, was designed by engineer Tommy Flowers and a team at the Post Office, Dollis Hill. The prototype was in operation at Bletchley Park by February 1944 and Colossus II first worked on 1 June, just in time for the Normandy landings.

There was a conflict between the Armies' and Air Forces' need for a full moon and spring tides and the two Navies' preference for approaching the coast in darkness. It was thought that the Germans would expect a landing at High Water, giving the troops the minimum of open beach to cross. But the Allies chose Low Water, as this meant that the beach defences and tank traps would be exposed. The compromise conditions existed on the 5, 6 and 7 June, with the full moon on the evening of 6 June. General Eisenhower settled for an invasion date of the 5 June. In the event, bad weather caused a one day postponement.

The area chosen for the landings was in the Seine Bay. From the east, at the small port of Ouistreham, the beaches were named Sword (Canadian), Juno (British), Gold (British) and Omaha (American). The fifth beach, the American Utah, was on the Cotentin Peninsular. The peninsular protected all the beaches from the worst of the Atlantic gales. But they were struck by an unseasonably severe summer depression in the middle of June, with a north-east gale.

As there were no ports big enough to take the enormous amount of traffic, it was decided to prefabricate two complete harbours. Sections were built in sites all over the UK. Five breakwaters were to be established by sinking lines of block ships, called Gooseberries. The chosen vessels were mostly merchant ships that had been damaged beyond repair. *Gooseberry One*, made up of nine US flag ships, was to protect Utah beach. *Gooseberry Two* was to be laid off St Laurent, using an old British Battleship and eight US flag and five Panamanian flag cargo ships. This breakwater protected the eastern entrance to *Mulberry A*. *Gooseberry Three* was to be made up of fifteen cargo ships; eight were British and the balance came from various European Allies. This was to be off Gold Beach, protecting the two entrances to *Mulberry B*. *Gooseberry Four*, made up of ten ships, was to provide shelter to Juno Beach; it included one Greek and one Belgian ship. *Gooseberry Five* was to be on the extreme left flank of the British sector; it was made up of six British cargo ships and three old Allied warships.

The sixty Gooseberry ships had been stripped of everything of value by the frugal British. Holes had been cut in their watertight bulkheads and they had been wired for scuttling charges. Their only identifying marks were numbers painted on their sides. The bulk of the ships were assembled at Methil, on the east coast of Scotland, from where they sailed on 23 May. Progress was painfully slow, and as their maximum speed was just over 5 knots, getting safely through the Pentland Firth was an achievement in itself. One ever present fear was that two of these unmanageable ships would collide. Had they done so, they would have sunk quickly. After three days they reached Oban, on the west coast of Scotland. They sailed from there, picking up a few other ships on the way, and arrived in Poole Bay the day before D-Day. On D + 1 the three sad CORNCOB convoys sailed to 'the far shore' on their final voyage.

Each Mulberry harbour was to be protected by concrete caissons and chained steel floats. The 'quays' inside would float up and down with the tide and would be joined to the shore with floating roadways. The finished units had been 'parked' along the British coast from Selsey eastwards to Dungeness; one still remains east of Dungeness. Twenty-two pumping ships were allocated to re-float them and over 200 harbour and coastal tugs were employed moving them to France.

For some months prior to the invasion, merchant seamen signing off or on ships were asked if they would be willing to have a 'V' stamped in the front of their Discharge Books. Those who enquired what it was about were told that the 'V' indicated that they were prepared to volunteer for the Mass Invasion of Europe and that they would be required to work on any merchant ship or ashore. Those who did not enquire were just told that it would entitle them to an additional weekly ration of 200 cigarettes. Over 90 per cent of the seamen volunteered, but there are no figures to indicate how many did so purely for the cigarettes! Young officers who qualified for their certificates early in 1944 were told that they might be required to command landing craft; again the numbers who did, if any, have not been recorded. Some young MN officers have unexplained gaps in their service records. Were they in naval service then? Some of the remaining 10 per cent had been rejected because of their age.

Ships assembled in bays and harbours all over the southern part of the country. The greatest concentration was in the Solent where over 500 ships were eventually anchored. The first had arrived as early as Y − 21 (Y = 1 June) four weeks before the landings; many of these early ships ran out of food. The ships that were loaded in the Thames ports waited at the Nore, while the ships destined for the American beaches assembled in ports and bays to the west of Southampton.

The invasion fleet consisted of seventy-five ships; they were the Infantry Assault Ships, Troopships and Attack Transports. The biggest group were the forty-two ships that flew the Red Ensign, including two from Canada and one from New Zealand. Twenty ships flew the Stars and Stripes, one the Dutch tricolour, and another the Belgian Ensign. The rest were former merchant ships commissioned by the Royal Navy. Three newspaper correspondents joined the merchant ships for the journey. Peter Duffield, the '*Evening Standard* Merchant Navy Reporter' joined what must have been the trooper *Neuralia* in the London Docks. Duffield said that there were 1,000 merchant ships manned by 50,000 Merchant Navy men, all volunteers. This must have been from a Ministry of Information hand-out, as *The Times* 'Special Correspondent with the Merchant Navy' quotes the same figure. *The Times* man gives an outline of the service's involvement from Norway in 1940 to Italy in 1944. He also correctly describes the thirteen Empire Anvil type LSI(L)s as 'designed by the Sea Transport Division of the Ministry of War Transport and built in California under the Lend Lease Agreement.' In a paragraph about the 'V' Articles and notes that 'at least one British woman – a certificated engineer' – had signed them, presumably Victoria Drummond.

Naval and Merchant Shipping forces taking part in NEPTUNE were as follows:

(a) Heavy Units: 7 Battleships, 25 Cruisers, 105 Destroyers , 2 Monitors,
     2 Gunboats   139
(b) Escort Vessels: 26 Escort Destroyers, 27 Frigates, 71 Corvettes,
     18 P.C.   142
(c) Coastal Forces: 145 M.L.s, 54 H.D.M.L.s, 82 Large M.T.B.s,
     84 Small M.T.B.s & others   316
(e) Tugs: 125 British, 91 American, 9 Rescue (3 elsewhere)   225
(f) Warship Blockships: 2 Very Old Battleships, 2 Very Old Cruisers   4
(g) Miscellaneous: 39 Salvage and Wreck Disposal Ships,
     60 Smoke Making Trawlers   99
(h) Landing Ships and Craft   4,021

Manned by:-	British	U.S.	Total
Landing Ships (L.S.I., AP.A. and L.S.T.) (43 Red Ensign)	126	185	311
Major Landing Craft Including Support Craft	777	434	1,211
Minor Landing Craft and Barges	1,570	929	2,499

Merchant Ships (US figures)

61	Personnel Ships and LSI
224	M.T. Ships
64	M.T. Coasters
122	Store Coasters
150	Tankers & Colliers
136	Cased Petrol Carriers
55	Blockships
76	Ammunition Carriers
18	Ammunition Supply Issuing Ships (ASIS)
78	Liberty Store Ships
10	Hospital Ships and Carriers
10	Accommodation Ships
295	Miscellaneous (inc. 225 tugs and 39 salvage vessels?)

Total Merchant Ships (including 43 merchant LSI)	1,416
Total Landing Ships and Craft	3,978
Total Naval Forces	1,089
Accumulative Total	6,483

The percentage of American and British (Including Allied) Ships in these totals is:

Type of ship	Total	American	British	Included in British
Battleships	6	50%	50%	+ HMS *Nelson*
Cruisers	23	15%	85%	1 Polish, 2 French
Destroyers	104	35%	65%	4 Canadian, 2 Allied
Landing Ships & Craft	4,021	40%	60%	Includes Allied
Coastal Forces	316	30%	70%	" "
Minesweepers	277	10%	90%	" "
Escort Vessels	152	15%	85%	28 Canadian, 8 Allied
Monitors & Gunboats	4	0%	100%	2 Dutch Gunboats

Ancillary Forces	324	30%	70%	Includes Allied
Merchant Ships (MT)	224	50%	50%	" "
Coasters (blockships included)	1,032	2%	98%	" "
Total Percentage of all Vessels	6,483	30%	70%	

If the smaller landing craft carried on the assault ships are omitted, the total is 5,015. John de S. Winser has seventy-seven Assault, Troop and Attack Ships/Transports, 326 Military Stores Ships, 415 Coasters, 237 Tank Landing Ships and 1,464 Assault Landing Craft, 1,633 Naval Craft of all types and 863 Other Vessels which comes to a total of 5,015. Young, in *Britain's Sea War*, says that 'on the first three days, thirty-eight convoys, comprising 743 ships, had been sent across the Channel. By the tenth day, 500,000 men and 77,000 vehicles had been landed' – truly the largest amphibious operation ever undertaken.

In peace time, 'coasters' traded around the British coast and between the River Elbe and Brest. For four years after Dunkirk, most had been confined to the British coast, but they saw as much of the War as anyone. On their short voyages, they faced attacks from E-boats and aircraft. Deep sea vessels did not pass through the Dover Straits, where the enemy could shell them, but the coasters continued to do so. This was the dreaded 'Hell Fire Corner'. Many who regularly made the trip carried coal for power stations, gas works and domestic fires. They became known as 'The Coal Scuttle Brigade', but they may have acquired this name years after the event. For the landings, these small ships carried every kind of stores, equipment, fuel and ammunition needed by the troops. It was decided that the coasters should be beached and discharged when the tide was out. This left these many ships in a most uncomfortable position; if the wind increased while they were beached, they stood a chance of broaching to when re-floating. Broaching is a seaman's word for being pushed round by the sea so, in this case, as to be parallel to the beach and in danger of capsizing. The ability of the German guns crews to get the range of the ships and shell them was of even more concern.

Each of the 224 larger ships had been loaded with the same lethal combination of stores, food, tanks, vehicles, petrol and ammunition as the coasters. The staff at the Sea Transport Division of the MOWT had planned the loading so that the loss of several ships would not deprive the forces of any particular item. Many of the cargo ships also carried troops. The only loss from among this group on D-Day was the British Liberty *Sambut* MT2 (numbers were displayed on a board mounted on the midship superstructure abaft the bridge). She had loaded her cargo in London and also carried 560 troops. *Sambut* was part of the twelve SAM ship convoy ETM 1. At noon on the 6th, only six hours after sailing from London, *Sambut* was hit forward by two shells fired from the shore batteries on the French side of the Dover Strait. She was set on fire and abandoned; she sank at 1900 that evening.

Most of the tugs that were employed are described as 'Requisitioned'; some were, some weren't. Whatever flag they flew, most of the British vessels still had their Merchant Navy crews. For the most comprehensive list of the tugs, see the Thames tugs website. There were also a dozen rescue tugs employed on various tasks and available to move larger units. These were deep sea tugs, mostly naval tugs or Dutch salvage tugs. Despite the White Ensign that many flew, the British vessels were crewed by merchant seamen and fishermen working under a T124T arrangement. The officers were given commissions in the RNR.

Another problem that the British anticipated was the need to get vast amounts of fuel across the Channel without using vulnerable tankers, which in any case were sorely needed elsewhere. Prototype submarine pipes were developed in 1942 by scientists and engineers from British oil and submarine cable companies. The two types were a flexible HAIS pipe and a less flexible steel HAMEL pipe of a similar size. It was discovered in testing that the HAMEL pipe was best used with final sections of HAIS pipe each end. Because of the rigidity of the HAMEL pipe, a special barge called *Conundrum* was developed to lay it. Twenty-one requisitioned merchant ships were allocated to Operation Pluto (Pipe-Line-Under-The-Ocean). The novel system was a great success. By January 1945, 300 tons of fuel was pumped to France each day, by March this was increased to 3,000 tons per day, and eventually to 4,000 tons a day. The vessels that carried out the work had been merchant ships, but were RNR manned and commissioned for the operation. At the end of the operation, the SNP PLUTO wrote 'I am proud to have commanded so fine a force, largely drawn from the Merchant Navy.'

Many other merchant vessels were pressed into service. They included:

Anti-Aircraft ships – eight 'Eagle' ships which took their name from *Golden Eagle*.
Buoy Laying – six Trinity House (the UK buoyage and lights authority) and French ships.
Cable Vessels – three vessels from the Post Office cable ship fleet and one MWOT.
Colliers – eleven coasters used to carry coal for the forces.
Hospital Carriers – ten packets plus the hospital ships *El Nil*, *Llandovery Castle*.
Mooring Craft – thirty-three, both HM Boom Defence vessels and merchant ships.
Naval Store ships – fourteen, mostly merchant ships.
Wreck Dispersal Vessels – a number of trawlers fitted out for the work, as HM ships.
Dutch schuyts – thirty-five at least twenty were working for American forces.
Miscellaneous ships – including Depot, Accommodation, Headquarters, Repair Ships, Dredgers, Fire boats, Trawlers and Lightships.

Though the *Sambut* was the only merchant ship lost on D-Day itself, more were lost in the months that followed. On 10 June, E-boats attacked ships at the convoy assembly point off the Isle of Wight, sinking the coasters *Ashanti*, *Brackenfield* and *Dungrange*. On 16 June, the Trinity House vessel *Alert* was sunk by a mine. The Canadian vessel *Albert C Field* was attacked and sunk off the Dorset coast on 18 June. The coaster *Westdale* sank after hitting a mine on 20 June. Several merchant ships suffered substantial damage.

The Hospital Carriers *St Julien* and *Dinard* hit mines on the 7th, but both were towed to Southampton and repaired. On 11 June, the *Fort McPherson* was damaged by aircraft. The tanker *British Engineer* and the coaster *The Viceroy* were mined later in the month.

Between 19 and 22 June, gale-force winds that veered to the north-east – the worst possible direction – wrecked the American Mulberry harbour. Ships dragged their anchors, some unintentionally beached, while others drifted causing damage to the piers. Many casualties were assisted by the salvage teams and tugs, or managed to make repair ports under their own power. The Phoenix breakwater was rendered almost useless, drifting Bombardons were a great hazard and a number of blockships were wrecked. The British *Mulberry B* was less damaged, but had to be repaired and reinforced with extra blockships; it was re-named Arromanches.

The cargo ship *Derrycunihy* had brought military stores and troops who were crammed in the ships holds. Captain Richardson had anchored his ship off Sword Beach waiting for the weather to improve. June 24 dawned fine and calm, so the anchor was weighed. The ship's movement triggered an acoustic mine, which split the *Derrycunihy* in two. The stern section sank very quickly. An ammunition truck on the ship exploded, igniting the spilled oil on the surface of the surrounding water. Of the 600 troops, 189 died and 150 were injured. Twenty-five of the crew, including a number of DEMS gunners, lost their lives. It was the heaviest single British loss of life off the invasion beaches.

The landing ship *Maid of Orleans* was sunk by U-988 in the English Channel on 28 June. Both the *Empire Broadsword* and the *Empire Halberd* were sunk in early July. The *Empire Broadsword* and her sister the *Empire Javelin*, which was sunk by a submarine on 28 December, appear in both the Naval and Merchant losses in the HMSO book *British Vessels Lost at Sea 1939-1945*. This shows the unusual status of this class of vessel. A number of them were transferred to the Navy during 1944 and 1945; they were given the names of Derby winners. Other merchant losses in the month of June included the *Dunvegan Head*, the *Fort Norfolk*, the *Empire Lough* and the *Empire Portia*.

South of France – Operation Dragoon

The landward side of this operation was the responsibility of the US Army who provided three divisions. They were assisted by seven French divisions and a significant number of Canadian troops. This was the first operation where the bulk of the merchant ships were from the US Merchant Marine, possibly because Winston Churchill had continually argued against Operation Dragoon (formerly Operation Anvil). But the British maritime services still made a contribution. Admiral Cunningham RN was C in C. Ninety British merchant ships – about a quarter of the Dragoon fleet – were involved in the landings and the follow-up convoys. A similar proportion was in the assault fleet, though by now several of the landing ships had been transferred to the Royal Navy.

The four landing areas extended for 30 miles along the Cote d'Azur. The landings started on 15 August. HM Landing Ships *Prince Baudouin, Prince David, Prince Henry, Prins Albert* and *Princess Beatrix*, the first four recently arrived from Normandy, were at Sitka. The *Keren* was part of the landing force at Camel beachhead. The *Ascania* and *Dilwara* were part of the force at Delta. The *Derbyshire* and *Dunera* were at Alpha. Special Assault convoy No. 2 included the LSI *Winchester Castle* and the two HM LSTs *Bruiser* and *Thruster*. Two French infantry divisions were landed by the eleven LSIs and personnel ships in convoy TF 1. The British contributed *Cameronia, Cirassia* and *Durban Castle*, the Dutch the *Volendam*, and the Polish the *Batory* and *Sobieski*. All were veterans of previous landings; the Polish ships had completed six.

Convoy TM 1, which included forty British cargo vessels, delivered the equipment and supplies to the beaches. Soon after arrival, the *Fort Maisonneuve*, with 168 personnel, 124 vehicles and 1,080 tons of stores, and *Essex Trader*, with 295 personnel, 120 vehicles and 53 tons of stores, were each hit by a number anti-personnel bombs. Both ships were saved, but there were many casualties on the *Essex Trader*. The *Fort Maisonneuve* was, however, lost in the Scheldt Estuary in December 1944. The Dutch *Van der Capelle* (ex-*Empire Ruskin*) grounded at the Delta beachhead on 17 Augusat, but was re-floated next day.

The operation suffered from a shortage of smaller landing craft, as most of these ships were employed at Normandy. Despite this, over 60,000 troops and 7,000 vehicles were landed on the first day, and within a day the Allies had penetrated 20 miles inland. They were then slowed by a shortage of fuel and other supplies, but their advance triggered an uprising by Resistance fighters in Paris. From a maritime perspective, the major ports of Marseilles and Toulon were the principal gains, but before these ports could be used, the salvage teams had to clear block ships. It was necessary to remove numerous wrecks and obstructions, in waters that were known to be mined, before the ports could be thoroughly effective.

Return to South East Asia

On 7 May 1945, Germany surrendered, and 8 May was designated as VE Day (Victory in Europe). Most people in Britain thought that this was the end, but full-scale war against the Japanese was still being fought East of Suez. The Japanese advance in 1942 had been halted on the Indian border, but the whole of South East Asia was still occupied after three and a half years. British Special Forces (SOE) had infiltrated behind enemy lines in Burma and Malaya. With them went a number of brave Chinese civilian men, including some from Canada. The SOE cooperated with Chinese communists against the common enemy, even though both sides knew that they would fight one another after the War. From the beginning of 1945, regular forces had made a number of landings in Burma and land convoys had entered Burma from India. But it was decided that it would be necessary to seize the port of Rangoon from the enemy; this was to be Operation Dracula.

Operation Dracula was timed to begin on 2 May to ensure that Rangoon and its hinterland were re-occupied before the start of the south-west monsoon. Fifty-two merchantmen were employed in the assault convoys and the follow-up. Six invasion convoys sailed from Northern Burmese ports to the Rangoon River entrance between 27 April and 30 April. Several of the merchant LSI(L)s had by now been transferred to the White Ensign, with many of their civilian crews remaining. The ships that were still under the Red Ensign included *Barpeta*, *Dunera* and *Rajula*, plus MT and Store ships.

When no opposition was encountered, it was realised that the Japanese forces had left several days before. The assault troops re-embarked and went up-river to Rangoon itself, where again there were no defenders. By 8 May, the merchant ships of the follow-up convoys were able to berth in Rangoon Harbour. The only casualty was when the *Silvio* (ex-*Empire Halberd*) struck a mine on 8 May and the ship was so badly damaged that she had to return to the UK for repairs.

With victory in Europe, available resources were allocated to re-take Malaya. The operation, codenamed Zipper, was to start with Port Dickson and Port Swettenham. This would be an all-British operation, as the Americans were committed in the Pacific. The Americans did not approve of the British and other

Europeans 'rebuilding' their Empires, though it could be said that the Americans themselves were doing just the same with General MacArthur's re-occupation of the Philippines.

September 9 was chosen as D-Day for Operation Zipper. The south-west monsoon was still blowing. This, and the week to twelve day journey for the troop carrying ships, put a strain on all concerned. In all, 188 merchant ships were involved and all but four completed the operation; those that did are listed in the table on Convoyweb, as are many who were later diverted to Singapore and Hong Kong.

The majority of the ships were at sea when the news of the Japanese surrender was received, so it was decided that it was too late to cancel the operation. Many of those in the follow-up convoys reached the beachheads around the nineteenth, but did not get to Singapore, a day and a half away, until the end of the month. The collier *Bushwood*, and others, had been built to work on the British coast and would have not had any form of blown air cooling. Few, if any, would have had air conditioning.

Among the merchant arrivals at Singapore were: *Highland Brigade* (2 September); *Dilwara* and *Ekma* (4 September); *City of Derby* and *Karapara* (5 September); *Karoa* (6 September); *Corfu* and *Monowai* (7 September); *Samvannah* (8 September); *Derbyshire* (9 September); *Fort Frontenac* (10 September); and *City of Canterbury* (11 September). When the *Dilwara* and *Karoa* sailed on the 10th, the *Fort Turtle, Islami, Samconon* and *Samvannah* sailed with them. No arrival dates are given for the last four. Similarly, when the *Monowai* sailed on the 11th, she was accompanied by the *Baharistan* and the *Samsteel*.

In a letter to his family, Major General Sir C. Lanes wrote:

Wednesday 12th September was the day of the Surrender Ceremony. The surrender took place in the very fine Municipal Buildings which Singapore possesses. The Guards of Honour were drawn up in front of the building, as were representatives of the services that had taken part in the campaign, British, Australian, Indian, R.N., Marines, Chinese, Dutch and French. The setting was very picturesque as the Municipal Buildings look out on to the Harbour where, of course, were our warships.

Yet again, the Merchant Navy had reason to turn their MN badges upside down, but they quietly went about their business.

Epilogue

The part that merchant seamen played in both wars has largely been ignored. Official figures show that one in seven British merchant seamen lost their lives during the Second World War. Comparable figures for the fighting services are: the Royal Navy, one in ten, and the Army and the RAF, about one in sixteen. Some have pointed out that losses in, for instance, Bomber Command, were much higher than the Air Force average; but so were losses on ore and ammunition ships and those on the North Atlantic and Arctic runs higher than for the Merchant Navy in general.

The Registrar General of Shipping and Seamen put the number of deaths at 29,180, plus 814 lost on fishing vessels. These figures include British Seamen on foreign ships and vice versa. The Trade Division of the Admiralty gives a total of 30,129; the real figure is probably nearer 40,000. As many as 12,000 died shortly after leaving their ships, or had their health so ruined that they were invalided out. The Army and Navy gunners who served on merchant ships suffered in the same proportion.

Figures from: *Merchant Seamen during the War*:

Services Table 9. MN Table 1.	Average strength x 1,000	Annual average war deaths x 1,000	% p.a. war deaths to strength	Annual average deaths by natural causes x 1,000	% p.a. deaths by natural causes to average strength
Royal Navy	550	8.5*	1.55*	1.2	0..21
Army	2400	24	1	3.3	0.14
Royal Air Force	775	11.6†	1.5†	7	0.09
Merchant Navy#	190 (assumed)	5.6	2.96	1.04	0.55

---

* Including deaths from disease attributable to war service. (MN figures do NOT include these deaths?)

† Including suicides. # Merchant Navy figures calculated from Table 1.

Mr Billy McGee has devoted a great deal of time and energy to compiling figures from around the world. His totals are: known losses 37,857; missing 4,654; wounded 4,707. An extra 5,720 were held as prisoners of war. At least 372 British Merchant Seamen were executed by machine gun, bayonet or sword. There were other reports of some enemy submarines machine-gunning merchant crews as they took to the boats; in some cases no one survived to make a report. The Japanese executed crews and escapees from at least eight ships; they were the *Behar, Daisy Moller, British Chivalry, Sutlej, Ascot, Nancy Moller, Nellore* and *Vyner Brooke*.

Commemorations are:

Tower Hill Memorial, 24,000 (including 139 Australian and sixty-nine New Zealand Merchant Seamen)
Buried Ashore, 2,594 (includes Canadian, Australian and New Zealand MN)
Canadian, 1,554 (Halifax Memorial, Tower Hill and Buried Ashore)
Bombay/Chittagong Memorial, 6,048
Hong Kong War Memorial, 1,400
Liverpool Naval Memorial, 1,400 (those who served on RN vessels under the T124T and T124X)
Australian War Memorial, 359

Royal Navy DEMS, 3,000 lost in MN Service
DEMS Maritime Regiments, 1,222 lost in MN Service
DEMS other Regiments, fifty lost in MN Service
Naval Staff, 699 lost in MN Service
Missing, presumed Dead, 4,654

Billy McGee's book, *They Shall Grow Not Old*, is dedicated to over 500 boys aged 16 and under who were killed while serving in the Merchant Navy. Fifteen of these were known to be only 14 years old. Within the service there was always talk of others who were even younger, having falsified their ages to join up. The CWGC have now acknowledged Cabin Boy Reggie Earnshaw as the country's youngest service casualty. Reggie was 14 years and 152 days old when he was killed during an attack on the cargo ship *North Devon* in 1941. As a result of a lot of hard work, especially by Alf Tubbs who was a DEMS gunner on the ship and, again, Billy McGee, Reggie's grave has now been marked with a CWGC headstone.

The oldest UK seafarers known to have been killed in service were Second Engineer Frederick Perry of the *Polzella* and Greaser James Killey of the *Fenella*; both were 74. Older still were Rahman Khalil, Serang of the *Gairsoppa*, at 75, and Santan Martins, Chief Cook of the *Calabria*, who was 79. Thomas Bryan, 81, was described as a civilian when he was killed by an air raid on his home, but he may have been a merchant seaman on leave.

A HMSO study, 'Merchant Shipping & the Demands of War', published in 1955, says that between 1942-44, as many as 11,600 Merchant Seamen died shortly after leaving their ship, or had their lives permanently damaged, either physically or mentally. Mr McGee says, 'whether or not all these numbers were ever taken into account for the final count is anyone's guess.' There are no figures for those similarly afflicted before 1942 or after 1944.

For the majority of the merchant seaman there was no 'de-mob', no gratuity (or gratitude) or 'civvy' suit; they just carried on supplying the nation. Another nasty surprise awaited those who were no longer needed at sea; anyone who had served for less than five years of the War became liable to serve for two years on National Service, mostly in the Army. There was very little support available for the injured, or for the families. The British Legion would not accept merchant seamen as members, classing them as 'non-combatants'.

Other charities did what they could. One, The Merchant Seaman's War Memorial Society, had been set up in 1920 by Havelock Wilson, the founder and president of the National Union of Seamen (NUS), to provide help for merchant seafarers. In 1920, the Society opened the Henry Radcliffe Convalescent Home in Surrey. It was named after the shipowner who was the principal benefactor. After the Second World War, the people of South Africa collected a large sum of money that they gave to the NUS to build a living memorial to the seamen who had done so much to keep the shipping lanes open during the conflict. The Society used the money to fit out Sachel Court in Surrey, on what became known as the Springbok Estate. Other maritime unions have established retirement homes for seafarers, but there are still instances of merchant seamen of all ranks who are unable to find sheltered accommodation that they can afford.

During the war years, the Seamen's Welfare Board maintained a London hotel in Bayley Street, off Tottenham Court Road. The history of seafarers' hotels goes back to the 1930s when the Board was funded by the government to set up hotels in the major ports. These included Cardiff, Glasgow, Liverpool, London, Middlesbrough, South Shields, Southampton and Swansea. In addition, it ran Seaman's clubs in Avonmouth, the Isle of Grain and Milford Haven.

During the Second World War, seafarers, including foreign nationals from the occupied countries, used the hotels when going to and from their ships, standing by vessels in refit, or studying for examinations in the colleges. For some they became home between voyages and for others a place where wives and families could stay while their ship was in port. Merchant seamen were not allowed to use the NAAFI canteens at railway stations or for that matter at the Normandy beaches, even though it was they who had delivered the stores.

A group of dedicated people ran the Merchant Navy Comforts Service. They knitted and made clothing for seafarers. It was largely because of their good work that the rescue ships were stocked with clothing for survivors.

The Merchant Service was further stretched as ships, and in many cases their crews, were requisitioned for naval service. They served as minelayers, minesweepers and danlayers, armed merchant cruisers (fifty vessels), armed boarding vessels, stores carriers and weather ships. The Royal Navy was equally over-extended. Captain S. W. Roskill RN says that 'the country had not provided itself with adequate naval forces to meet [the situation].' Roskill goes on to say: 'In those circumstances all that could be done was to meet the most vital requirements; and they were judged to be the defeat of invasion and the maintenance of our hold in the Mediterranean. Trade protection had to take third place and the Western Approaches Command was therefore stripped almost bare of escort vessels.' In his book, *A Merchant Fleet in War*, he says: 'The real tragedy lay in the fact that a nation which was – and is – utterly dependant on seaborne transport, had not provided itself with the means to defend its merchant ships; and much of the price was, as so often before, paid by its merchant seamen.'

To deal with the shortfall in naval manpower, a number of officers and men of the Merchant Navy served with the Royal Navy under the terms of a T 124 agreement, which made them subject to Naval discipline while generally retaining their Merchant Navy rates of pay and other conditions. More than 13,000 seamen served under these terms in various types of auxiliary vessels, at first mainly in armed merchant cruisers and later on armed boarding vessels, cable ships, rescue tugs (T124T) and others on special service (T124X). When the tug HMS *Saucy* sank after hitting a mine in September 1940, all of her twenty-eight-man crew were lost. Eighteen were Merchant Navy men from Brixham (five from one family), the rest of the ratings were described as Naval Auxiliary Personnel (Merchant Navy), while the three officers were Sub Lieutenants RNR, again from the Merchant Navy. This sort of manning was not unusual.

The great majority of the Merchant Navy dead have no grave. As their U-boat adversaries sang, *'Auf einem Seemansgrab, da bluhen keine Rosen'* – 'On a seaman's grave, no roses bloom.' These are the men who are commemorated on the Merchant Navy Memorial at Tower Hill in London. The merchant seamen who were buried ashore have graves marked by the Commonwealth War Graves Commission. Plaques have been placed at Arromanches, Normandy, and in the grounds of the former Bidadari Cemetery in Singapore. Both were paid for by people who are connected with the industry. In the National Memorial Arboretum, 2,535 oak trees have been planted, one for each UK merchant ship lost.

Almost 5,000 Allied merchant seamen and DEMS captured by the Germans during the Second World War were at first housed in The Marine Internierten Lager (MILAG), one of two compounds inside Sandbostel Concentration Camp south of Bremervorde, Germany. The adjoining Marine Lager (MARLAG) was for captured Royal Navy personnel. Both groups were later transferred to camps at Westertimke, near Bremen, Germany. The Merchant Navy camp then became known as MILAG NORD. Near the end of the War, those who were fit enough were marched towards Lübeck, or to Krakow, in Poland. They both narrowly escaped being 'liberated' by the Russians.

A committee handled the internal organisation of the camps. Most of its members were ship masters, of whom there were a disproportionate number as U-boats would often take the master prisoner after sinking his ship. Most former prisoners remember their stay as being hard, but the International Red Cross did what they could to make conditions bearable.

During the War, when some British and Allied merchant seamen were landed in Iceland after being shipwrecked, they were sent to a British Army-run transit camp. There were only benches to sleep on; there were no mattresses or pillows, though they were given blankets. The food was extremely bad, mostly hash stew and if the seamen were even minutes late they had to go without. Washing facilities were very limited and the water was 'usually turned off in the midst of our wash.' When one of the masters brought the conditions to the attention of the British Consul, he was told that 'he [the Consul] considered the conditions for the survivors to be quite satisfactory'. As many of these men were off pay from the moment their ship was torpedoed, they were not even able to draw money and go into town to buy food. When, or if, they eventually got back home, usually as DBSs (Distressed British Seamen), they were given a Rail Warrant and left to find their own way.

There were debates in Parliament regarding conditions in the service. The discussions spilled over into the letters column in *The Times*. Hansard of 8 July 1941 records a debate on the subject of hospital rations for the Mercantile Marine. On 10 September 1941, Lord Marchwood moved a motion to have a Royal Commission appointed to inquire into the conditions of service in the Mercantile Marine. In this he was supported by the Earl of Cork and Orrery and Lord Chatfield. Lord Marchwood was a Master Mariner and both the Earl of Cork and Orrery and Lord Chatfield were retired Admirals of the Fleet. Other Lords with experience in one or other of the sea services spoke in favour. Lord Thurlow had been on the Pacific coast in the days of sail and remembered that 'the conditions of a merchant sailor were probably as bad as anything you can imagine. The masters did their very best to make them better.'

The motion was strongly opposed by Lord Leathers, who was the Minister of War Transport. He contended that 'A Royal Commission is unnecessary because there already exists, in the form of the National Maritime Board, an organisation representative of the officers, seamen and employers which is fully competent to deal with the problems relating to the well-being and conditions of seagoing personnel.' In fact, throughout its existence, the NMB had not made an effort to improve conditions in the Merchant Navy.

In March 1942, the subject of a Royal Commission was debated in the Lower House. Petty Officer Herbert, the Senior Burgess for Oxford University, dealt fully with the subject. He said that 'I did not yield to the temptation to send all these letters (from seafarers in support of a Royal Commission) to the press when Lord Marchwood and I were so much abused.'

In the course of his lengthy speech he also said:

It has been my privilege during this war to see from time to time ... the convoys coming home, ships of all sorts and sizes. Their paint is battered, and they have wounds on their sides sometimes. They have come through every imaginable danger, but their flags are flying, and no man can look at them without a lift of the heart. But they go by ... as strange and silent as ghosts. How little we know about the lives of these men. The seamen look over the side with that remote, sardonic look which they reserve for all miserable mortals who are not sailing in their own particular ship. They seem to say to me 'You will never know anything about us, and you will never really do anything for us. We are the pets of all the world today. Tomorrow you will forget us, as you did last time.'... I hope that this will not be true.

Mr Noel-Baker, the Joint Parliamentary Secretary to the Ministry of War Transport, thanked his 'Honourable and Gallant friend', but said that 'a Royal Commission is unnecessary'. The Lords returned to the subject on 16 June 1942 with the Second Reading of the Pensions (Mercantile Marine) Bill.

The Merchant Navy Association was formed in 1989 to promote interest in the Merchant Navy and its seafarers and keep the memory of their contribution alive. It works alongside the British Legion, which has changed its stance in recent years. The MNA organised a Merchant Navy Day on 3 September. This day is observed in much of the Commonwealth, but has largely been forgotten in the UK.

Had it not been for the steadfastness of her merchant seamen, the 1939-45 war that the Allies won would have been the 1939-42 war that Britain lost. By hauling enough food, fuel and materials to enable the nation to hold on, and by saving troops and civilians to carry on the fight, they lengthened the War long enough for the Americans to come in on Britain's side after the invasion of Pearl Harbor. They brought vital supplies and troops from America and elsewhere, both to Britain and to her allies. From the beginning, the British effort was strongly supported by Allied and neutral merchant ships; many of the seamen manning these ships came from territories occupied by the Axis including Norway, Denmark, Holland, Belgium and Greece, and faced the added threat that their families could suffer if they assisted Britain.

Today the British Merchant Navy is only a shadow of what it was, and most of our seaborne trade is now carried in foreign ships. Some years ago there was a move to arrest the decline, which gave the illusion of a substantial increase, but the 'new' ships were mostly using the Red Ensign as a Flag of Convenience. The only British crew members on some of these ships are cadets, usually only two. One feels for these lads and lasses, alone with a foreign crew. Most British shipping companies are no more; famous names like Cunard and P&O are merely 'brands'.

... Some, reaching harbour, maimed and battle-scarred,
Some, never more returning, lost to us.
But, if you 'scape, tomorrow you will steer,
To peril once again, to bring us bread,
To dare again, beneath the sky of fear,
The moon-moved graveyard of your brothers dead.
You were salvation to the army lost,
Trapped, but for you, upon the Dunkirk beach;
Death barred the way to Russia; but you crossed;
To Crete and Malta, but you succoured each.
Unrecognised you put us in your debt;
Unthanked, you enter, or escape, the grave;
Whether your land remember or forget,
You saved the land, or died to try to save.

'For the Sailors' John Masefield O.M., LL.D.
(1891-1994) a former sailing ship apprentice.
(*Courtesy: The Society of Authors as the
Literary Representative of the Estate of John
Masefield*)

Cartoon by Illingworth, April 1942,
(*Courtesy:* Daily Mail)

Abbreviations

AA	Anti-Aircraft
ADC	Aide de Camp
A/S	Anti-submarine
ANCXF	Allied Naval Commander, Expeditionary Force
ARS & BARS	US Naval Salvage Vessels
ASDIC	Anti-Submarine Detection Investigation Committee (Sonar)
ASV	Admiralty Salvage Vessel
BAR	Boom Defence Vessel – the names began with BAR
BDV	Boom Defence Vessel
BEM	British Empire Medal
BHP	Brake Horse Power (motor ship) & IHP Indicated Horse Power (steamer)
BI	British India Steam Navigation Co. (also BISN)
BNLO	British Naval Liaison Officer
C in C WA	Commander in Chief Western Approaches
C in C XF	Commander in Chief, Expeditionary Force
CS2	Commander Cruiser Squadron?
CSV	Coastal Salvage Vessel
CTL	Constructive Total Loss – where the cost of repair would exceed the sound value
CWGC	Commonwealth War Grave Commission.
D9	Commander destroyer Squadron 9?
DEMS	Defensively Equipped Merchant Ships, also Army or Navy gunners these ships
DSC	Distinguished Service Cross
DSO	Distinguished Service Order
DUKW	'Duck' an amphibious vehicle US
GC	George Cross – the highest British award for civilian bravery
GRT	Gross registered tonnage – the internal cubic measurement of a merchant ship

HMS	His Majesty's Ship, now Her Majesty's Ship – I have used this in the first mention of the warship
LCA	Landing Craft, Assault
LCI	Landing Craft, infantry
LCT	Landing Craft, Tank
LCT (R)	Landing Craft, Tank (Rocket)
LCVP	Landing Craft, Vehicle and Personnel
LMC	Lloyd's Machinery Classification
LSI	Landing Ship, Infantry
LST	Landing Ship, Tank
MBE	Member of the Order of the British Empire
MOWT	Ministry of War Transport
mv	Motor Vessel (British)
ms	Motor Ship (Continental)
MT	Military Transport, Mechanised Transport or Motor Transport (in MN = empty)
NOI/C	Naval Officer in Charge
OBE	Officer of the Order of the British Empire
OTS	Overseas Towage & Salvage
P&O	Peninsular & Oriental Steam Navigation (also POSN)
RA	Royal Artillery
RAF	Royal Air Force
RFA	Ships, mostly tankers, owned by the Admiralty, manned by merchant seamen
RN	Royal Navy
RNR	Royal Naval Reserve (a reserve of professional seamen – i.e. Merchant Navy)
RNVR	Royal Naval Volunteer Service (mainly non-seafarers)
SNO	Senior Naval Officer
ss	Steam Ship – used by the Navy as a prefix for any merchant ship
STO	Sea Transport Officer
T124	Arrangement under which merchant seamen served on RN ships, also T124T
UXB	Unexploded Bomb and therefore Bomb Disposal teams
V/l	Vessel

Bibliography

General Reference

Blair, C., *Hitler's U-boat War, Volume one, The Hunters 1939-1942*, Cassell & Co., 1996

Cantwell, J. D., *The Second World War, A Guide to Documents in the Public Record Office*, PRO, 1998

Colledge and Lenton, *Warships of World War II, Part 5 – Auxiliary Support Vessels*, Ian Allan, 1962

Cooley, R., *The Unknown Fleet, the Army's Civilian Seamen in War and Peace*, Alan Sutton, Royal Naval Museum, 1993

Hessler, G., *U-boat War in the Atlantic 1939-45* (English translation by HMSO for the MOD), 1989

HMSO, *British Vessels Lost at Sea*, Patrick Stephens, 1988 – combined volume of HMSO publications

HMSO, *British Coaster 1939-1945, The Official Story*, 1947

Macmillan, H., *The Blast of War 1939-1945*, Macmillan, 1967

Mitchell and Sawyer, *The Empire Ships*, Lloyd's of London Press Ltd, 1990

Roberts, A., *The Storm of War*, Allen Lane, 2009

Roskill RN DSC, Captain S. W., *The War at Sea 1939-45*, HMSO, 1976

Slader, J., *The Fourth Service*, New Era, 1995

Talbot-Booth, E. C., *Merchant Ships 1943*, Sampson Low, Marston & Co. Ltd

Winser, J. de S., *Short Sea: Long War, Cross Channel Ships ... in World War Two*, World Ship Society, 1997

Woodman, R., *The Real Cruel Sea*, John Murray, 2004

Woodman R., *A History of the British Merchant Navy, Volume Five. Fiddler's Green,* The History Press, 2010

Young, J. M., *Britain's Sea War*, Patrick Stephens Ltd, 1989

www.ibiblio.org/hyperwar/UN/UK/londongazette.html, Index Despatches written by commanders

Flight from Singapore

Simkins MBE, Radio Officer T., 'BBC Peoples War' – S/T *Pinna* (filed under Royal Navy)

www.angellpro.com.au/Hamilton.htm (etc.) – Australian nurses

www.bluestarline.org/empire2.html – *Empire Star*
www.diggerhistory.info/pages-battles/ww2/singapore.htm
www.historylearningsite.co.uk/fall_of_singapore.htm
www.members.dodo.com.au/~mervynw/Giang%20Ann%20and%20Darvel.htm
www.mercantilemarine.org – Especially Prudence and Hugh
www.merchantnavyofficers.com/straits2.html – Straits Steamship Co. www.
    singaporeevacuation1942.blogspot.com
www.Naval-history.net
www.naval-history.net/xDKCas1942-02FEB.htm – Royal Naval Casualties
www.qaranc.co.uk/bmhsingapore.php – *Wu Sueh*
www.seawaves.com/newsletters/TDIH/february/06Feb.txt

TNA: WO 106/2534 *bouches inutiles* /2552 Chronology /2569 Fall /2610 Escapees;
    WO 41/100 Evacuation, WO 222/1378 British nurses WO361/164 *Roosenboom*
    /178 *Dragonfly* /184 *Chau Tee* /187 *Ban Ho Guan* /383 *Gorgon* /404
    Grasshopper /421 *Sui Kwang* /446 *Felix Roussel* /462 *Tanjong Pinang*.

The Norwegian Campaign and the Fall of the Low Countries

Bernaerts, A., *Naval War Changes Climate*: *Arctic winter 1939/40*
New York Times, James Aldridge's report, 25 December 1939

www.1ocean-1climate.com/pdf/b9.pdf
www.polandinexile.com/norway.htm
www.naval-history.net/xDKWW2-4004-13APR03.htm
www.bluestarline.org/arandora.html

Operation Dynamo – Dunkirk

Gardner, W. J. R. (editor), *The Evacuation from Dunkirk: 'Operation Dynamo'* 26
    May-4 June 1940, Frank Cass, 2000
Looseley R., dissertation, http://www.francobritishcouncil.org.uk/publications.php/51/
    le-paradis-apres-lenfer-the-french-soldiers-evacuated-from-dunkirk-in-1940
The London Gazette, supplement 17 July 1947 – the evacuation of the allied armies
    from Dunkirk etc.
Winser, J. de S., *B.E.F. SHIPS before, at and after Dunkirk*, World Ship Society,1999

TNA: MT 40/66, WO 215, ADM1/11144, ADM 116/4504, ADM 199 786796B.

Operations Cycle and Aerial

BBC, 'The Dragon's Opponent', 1973
Comer, B. and Chaim Even-Zohar, 'Paul Timbal's Diamond Odyssey' in *Financing
    the World's Most Precious Treasures*, Antwerp Diamond Bank N V, 2009
Fenby, J., *The Sinking of the Lancastria, Britain's Greatest Maritime Disaster and
    Churchill's Cover-Up*, Simon & Schuster, 2005
Freeman, K., *Jack Howard's War*, 2012, Awaiting Publication
Howard, G., *My Elizabethan Brother, the Earl of Suffolk*, Reader's Digest, November 1969
Kowarski, Dr L., *Oral History Transcript*, American Institute of Physics, 1969
Letter from Weymouth, 28 June, University of Manitoba – Special Collections, also

Rhiannon Looseley's dissertation

Mount, J., *My First Ninety Years*   (unpublished)

Reception of Refugees in Weymouth (the Dorset Women's Institute paper), Dorset County Records Office, Dorchester

Rickard, J. *Operation Aerial, the evacuation from north western France, 15-25 June 1940*, www.historyofwar.org/articles/operation_aerial.html

'The Plymouth Journal' via Bob Kindell. Also see: http://www.naval-history.net/xDKWDa-Aerial.htm

Winser, J. de S., *B.E.F. Ships before, at and after Dunkirk*, World Ship Society, 1999

www.radley.org.uk/OR/OldRadleian/2009/PDFs/7%20Incredible%20Earl%20of%20Suffolk.pdf

www.trove.nla.gov.au/newspaper/result?q=Earl+of+Suffolk

www.ww2talk.com/forum – Marguerite Nicolle's itinerary and diary (from 10 June in Paris to 8 July)

TNA pieces AB1/569, ADM 267/126, ADM 179/158, ADM 1/10481, ADM 1/10756, ADM 1/11408, ADM 1/11650, ADM 1/12442, ADM199/2207, BT 381/1672, WO106/1739, WO106/1615.

TNA: AVIA 22/2288A, AVIA 22/3201. Official Log of the *Broompark*.

Evacuations from the South of France through, and from, Gibraltar

Somerset Maugham, W., *Strictly Personal*, William Heinemann Ltd, 1942

www.webspace.webring.com/people/fc/czechandslovakthings/WW2_aguide.htm

Children's Overseas Reception Board and Other Civilian Evacuations

Fethney, M., *The Absurd and the Brave*, Book Guild Ltd, 2000

Innocents Abroad

Jacks, C., *Who Will Take Our Children?* McFarland, 2008

First Low Water, 1941

Black Eight (magazine of the Stanier 8F Locomotive Society) – various editions, Stanier 8F Locomotive Society

Bletchley Park Trust, *Convoys and the U boats, The First Breaking of Enigma & Breaking Naval Enigma*, Bletchley Park Trust

Conyers Nesbit, R., *Ultra versus U-boats*, Pen & Sword, 2008

The London Gazette, supplement 18 May 1948

Tourret, R., *Allied Military Locomotives of the Second World War*, Tourret Publishing, 1995

http://en.wikipedia.org/wiki/Enigma_machine

TNA: LIB 5 197 *The 2-8-0 and 2-10-0 Locomotives of the War Department 1939-1945*, The Railway Correspondence and Travel Society, 1946

Second Low Water, 1942

Carter, F., *Breaking the Naval Enigma*, Bletchley Park Trust
Hague, A. and Bob Ruegg, *Convoys to Russia 1941-1945*, World Ship Society, 1992
Hutson, H. C., *Arctic Interlude, Independent to North Russia*, Merriam Press, 2000

www.en.wikipedia.org/wiki/Japanese_Invasion_of_Malaya
www.ww2talk.com/forum/war-sea/19579-merchant-navy-awards.html
www.ww2talk.com/forum/war-sea/19579-merchant-navy-awards-38.html

First of the Flood

Stone, B., *Operation Ironclad: Invasion of Madagascar,* Stone & Stone, 1998
Winser, J. de S., *British Invasion Fleets: The Mediterranean and Beyond 1942-1945,*
    World Ship Society, 2002

www.combinedops.com/Torch.htm.
www.en.wikipedia.org/wiki/Convoy_SL_125#cite_note-Rohwer_.26_Hummelchen_
    1992_p.172-2
www.naval-history.net/WW2CampaignsNorthAfrica.htm.

Normandy Landings – Operation Neptune

Craigie-Halkett, L. and Roy Martin *Risdon Beazley, Marine Salvor*, self published,
    2006
Sowden, D., *Admiralty Coastal Salvage Vessels*, World Ship Society, 2005
Winser, J. de S., *The D-Day Ships*, World Ship Society, 1994

www.history.navy.mil/library/online/comnaveu/comnaveu_index.htm, p. 291-93
www.thamestugs.co.uk/MULBERRY-TUGS-%5B1%5D.php
www.timesonline.co.uk/tol/system/topicRoot/D_Day/ – 'Merchant navy's role'

Return to South East Asia

www.burmastar.org.uk/willy_chong.htm Force 136
www.fepow-community.org.uk/Japanese_Surrender_at_Singapore/html

Epilogue

www.actuaries.org.uk/__data/assets/pdf_file/0011/25679/0250-0284.pdf
www.gordonmumford.com/m-navy/memorial4.htm
www.hansard.millbanksystems.com

Ship List